Resistance and Ideology in Settler Societies

Southern African Studies Volume 4

Resistance and Ideology In Settler Societies

Southern African Studies
Volume 4

Edited by Tom Lodge

Ravan Press

Johannesburg

Published by
Ravan Press (Pty) Ltd
P.O. Box 31134, Braamfontein 2017
in association with
The African Studies Institute
University of the Witwatersrand, Johannesburg

First impression 1986
Cover design: Carla Lodge
ISBN 086975 304 5
Printed and bound by Sigma Press (Pty) Ltd.

This volume is dedicated to the historian

MASHOALA MOSES MOLEPO

killed by a police Casspir vehicle in
Soweto, 21 August 1985

Contents

Contributors

1. Helen Bradford has just received a Ph.D from the University of the Witwatersrand for her thesis on the ICU. She is a member of the Department of Economic History at the University of Cape Town.

2. Ronald Ellsworth is a Ph.D student at the University of British Columbia, Canada.

3. Tony Emmett is a researcher at the Human Sciences Research Council, Pretoria. He recently completed a doctoral dissertation on the rise of African nationalism in Namibia for submission to the University of the Witwatersrand.

4. Tom Lodge is a member of the Department of Political Studies at the University of the Witwatersrand. He is the author of *Black Politics in South Africa since 1945* (Johannesburg, 1983).

5. John Lonsdale is Lecturer in History and Fellow of Trinity College, Cambridge. He has written extensively on Kenyan history in addition to his Ph.D thesis, 'A Political History of Nyanza, 1888-1945' (Cambridge, 1964).

6. Mirjana Roth is a Ph.D student registered with the Department of History, University of the Witwatersrand. Her research is on the history of the Natives Representatives Council.

7. Raymond Suttner is a senior lecturer in the School of Law at the University of the Witwatersrand. He is Education Officer for the Transvaal Executive of the United Democractic Front.

8. John Wright is a senior lecturer in the Department of Historical Studies at the University of Natal (Pietermaritzberg). He is working on a Ph.D thesis which will examine the history of Natal chiefdoms between 1750 and 1850.

Introduction

This is the fourth volume of papers in Southern African studies published in this series.[1] As in the cases of its predecessors, any unity of theme or approach in the papers published here is more a reflection of the intellectual environment in which they were produced than the consequence of a deliberate process of selection by the editor. It is striking, therefore, that six of the papers are concerned with acts of resistance, whether by whole communities, or organisations, or individuals. Conversely, the two other papers discuss attempts, both ideological and coercive, to contain resistance. Notwithstanding their scholarly character, the themes and issues explored in the papers are inspired as much by the conflicts of South Africa's contemporary history as they are by the topics and periods which form their subjects. The papers are evidence of the growth of a tendency among English-speaking South African social scientists and historians to concentrate their analysis upon the dominated sections of South African society.

The papers are arranged in historical sequence. The first three are focused on developments in South Africa and Namibia in the aftermath of the First World War. The next two examine responses by the dominant classes to popular political assertions during the interwar period. The last three discuss African political activity in the wartime and post-Second World War eras in South Africa and Kenya.

This volume is entitled 'Resistance and Ideology in Settler Societies' in an effort to capture the essential unifying preoccupation of the papers. All the papers describe social movements which are part of the history of the early stages of the imposition of a capitalist industrial order. But not just any capitalist order: these are settler societies, and the backdrop they provide to the historical dramas contained in these papers presents an explosive combination. Here relatively advanced economies develop in conjunction with colonial hierarchies of privilege and rightlessness. In such societies little or no provision is made for the political accommodation and ideological incorporation of underclasses. In consequence, rebellion and revolt reflect this incomplete involvement of popular classes in a capitalist social order: they seek more frequently to re-establish the integrity of a community or a nation than advance the interests of a particular class. In the papers collected here we have different expressions of the same historical process. Namibian and South African farmworkers through their adherence to nationalist movements articulate a rejection of a recently imposed rural capitalism, a rejection which was echoed in the discourse of the newly emergent African middle class frustrated by racist barriers to its promotion. In a later context, populist movements in Kenya during the 1950s and in South Africa after 1960 still embody pre-capitalist communal reactions to the advance of industrial society, once again finding their spokesmen amongst a rightless urban middle class. The new social identities normally formed by the progress of a non-colonial capitalist society are here subject to physical resistance and moral challenge. Complicating matters still further are the actions of ruling class bureaucrats and intellectuals. These are directed at re-ordering and neutralising concepts of community and nation, as well as holding up the genesis of a proletarian consciousness. In only one of these papers does an industrial working class have a significant role in the narrative, and even then it has not yet begun to generate its own leadership, functioning instead as a radicalising pressure below the surface of organised politics. The nationalism of this phase of Southern African history is not a proletarian nationalism; it is a movement which often emerges on the fringes rather than from the centre of an embryonic industrial society. This is a book about national struggles but these are not the struggles conducted by modern proletarian mass organisations such as the African National Congress, the Communist Party, or industrial trade unions. These are the struggles of communities which only have a past, not a future.

The main convergences in method and conclusion between the papers will be evident from the condensations of their contents which follow. In Tony Emmett's study of popular Namibian resistance during the 1920s, disappointed expectations of social reform, economic recession, deteriorating agricultural conditions, and increased taxation all contributed to a rising tide of resentment. This provided the environment for an unparalleled variety of forms of anti-colonial protest. These included armed rebellion, stock-theft, banditry, and efforts at formal political organisation. The paper's emphasis is on the last, tracing the emergence and evolution of the Garveyist Universal Negro Improvement Association (UNIA). From its inception as the vehicle for elitist concerns of West Indian and West African ex-patriates in Luderitz, the UNIA was to find a more generalised resonance in the millenarian anticipation of farmworkers in the Herero hinterland. The UNIA's popular influence testified to the existence of a widespread climate of discontent in the territory. The impetus for revolt was, nevertheless, uneven. Black Namibian society was too scattered and fragmented. The existing political organisations with their petty bourgeois orientation were not predisposed to play out the insurrectionary role assigned to them. The state was swift to suppress resistance with an intimidating exhibition of military technology. Emmett's paper breaks historiographical ground in setting the two most well known episodes in this unrest, the rebellions of the Bondelswarts and the Rehobothers, within a wider context of protest and resistance, much of it interconnected. The confluence of ideological themes, usually associated with either 'primary' or 'secondary' resistance, within one social movement, points to the need for a revision of the teleological concepts which still remain influential in much of the contemporary discussion of African nationalism.

Helen Bradford's view of petty bourgeois African politicians is more favourable than Emmett's. The failings of the Industrial and Commercial Worker's Union (ICU) have often been imputed to the narrow sectional interests of a middle class steeped in Victorian bourgeois culture. Bradford dismisses this argument as superficial and draws attention to the essential ambiguity of the ICU's discourse. Certainly the rural ICU's efforts seemed at times to be directed mainly at the 'creation of an elite independent of wage labour' but this was not uniformly so. Simultaneously with the advocacy in the ICU newspapers of independent black businesses, ICU organisers were urging preparations for a 'socialist commonwealth' and the downfall of capitalism. The inconsistency reflected the complexity of the class position of a black sub-elite standing between capital and labour and pulled in both directions by each. As Bradford argues, developments in the late 1920s increased the likelihood of a petty bourgeois finding common cause with the popular classes. Increasing occupational discrimination, the impoverishment of the white collar professions, land shortage, and curbs to their political rights made the more vulnerable members of the middle class susceptible to socialist ideology. In such circumstances, they functioned more frequently as organic intellectuals of the underprivileged than lackeys of the propertied.

The next paper is about individual rather than collective forms of resistance. Ronald Ellsworth's examination of African railway passenger transport during the 1920s confronts a common racist stereotype: the incapacity of Africans to respond rationally to modern technology. White railway staff attributed to the 'simplicity of the native mind' the misuse of tickets and the apparent inability of African passengers to identify the trains to which they were permitted access. Ellsworth perceives in this behaviour deliberate attempts to evade regulations which subjected Africans to uncomfortable and inconvenient travelling conditions. The pressure on the railway administration from low-wage employers in mining and agriculture to introduce concessionary fares was symptomatic of the sensitivity of Africans to transport costs. Contrary to official assumptions, African railway passengers behaved with calculation and discrimination.

The subject of white beliefs about Africans is also central to John Wright's investigation of the historic usage of the generic term 'Nguni' as he separates the layers of ideology which can be discerned beneath the word's ostensibly scientific function. 'Nguni' as an appellation for the African people of east South Africa became entrenched in scholarship only in the 1920s. Wright traces the establishment of 'Nguni' as a generic term to three ideological impulses. The first two of these were interlinked: the 'developmental' ideology of a rising national bourgeoisie and the efforts to check and deflect the challenge of African national and class consciousness through a policy of 'retribalisation'. These helped to spur the growth of ethnographic scholarship. The term 'Nguni' owed its prominence at the time to the third impulse referred to by Wright: the creation of a wider ethnic identity for Africans in Natal by the ruling Zulu house; it was in this process that the word began to acquire its current meaning. According to Wright, then, as an ethnic lable 'Nguni' is historically invalid and politically contentious.

Part of the process of 'retribalisation' referred to by Wright is evident in Raymond Suttner's description of the special legal system established to deal with civil cases between Africans. Commissioner's Courts from 1927 have had the discretion to apply 'Black Law' - a form of pseudo-traditional customary law. Purportedly set up to meet the particular needs of Africans, the courts are widely perceived today to be unsatisfactory. The real purpose of 'Black Law', contends Suttner, has never been to provide for the special requirements of African litigants. Instead it has had two main functions. The first of these has been the consolidation of a tribal family-centred redistribution system and hence the subsidisation of the capitalist mode of production in the reserves. The second function has been ideological: to help incorporate Africans as tribal subjects and thus disrupt the formation of a national consciousness. As long as these purposes remain, reforms of the system will not significantly alleviate its inadequacies. A just legal system will emerge only when Africans are politically represented and can participate within the judicial hierarchy itself.

African political representation forms the subject of the following paper. Mirjana Roth's study of the 1937, 1942, and 1948 native representative elections suggests that, notwithstanding their origins in unpopular legislation, the elections had considerable political significance. Through a cumbersome system of indirect voting, representation was weighted in favour of urban Africans and increasingly reflected their political preoccupations. The supplicatory posture of the Native Representative Council and the paternal liberalism of white native representatives encountered growing criticism in the years which followed. The successful candidates of the 1942 and 1948 elections were more radical and more militant as a result of the economic and political advances of the war years[2]. The electoral choice of representatives became more frequently governed by considerations of ideology and less often by the characteristics of individual personalities. By 1948, Roth asserts, African voters finally repudiated liberalism with their election of a communist member of parliament. In their composition and principles the transformation of the native representatives signified profound shifts in the nature of African politics.

The two final papers offer illuminating comparisons with each other. John Lonsdale's historiographical survey examines two sets of explanations for the Mau Mau insurgency. Until the 1970s treatments of the movement tended to discuss it as a homogeneous entity and historians differed in their interpretations mainly in how they understood the behaviour of its leaders. Early settler-oriented accounts presented the Mau Mau as a selfish conspiratorial elite manipulating barbaric themes drawn from pre-colonial Kikuyu ideology. Later nationalist history reversed the terms of this analysis depicting the Mau Mau as the 'militant wing of modern nationalism'. A recent evaluation has been provided by American scholars who have recast the revolt in the form of a leadership struggle between dominant and emergent elites in Kikuyu society. An alternative line of investigation is followed by those analyses which examine the different regional bases of Kikuyu politics before attempting to reconstruct from the bottom upwards an impression of the movement's character. Here the evidence suggests that the Mau Mau was the crystallization of several distinct social processes. These are linked through an ideology drawn from a highly formalised and elaborate communal culture. They are brought into collusion with each other through shifts in the relationship between the state and rural notables. These promote a switch in popular allegiances from traditional Kikuyu leadership to those elements emerging from the 'advancing line of class formation'.

There are telling similarities between this conception of the Mau Mau and Tom Lodge's description of the South African Poqo movement of the early 1960s. As with the Mau Mau, the Poqo insurrection encompassed a combination of different communal struggles and was united more in an ideological sense than an organisational one. Its ideology too was shaped by a communal intellectual heritage as much as externally derived ideas. Unlike the Mau Mau, though, the Poqo movement embraced only some of the constituents of militant African opposition. The development of a modern industrial economy in South Africa was by the 1960s too advanced for Poqo millenarian populism to attain an ideological hegemony over the dominated classes.

Despite their differences in subject matter a number of common strands can be detected in the arguments proposed in most of the papers. There is a shared aversion towards rigid forms of social classification. The sociology of the communities under discussion is commonly portrayed as fluid, emergent, fragile, and historically hybrid. Class concepts are employed with a consciousness of their ambiguity and the blurred nature of their boundaries. Reflecting the subtle and qualified deployment of class analysis, much of the argument in this volume ascribes to ideology an important function in shaping and determining historical action and political behaviour. The power of ideas to take on fresh meanings and outgrow the significance and content attached to them by their original advocates is a recurrent theme throughout the collection. This is not always easy to document; often the popular interpretation of ideology is not given expression in the kind of archival material which provides the staple sources for much of the scholarship reproduced here. The academic examination of South African popular culture still takes place at a considerable social distance from its bearers and participants. This is not a unique problem - proletarian historians are an unusual phenomenon the world over - but in South Africa the chroniclers of popular history are additionally isolated from their subjects by barriers of race, language, and culture, as well as those of class. Much still needs to be accomplished before those barriers can be overcome.

Tom Lodge
Johannesburg, August 1985.

NOTES

1 Previous volumes: P. Bonner ed., <u>Working Papers in Southern African Studies, Papers Presented at the A.S.I. African Studies Seminar</u> (Johannesburg 1977); P. Bonner ed., <u>Working Papers in Southern African Studies, Volume 2</u> (Johannesburg 1981); D. Hindson ed., <u>Working Papers in Southern African Studies, Volume 3</u> (Johannesburg 1983).

2 Though contrary to popular belief, Roth argues, their decision to adjourn the Native Representative Council pre-dated and was not prompted by the 1946 African mineworkers' strike.

The drawing reproduced on the cover is from the Africana Collection at the Johannesburg Public Library. The artist is David Mogano.

Popular Resistance in Namibia, 1920-1925

Tony Emmett

The first five years of the South Africa mandate marked an important milestone in the development of resistance in Namibia. Between 1920 and 1925 resistance against colonial rule assumed a variety of forms unparallelled in Namibian history. The Bondelswarts rebelled in 1922 and the Rehoboth Basters, with their Herero, Damara and Nama allies, in 1925. Further smaller-scale outbursts of violence erupted in other parts of the territory, and rumours of a general black rising were rife amongst both black and white communities. Even the San, who were usually isolated from other black communities by their nomadic existence in marginal parts of the territory, resorted to stock theft and banditry on an unusual scale, becoming embroiled in skirmishes with the police and administrative officials. This period also saw the introduction of new forms of political organisation that transcended pre-colonial divisions and began laying a basis for national unity. Among the organisations that were established during this period were the Universal Negro Improvement Association (UNIA), the Industrial and Commercial Workers' Union (ICU), the African People's Organisation (APO) and the South West Africa National Congress (SWANC). In particular, UNIA with its pan-Africanist platform proved remarkably successful, spreading from the industrial centre of Luderitz to other urban centres, and then to the countryside.

The resistance movements of this phase of Namibian history have thus far received little attention from researchers. The few studies of resistance during this period have concentrated almost exclusively on the two rebellilons[1] and, for the most part, treat these outbursts as discrete episodes unconnected with other manifestations of protest. Very little has been written about the various political organisations that came into being during this period, and where these are mentioned, it is usually in the context of urban centres such as Luderitz and Widhoek.[2] Some of the most striking features of this period such as the diversity and scale of popular involvement and the rich network of relationships connecting the different strands of protest, have therefore gone largely unnoticed.

However, what was especially noteworthy about this phase of resistance was not only its intensity and scale, but the qualitative changes in the prevailing forms of social consciousness and political mobilisation. The early 1920s saw for the first time concerted efforts to transcend the narrow communal divisions of pre-colonial Namibia and to forge a new popular unity by means of innovative ideologies and organisational structures. Prior to this, attempts had been made to limit conflict between indigenous communities and to forge alliances against the colonial incursion, but these alliances had always been between discrete communities and, on the whole, appear to have been tenuous and unsuccessful. One of the tragedies of the great rebellions of 1904-1907 was the failure of the Namas and Hereros to coordinate their revolts. Following the resistance of the early 1920s, the innovative organisations and ideologies that originated during this period disappeared and were replaced by predominantly communal and ethnic forms of mobilization. Defiance and confrontation gave way to accommodation and, where it manifested itself, resistance took more covert and symbolic forms.[3] Although colonial opposition gained momentum during the mid-1940s, it was not until the late 1950s that formal political organisations based on national and popular identifications emerged.

This pattern of resistance raises some general questions about the development of anti-colonial protest. There has been a clear trend in African (and other Third World) studies to emphasise continuities in the development of resistance. Whether this is linked to a unilinear model of progressive westernisation or associated with the process of imperialist and capitalist penetration, the tendency is to depict the development of social movements as a succession of stages or as a progressively unfolding consciousness. The long-surviving notion of "primary" and "secondary" resistance, for example, suggests a clearly defined sequence of stages. Although this distinction originated from the ethnocentric and teleological framework of modernisation theories,[4] slightly modified versions still enjoy respectability, even among "progressive" writers such as Basil Davidson.[5] A related approach is to see early millenarian movements as precursors or progenitors of more "advanced" social movements like nationalism or socialism.[6] Thomas Hodgkin, for example, maintains that African millenarian movements "represent a relative primitive phase in the development of nationalism", while Eli Kedourie argues that "the mainspring of nationalism in Asia and Africa is the same secular millenialism which had its rise and development in Europe ..."[7] More sophisticated analyses of socialist writers like Peter Worsley,[8] Eric Hobsbawn,[9] Allen Isaacman[10] and Charles van Onselen[11] tend to depict early social movements such as millenarianism and "social banditry" as foreshadowing more class-conscious and politically-directed movements.

While a critique of evolutionary perspectives of social change is clearly beyond the scope of this paper, it might tentatively be suggested that more attention needs to be devoted to the discontinuous features of change in Third World formations. As Sholto Cross suggests in a paper on African social movements during World War I, the search for continuities in the development of protest and social consciousness may have helped to obscure qualitative and discontinuous changes.[12] In this paper special emphasis has been placed on the discontinuous features of both colonial policies and resistance in Namibia. The first part of the paper is devoted to an analysis of the social conditions that gave rise to the resistance of the early 1920s, while the latter part deals with the various manifestations of resistance, focusing in particular on the Garveyist movement. The paper closes with a brief analysis of the major reasons for the failure of the resistance during this period.

****

On July 9, 1915 the last German troops defending the colony of South West Africa surrendered to the numerically superior South African forces at Khorab, ending thirty years of German colonial rule and initiating a new phase in Namibian history. With a few limited exceptions,[13] historians have devoted little attention to the five years of military occupation which followed and helped to lay the foundations for permanent South African control of the territory. At the basis of this neglect has been a widely held assumption of an essential continuity between the German and South African administrations of the territory. Although this assumption has taken various forms and been incorporated within a variety of different analytical frameworks, its implications have been consistent: Namibia merely passed from one set of imperialist interests to another, and it continued to evince the typical characteristics of imperialist subjection and capitalist exploitation;[14] the "mode of exploitation" did not "change in the slightest, and its form only in minor aspects";[15] South African rule in Namibia "emulated" that of the Germans;[16] the repression of the Bondelswart rebellion of 1922 demonstrated to the colonised that "under the new rulers nothing had changed for them";[17] the South African administration "reproduced, if in slightly less draconian form, the essentials of the German labour code".[18] As with most misleading propositions, there is an element of truth in the assumption of continuity. The goals and interests underlying South African rule were indeed similar to those of the preceding regime, and South Africa was the direct beneficiary of German policies of domination and expropriation. Exploitation and a highly repressive labour system were the hallmarks of South African rule in Namibia as they were of German rule. These similarities, however, provide only part of a more complex picture which includes some significant breaks with the past.

The change of regimes in Namibia was not simply an isolated event, but was played out against the global shifts of power of the First World War. Capture of the German colonies had been one of the war aims of the allies, and the disposal of these colonies by means of the mandate system was a product of the new alignments of power of the post-World War period. Richard Rathbone has aruged that World War I was a "period of immense and significant change" for Africa. More specifically, the war accelerated the process of political and economic change in colonial Africa, bringing the colonies into more centralised relationships with the metropolitan powers and radically altering the "style" of coloniailism.

> Before 1914 Africa was for the most part a dream for the greedy speculator. From 1918 it seems likely that her role was more centrally related, as part of the empire, to the very heart of the metropolitan economies.[19]

A number of divergent, and sometimes incompatible, requirements and influences helped shape South African policies in the territory during the military occupation. Notwithstanding South Africa's long-standing interests in the German colony, its legal hold over the territory was tenuous. The invasion of German South West Africa had been undertaken on an official understanding with Britain that all occupied territory would be put at it's disposal for an indeterminate settlement at the end of the war. After the successful conclusion of the military campaign, South Africa thus set about establishing its claim to the territory. This was based on two major arguments, that South West Africa was essential for South Africa's national security and, secondly, that the Germans had proved themselves unfit to rule the colony.[20] In order to lay the foundations for its second claim, the South African administration in Namibia began collecting evidence of the injustices and atrocities of German rule of the colony. The evidence was published in an Imperial "Blue Book" in 1918. However, this strategy imposed certain conditions on South Africa's administration of the territory. Clearly it was not only necessary to persuade the world of the inadequacies of German colonial policy, but also to establish that South African rule represented an appropriate improvement on German rule. Certain minimal reforms were thus necessary in order to secure control over the territory.

Besides these requirements there is evidence that South African officials actively disapproved of German colonial practices. While the two regimes shared common interests in exploiting the colony, the South Africans were critical of the costs and efficiency of German policies. As administrator Gorges pointed out to Smuts, it was regrettable that "so many white lives had been lost and so many millions of pounds wasted" on colonial wars which were a result of inappropriate colonial policies. These wars had not only succeeded in destroying large parts of the colonial labour supply, but posed a direct threat to South African interests as "unrest" might spread across the borders into South Africa.[21] The Germans had themselves come to realise the counter-productivity of their policies, and shortly before World War I had begun to introduce reforms in a bid to stabilise the labour force.[22]

The changeover also altered the relationship between administration and settlers. The South African administrators found themselves in the unusual situation of being faced not only with a hostile, or potentially hostile, black population, but also a hostile white population. In the other German colonies, most of the German settlers were expelled or repatriated. Namibia was unique among the mandated territories in retaining a large German community.[23] The possibility of a black rebellion therefore posed a double threat to the military administration, because the German community might take advantage of the opportunity to rebel against the occupying forces and reintroduce German rule.[24] In part therefore, military insecurity favoured a more conciliatory approach to the black population. Far more important, however, was the lack of identification between administration and settlers. Especially during the closing phase of German rule, the settlers had wielded considerable political influence. With the change in colonial regimes, however, the settlers were reduced to the status of enemy subjects, and this allowed the new administration greater freedom to pursue alternative goals and interests. It was not until after the granting of the mandate that the settlers, and in particular the farmer, were able once again to impose their influence on colonial policy.

In spite of a perceived need for change, a number of constraints operated to produce a degree of continuity with the past. For example, the Hague Convention required the occupying power of a conquered territory to limit changes to existing legal and governmental structures. South Africa's tenuous hold over the territory was also a factor limiting change. Not only was the future of the territory undecided, but the new administration experienced a variety of difficulties in the implementation of its policies. These difficulties were associated with the newness and temporary nature of the administration during the period of martial law, and included staff shortages, lack of experience and information on local conditions and the incompetence of local officials and police. Under these circumstances, policy options were severely limited.

A prominent feature of German colonial rule was that it telescoped the colonial process into a relatively contracted period, achieving the expropriation of Police Zone blacks and the creation of a rigidly controlled labour force within little more than 20 years. The brutal suppression of the 1904-1907 rebellions and the dramatic finality of the expropriation of most Namibians in the southern and central parts of the country, were reflected in the laws promulgated in the post-rebellion period. Legislation introduced immediately after the rebellions aimed not only at the destruction of indigenous economic power (and thus the creation of a servile labour force), but also at the destruction of indigenous social and political organisation. With a few minor exceptions such as the Berseba Namas, the Bondelswarts and the Rehoboth Basters, blacks in the Police Zone were prohibited from owning or obtaining land and large stock. The law also forbade more than ten families or individuals from residing on any farm or property. The pass laws compelled all blacks above age of seven to register as labourers and to wear brass badges in addition to carrying a diensbuch (service book) with them. Blacks without labour contracts had no legal rights, and all whites had the power to arrest them. The police were empowered to administer direct punishment (without the control of a court) to black servants for a variety of offences including "laziness", "negligence", "vagrancy", "insolence" and "disobedience". As the simplest and least expensive form of punishment, flogging was used extensively during the German period. Between January 1, 1913 and March 31, 1914, for example, there were 2,787 "sentences" to lashes and 46,719 individual lashes administered. In terms of the semi-legal vaterliche zuchtigungsrecht ("right of parental chastisement"), employers were allowed to mete out beatings to their labourers. Questions were only raised in those cases where labourers were hospitalised or died from their beatings, and even then the situation was rationalised. As the German governor Leutwein saw it, "beating to death was not regarded as murder; but the natives were unable to understand such legal subtleties."[25]

Taken individually, the changes[26] introduced by the South African administration during the period of martial law appear both superficial and insignificant. The German system of registration, together with the diensbuch (service book) and brass badge, were abolished and replaced by a pass law. The age of those required to carry passes was raised from seven to fourteen, and "Certificates of Exemption from Labour" provided for those who could show "visible means of support". To qualify for this certificate the applicant had to own at least ten head of large or fifty head of small stock. As under the German law, blacks were barred from obtaining any right or title to fixed property without the consent of the administrator. They were, however, allowed to acquire and own livestock. This, the Deputy-Secretary of Native Affairs in Windhoek reasoned, would "tend to make the native more contented and law abiding".[27] The South African administration clearly did not envisage that the right to own cattle would be allowed to interfere with the flow of labour, rather it saw the right as an inducement to accept labour.

Although, ultimately, the South African authorities subscribed to the same objective of labour control, they insisted that this control should be more centralised and that there should be a stricter separation of magisterial and police functions. In other words, labour control was seen as the prerogative of the state, not of the individual employer backed up by the state. There was thus, during the period of martial law, a growing tendency for the central authority to define and regulate relations between blacks and whites, employers and employees. Between 1916 and 1920 the Masters and Servants law was revised twice, in order to make the regulation of labour relations more comprehensive and detailed. Besides carefully defining the respective obligations of employers and employees, the Masters and Servants laws outlawed the practice of "fatherly correction" (whereby white employers had the right to beat their servants) and put a stop to the practice of flogging which magistrates were urged to "make special efforts" to prevent.

> It should be widely made known to the native that masters and policemen have no power to flog, and any complaints of flogging must be carefully investigated and that the offender prosecuted without respect of person.[28]

Spurred on by the need to discredit the former German regime and to contrast German rule with its own, the South African administration actively enforced the new provisions of the law. Between September 1915 and January 1918 more than 310 cases involving ill-treatment of black servants were brought before the lower courts alone.[29] The more serious cases of murder and assault against white settlers were given prominent attention in the 1918 Blue Book and elsewhere.

The real significance of these changes, however, lay not so much in their direct contribution to reform, but in the effects produced by their combination with surviving elements of German policy. As already argued, South African policy in Namibia during the military occupation was shaped by a variety of contradictory influences and constraints, so that what finally emerged was a combination of both German and South African colonial policies. While these policies shared the common goal of exploiting the labour resources of the colony, they were not necessarily compatible as they differed in the means they employed to secure this common goal. Furthermore, the situation was complicated by two additional factors. The need to discredit German rule and project an image which would be acceptable to the international community was a factor which was extraneous to the normal concerns of a labour-extractive system. It helped to produce, in the upper echelons of the administration, a tentative liberalism which was out of step with the rest of the social formation and which quickly evaporated after the granting of the Mandate. A second set of complications resulted from the logistic difficulties associated with creating a new administration under the conditions of war.

While it retained the general framework of the German forced labour system, the South African administration removed some of the means by which labour had been extracted. German labour policy was dependent on a generalised and decentralised system of violence for its survival. When the South Africans administration prohibited the practices of flogging and "parental chastisement" strains occurred within the system of control. Instead of being able to "discipline" their labourers themselves, farmers were now obliged to travel to the seat of the district magistracy. This often involved the inconveniences of long journeys and of being absent from their farms for a number of days.[30] Besides the loss of time and other expenses entailed, the farmers feared that absence from their farms would result in other labourers deserting, stealing their stock, or neglecting to take proper care of their farms.[31] In addition, there was the uncertainty of whether the farmer would be able to secure a conviction against his servant as some of the magistrates were regarded as too "lenient".[32] However, in those cases where a conviction was secured and the labourer was sentenced to a term of imprisonment, the farmer would be deprived of his labour for that period. According to colonial officials, black labourers were aware of of their employers' dependence on them and took some satisfaction in serving jail sentences because this deprived their employers of their labour.[33]

A second policy conflict arose out of the relaxation of the German restrictions on the ownership of stock. While the ban on the ownership of large stock was repealed and provision made for the exemption of certain black stock-owners from the labour requirement, no clear policy emerged for the allocation of land to the colonised. The German law which prohibited blacks from obtaining "any right or title to fixed property" remained in force, and the question of reserves was held in abeyance until after the granting of the Mandate. This inconsistency in the policy of the military administration held a number of important implications. As the number of black owned stock increased, so obviously did the need for land. In order to meet the land shortage black stock owners adopted a variety of strategies. In some cases they simply moved onto vacant Crown land or unoccupied farms. Some of these squatter settlements were later recognised as temporary reserves by the administration. Squatting on white farms also became common during this period, particularly as it provided a source of labour at a time of severe labour shortage. In other cases government, municipal or private land was hired for grazing. Temporary reserves like Orumba and Okatumba in the Windhoek magisterial district soon became overstocked and overcrowded. As a result conflicts arose with the white farmers who complained of stock thefts and trespassing on their land.[34] When more permanent reserves were finally established in the early 1920s, the administration decided to close the temporary reserves and met with strong resistance from their occupants.[1] The accumulation of stock by blacks who had been formerly prohibited from doing so, also threatened the interests of settler farmers. Settlers complained that their farms were being overrun by the stock of their labourers. They claimed that if they tried to limit the number of stock kept by their servants, they ran the risk of losing them - a serious eventuality in a situation of chronic labour shortage.[35]

The incompatible influences at work in the transitional colonial policies of the military period led also to conflicts between the police and senior administrative officials. The police who had been recruited from South Africa and identified closely with the settler farmers, did not understand or share the views of senior officials who wish to present an enlightened image of the South African administration of Namibia.[36] The magistrate of Outjo complained to the Secretary for the Protectorate in 1920 that distrust between police administrative personnel had resulted in "a want of that harmony between magistrate and police which is so essential to the good administration of any District, while it also encourages the native to think that the police are in the wrong and are inimical to them thus leading to the insolent attitude complained of - an attitude in marked contrast to what it was under German rule".[37]

The problems experienced with the police were but one symptom of a more general malaise that permeated the administration. The magistrate of Okahandja succinctly summed up the situation in 1920:

> When one looks back at the past four and a half years with what we have had to contend - dealing with an hostile population, wholly insufficient and inefficient staffs, incompetent and almost useless police, a complete change of native policy, the disorder on active warfare, and, above all, an Administration which was necessarily unstable and to a certain extent temporary and uncertain - it is not to be wondered at that conditions today are still far from ideal or even satisfactory. The instructions laid down in the native memorandum (of 1916) ... were a big step forward in the right direction. Unfortunately - and here I think one touches on the crux of the whole matter - it has not been found possible in the absence of constant and firm supervision, with the staff and police at our disposal, to carry out the excellent directions laid down.[38]

This administrative malaise served not only to create friction within the ranks of the administration, but also impaired the control the colonial state was able to exercise over the colonised, preventing it from effectively executing those functions of dominance and control central to the colonial enterprise. Within this context the black work force was able to devise various strategies to resist or by-pass the system of forced labour. Although desertion had become a well-established tactic even under German rule, shortages and inefficiency of police, the removal of police powers from the settlers, and the general inefficiency and lack of control of the administration made desertion and the withholding of labour an even more attractive and feasible prospect during the period of martial law. The disruptions and confusion caused by the military campaign and change of administrations provided further opportunities for desertion and other forms of resistance. Following the Union's invasion and occupation of the territory, desertions, particularly from farms, reached unprecedented heights,[39] precipitating a severe labour crisis, especially among farmers. Another way of circumventing the repressive labour system was by accumulating enough stock to qualify for an exemption certificate. The magistrate of Otjiwarongo reported in 1920 that "the Herero" was "straining every nerve to acquire large and small stock, in order that he may again become independent and relieved of the necessity of working". He maintained that between 1914 and 1920 black-owned small stock had increased from "no more than a few hundred" to more than 4,000 in his district.[40] In the minds of both the settler and the authorities, the dramatic increase in black-owned stock was closely linked to increasing stock thefts during this period. Although the available evidence makes it difficult to confirm or refute this link, it would appear that losses of small stock in particular were very heavy. It was even alleged that because of stock theft small stock farming was no longer viable in the territory.[41]

However, for the majority of blacks in Namibia the strategies outlined above were not immediately available. At the low wages paid during this period, it would have been impossible for most blacks to obtain sufficient stock to qualify for exemption from forced labour. Strategies such as stock theft, desertion and living in the veld held their own limitations and difficulties. Even for those who were able to acquire exemption certificates, problems still arose as to where they could keep their stock as there was little land available to black stock-owners during this period. In the situation the majority of Blacks fell back on the widespread strategy adopted in other parts of Africa against forced labour, poor wages and other conditions of colonial repression. In the words of the settlers and colonial authorities, they became "insolent", "lazy", "inefficient", "unreliable" and "negligent". By 1920 complaints of this sort had reached a climax and permeated every level of the settler community.[42] The administration showed some awareness of the relationship between the inefficiency of the black labour and the repressive labour policy of the state. The magistrate of Otjiwarongo, for example, referred to "a passive resistance movement, at present confined to doing the work as badly as possible"[43] and the Secretary for the Protectorate pointed out that "large numbers" of blacks

> work only because the law compels them to do so, and in consequence they do their work with very little grace and with only so much effort as circumstances demand. This is the reason for the general complaint about the inefficiency of labour in this country ...[44]

Another unanticipated consequence of the change in colonial administration during the World War I was the generation of unrealistic, but firmly held, expectations of reform among the black population. The defeat of the German colonial power during the war helped foster the belief that their lands would be returned to them. As late as 1946, a Herero witness told Michael Scott:

> What we don't understand is that when two nations have been at war, such as Britain or Germany or Italy, and when one or other of those nations is defeated the lands belonging to that nation are not taken away from them. That nation remains a nation, and their lands belong to them. The African people although they have always been on the side of British people and their allies, yet have their lands taken away from them and are treated as though they had been conquered.[45]

Expectations like these appear to have been widespread among Police Zone blacks during the military period. It is probable that these beliefs were encouraged by reforms adopted during this period. Although these were only minor concessions, war propaganda, the prosecution of German employers, and the tensions that existed between settlers, police, and administrators undoubtedly made an impact on Namibians. These expectations were, however, to be rudely shattered in the period that immediately followed the military administration, and played a significant role in the concerted resistance to colonial rule between 1920 and 1925.

It was against this background that South Africa was granted the mandate over Namibia. The new security of tenure that came with the mandate meant that the colonial administration needed no longer to pander to international opinion by presenting a liberal image to the world. Colonial policies could now follow colonial interests, and the paternalism of the interim military administration could be stripped away to reveal the grim realities and requirements of the settler economy. With the end of the war and the international recognition of South Africa's right to Namibia, the German settlers could be welcomed back into the fold as fellow whites and colonial masters. There was no longer a need, as there had been in the earlier period, to depict them as brutal and vicious in their treatment of blacks.[46]

Changes in colonial policy in Namibia after 1920 were not only a response to the new international status of the territory, but also reflected the deepening political crisis in South Africa where the government was coming under increasing pressure from Afrikaner nationalists and militant labour.[47] From the beginning Botha and Smuts regarded Namibia as a potential safety-valve for the political pressures building up in South Africa. Even before the German forces in Namibia had surrendered, Botha wrote to Smuts about the possibility of using the lures of land and jobs to neutralise dissatisfaction, particularly amongst the Afrikaners.

> We shall have to make a point of it in the elections that the territory will now afford an opening particularly for acquiring land, as well as an opening in the police and administration.[48]

Following the South African occupation of the territory, the military administration devoted considerable attention to restoring farming, commerce and industry in the territory. Mining was resumed although on a smaller scale than previously and farming flourished owing to the ready markets for farm produce during and immediately after the war. Not only did the presence of the Union garrison provide a market within the territory, but there were also excellent markets for slaughter stock both in South Africa and overseas. The abnormal prices realised for stock resulted in high values being placed on land. Partly because of the high values of land and the uncertain future of the territory, few settlers entered the country during this period. The smallness of the settler population in turn ensured that the level of agricultural production would remain low, thus maintaining the high prices.[49]

However, within two years of the war the economic boom came to an end, and by 1922 the territory, along with other parts of the world, had entered the depths of the post-war recession. The disbandment of the military garrison after the war meant that an important local market for farm produce was lost. The end of the war had also seen the reorganisation of agriculture on a world scale and the consequent contraction of markets for slaughter stock and other produce both in South Africa and overseas. At the same time a severe drought overtook the territory. The situation deteriorated further with the reversal of the inflow of capital from Germany to the territory, and the severe slump in diamonds and other major mineral products of Namibia.[50]

With the establishment of the mandate, a more sympathetic policy was adopted to the settler community early in 1921 an Advisory Council was appointed to represent settler interests, and played a prominent role in shaping colonial policies of this period.[51] An extensive settlement scheme, based on the grossly over-optimistic recommendations of the Farmers' Produce Commission,[52] was launched in the second half of 1920. The scheme coincided with the onset of recession and drought, and by 1921 most of the new settlers and even some of the more established farmers were in serious financial difficulties. Rather than back down on its settlement policy, the administration continued to dispose of large quantitites of land to South African settlers, many of whom had neither the financial resources nor the farming experience to cope with the harsh demands of the Namibian environment. In support of this short-sighted scheme, the administration provided extensive financial aid to the white farming community, and increased pressures on indigenous communities to provide labour to the largely unviable farming operations.[53] Both strategies were to have disastrous consequences. The pressures put on indigenous communities were to provide a major impetus to the revolts of the Bondelswarts and the Basters, while the aid provided to settlers only succeeded in encouraging dependence on state aid and ensuring the short-termed survival of essentially unviable farming ventures.

The vigorous settlement policy also had implications for the allocation of reserves. Essentially, the reserves policy that was initiated in the early 1920s emerged out of the contradictory blend of South African and German policies that characterised the military period. In South Africa the major thrust of native policy had been to frame legislation and administrative devices to draw labour out of the reserves. German colonial policies in Namibia, on the other hand, had attempted the proletarianization of the majority of the population in the Police Zone by means of military force. The existence of a large landless population, however, posed problems of control for the South African administration in the territory. The policy that emerged during the early 1920s was therefore an attempt to steer a course between the two contradictory demands of establishing reserves (in order to facilitate control, reverse, or at least control, black urbanisation, and standardise administrative procedures) and, at the same time, ensure an adequate supply of labour. As the Native Affairs official Captain Bowker pointed out in 1916, the two goals were not necessarily incompatible:

> It may prove more economical to consider the possibility of establishing one large settlement for all the Protectorate Natives in an area such as the Kaokoveld, where the natives would be entirely segregated from the European Farming community, and from which, through economic pressure, they would be forced to seek employment, the labour market thus not being seriously affected; on the contrary, it is felt, that such a course would act as a stimulus to labour, for the natives would be under closer control and the payment of such taxes as may be levied could be effectually enforced and such money would have to be earned.[54]

In addition to these considerations, provision had to be made to accommodate the livestock accumulated by landless blacks and those in the overcrowded "temporary reserves". It was also hoped that the allocation of reserves would go some way towards meeting black land demands and the expectations generated by the change in regimes. In broad outlines therefore the policy of the early mandate administration made provision for the creation of reserves to accommodate the residents of the temporary reserves, squatters on both white farms and the Rehoboth Gebiet, and the "surplus" populations of the urban areas. The amount of land allocated was, however, strictly controlled. Furthermore, land was allocated largely in marginal areas of the country which were less suitable for farming. A variety of economic pressures such as grazing fees, dog taxes and the strict control of "informal sector" economic activities were imposed to facilitate the efflux of migrant labour. These measures were incorporated into an over-arching system of legislative and administrative controls which applied to all blacks in the country.

In terms of the 1921 recommendations of the Native Reserves Commission, 655,650 hectares would be allocated for the proposed reserves and a further 636,881 hectares "in case of future extension, or of unsuitability of the proposed reserves". Together with the reserves that had been created during the German period, the total allocation of land for Africans, as envisaged by the Commission, amounted to 2,237,874 hectares.[55] This was only slightly more than the 2,125,154 that had been allocated to 311 settlers in 1921 alone.[56] In spite of the meagreness of the proposed areas, the opening of the reserves was delayed by drought and inadequate water supplies.[57] By the end of 1923, 634,000 hectares had been allocated. The insignificance of this area can be gauged from a comparison with the more than 1,9 million hectares allocated for settlers in 1922 and 1923 at the height of the drought. A further 349,782 hectares were added to the reserves in 1924 and about 754,360 in 1925.[58] With the proclamation of Otjimbingwe (77,498 hectares) after 1925, the programme of the Reserves Commission was completed.[59]

Grazing fees were extended to all reserves with the exception of those granted under German treaty. Livestock was taxed on a sliding scale with the obvious intention of limiting the number of animals kept on the reserves. Thus large stock was taxed on the basis of 1 d. per head per mensem for one to twenty five head, and 3 d. for herds of twenty six or more. Similarly the grazing fee for small stock was 1/4 d. for herds of 100 or less and ½ d. for those above 100.[60] That the major aim of grazing fees was to ensure a steady flow of labour for the reserves is made clear by the report of the Native Reserves Commission 1928.[61] In the reserves recognised by German treaties, grazing taxes were not imposed. However, a dog tax , also based on a sliding scale, was levied under Proclamation No. 16 of 1921.[62] Particularly in the early twenties the tax proved an effective instrument for forcing labourers from these reserves onto the labour market and was an important contributory cause in the Bondelswart rising of 1922. To bolster the reserve system, a battery of laws and regulations were passed between 1920 and 1922.[63] These included amendments to the Masters and Servants laws, a vagrancy law, and a series of regulations making provision for the removal of squatters from Crown and Mission land, the control of movement of all blacks in the territory, the branding of black-owned cattle and the control of blacks in urban areas.

To sum up, the first five years of the mandate saw an important shift in colonial policies, away form the limited reformism of the military period and towards a more rigorous system of control. In part this shift was a result of the administration's need to rationalise its policies, both by bringing them more in line with those in the Union and by resolving the contradictions that had arisen from the blending of South African and German colonial policies during the military period. It flowed also out of the greater security of tenure provided by the mandate, the deepening political crisis in South Africa, and the ill-timed and short-sighted settlement policy to which these two developments gave rise. Perhaps the most crucial factor in the configuration of events that contributed to the resistance of the early 1920s was the extreme vulnerability of settler agriculture in Namibia during this period. The marginality of settler farmers made them heavily dependent on extra-economic coercion to ensure a supply of cheap and servile labour.

This is vividly illustrated by the conditions that gave rise to Bondelswarts rebellion of 1922. Conflict between the Bondelswarts and white farmers was evident from the beginning of South African rule. In 1915, for example, the Native Affairs Department reported that although the Bondelswarts were "anxious to obtain employment ... several absolutely set their faces against accepting work with farmers. On being asked the reason I was told in almost every instance, that farmers were used to dispense Justice without reference to anyone". There could be little doubt, the Department argued, that the "great shortage of farm labour" was a natural reaction to the "ill- treatment meted out to farm labourers in the past, by German and Dutch farmers alike". In spite of this the Department was using "every effort and persuasion" to induce the local black population to accept farm labour.[64] In the same year the officer in charge of Native Affairs reported that several incidents had been brought to his notice

> where farmers engage boys at 15/- per month, and when paying them off, they give them the equivalent in stock. The equivalent of a goat usually being 15/- ... I need need not point out that 15/- ... is much in excess of the value of an ordinary breeding goat, which is worth from 5/- to 10/- according to size.[65]

Nor had the situation changed for the better in 1920 when the military magistrate of Warmbad blamed deteriorating relationships between whites and blacks in the area on the "poor wages, improper treatment (and) poor food" to which farm labourers were subjected. The farmers, he said,

> look upon the Hottentots as a kind of animal, not a human being and his first impression is that a Hottentot because he is a Hottentot should have a hiding once a day.[66]

Many of the settlers attracted to the Protectorate by low interest loans, were farmers possessing little capital or stock and contemptuously known as "bokboere" (goat farmers) by the more established settlers. The portion of these already marginal settler farmers deteriorated further as a result of the poor rains between 1918 and 1920, and the severe drought of 1921-22. Complaints about poor wages and the withholding of pay were already common during the military period, and the situation could only deteriorate under the combined assault of the drought and recession of the early 1920s. The administrator, for example, reported in 1922 that because of the depression, "many farmers not of the really poor class, unfortunately find themselves unable to pay wages in cash and some are unable to feed their employees properly". Although the administration was opposed to the payment of wages in kind, the administrator said he saw no immediate "option but to countenance the payment of wages in kind where the native does not object".[67]

It is one of the ironies of the build up to the Bondelswart rebellion that at a time when the administration was sanctioning the payment of wages in kind, it should impose an absurdly high tax to force the Bondelswarts into the labour market. A dog tax of 5/- was first introduced in the rural areas in 1917, but under pressure from farmers, the administration in 1921 increased the tax to £1 for the first dog, £2/10/- for two dogs, £4/10- for three dogs, £7 for four dogs, and £10 for five dogs.[68] Dogs played an important role in the Bondelswarts economy. Not only were they used for hunting, but they were essential for the protection from, and destruction of vermin, particularly jackals. In those cases where the dog tax was not paid, the police were empowered to seize and destroy dogs. Prosecution of Bondelswarts for non-payment of the tax commenced in September 1921, and by January 1922 the Warmbad Magistrate had tried 140 cases.[69] The average sentence was a fine of £2 or fourteen days imprisonment. In addition to the dog tax, the Bondelswarts were subjected to a variety of other pressures and regulations such as the strictly enforced game laws, which put further obstacles in the way of hunting, and quarantine regulations which prevented the Bondelswarts from selling livestock on the most profitable markets.

Another key issue which helped to precipitate the Bondelswarts rebellion revolved around the appointment of a captain for the community. A labour extraction system of the type that operated in Namibia during the early mandate period, was not only dependent on the state to dislodge a labour force from the countryside, but also required the assistance of the state to counteract any political or military organisation (or even individual defiance) on the part of the labour force or potential labour force. In the case of the Bondelswart community, the past rebellions and military successes of the Bondelswarts were a potent source of anxiety for the settlers. As the Bondelswarts had been able to maintain a territorial base in spite of their rebellion against the German colonial authorities, they were able to retain a certain degree of communal identity and political organisation. Settlers and state thus sought to limit and control the political organisation of the BOndelswarts. These efforts largely took the form of preventing the Bondelswarts from obtaining effective leadership. Until 1918 the state resisted all moves to secure the appointment of a captain. The position of the administration was clearly stated by the magistrate of Warmbad in 1917:

> I cannot in my opinion too strongly advise the Administration not to appoint a Captain or Chief over the Bondelswarts as that would immediately combine the nation which could then give endless trouble.[70]

Although the administration continued to resist the appointment of Jacobus Christian, the most influential leader of the Bondelswarts, between 1918 and 1922 it sanctioned the appointments of three captains for the Bondelswarts. The first, Willem Christian, was described by the local magistrate as a "harmless idiot who was incapable of influencing his people in any way or even showing any interest in them". He was followed by Hendrik Schneeuwe, who had to be removed after he was accused of embezzling tribal funds. Timotheus Beukes, described by the Chief Native Commissioner as having "no desire or particular ability" to lead the Bondelswarts, then assumed the captaincy.[71] Ultimately, it was the return of the legitimate and effective Bondelswart leaders, Jacobus Christian and Abraham Morris, from Namaqualand, that precipitated the rebellion of 1922.

****

Having sketched in the context that gave rise to the resistance of the early 1920s in the first part of this paper, this section will examine some of specific manifestations of that resistance. As the rebellions of 1922 and 1925 have already been adequately documented,[72] they will not be dealt with here, except to place them within the broader context of resistance. Instead this section of the paper will focus predominantly on the Universal Negro Improvement Association (UNIA) which provided the ideological nexus around which the various strands of resistance coalesced and began to obtain the coherence of a movement.

The Universal Negro Improvement Association and African Communities League (UNIA & ACL) was launched in Luderitz in 1921. The catalyst for the formation of this branch of the Garveyist organisation was a small group of West Africans and West Indians who had settled largely in the coastal towns of the territory. The majority of this group originated from Liberia, the Cameroons, Sierra Leone and the Gold Coast, and had been brought into the territory by the Germans before and during World War I. In 1910, for example, fifty men and a number of women and children were deported from the German colony of Kamerun to Luderitz, following a mutiny among the black Schutztruppe in the West African colony. The majority of this group were returned to West Africa after the occupation of Namibia by South African forces, but a number who were working in Luderitz stayed behind.[73] Other West Africans, particularly the Liberians, had been brought to Namibia by the Woermann shipping company. Some of these had been deck hands on the Woermann ships and had been stranded in Luderitz and other coastal towns when war broke out in 1914.[74]

While they intermarried with the local people, the West Africans formed a distinctive segment of the Namibian population. As a group they had a higher level of education and greater urban and industrial skills than the local population and some earned relatively high wages. Others lived on the fringes of their communities supporting themselves by gambling or petty crime. The magistrate of Luderitz and Swakopmund complained frequently about the "gambling and thieving propensities" of the West Africans in their districts. The West Africans were "the cause of a lot of trouble", the magistrate of Luderitz complained in 1920. Many of them lived "by swindling the aborigines of their hard earned wages by card sharping".[75] The police believed that they were "corrupting" the local blacks and were the cause of an escalating crime rate in Luderitz, but perhaps most troublesome to the administration were the "political inclinations" of some of the West Africans.[76]

The first formal connection between Namibia and the Garveyist organisation occurred in 1919 when the UNIA sent commissioners to the Versailles Peace Conference in an unsuccessful attempt to influence the plans being framed for the former German colonies.[77] In 1922 a UNIA delegation was sent to Geneva to petition the League of Nations to turn the former German colonies over to black leadership. The League was also urged to appoint a black representative to the permanent Mandates Commission. Another petition relating to the mandates was issued by Garvey in 1928, but enjoyed as little success as the first attempt.[78] Although Garvey's ambitions for the former German colonies failed to have any impact on the international status of the colonies, the ideas propagated by his organisation were of considerable significance to political developments in Namibia. In fact Garveyism and its various mutant versions provided the first coherent, if somewhat fanciful, ideological framework within which the various Namibian communities could unite in their efforts to resist colonialism.

Towards the end of 1921 the Luderitz branch of UNIA had a membership of 311 and had collected £41/10/0 in subscription fees. Given the size of the black population of Luderitz (2,155 according to the 1921 census) and the low wages of the overwhelming majority, this was a considerable achievement. The organisation catered for both the welfare and the political needs of its members. Its welfare benefits included assistance in time of sickness, funeral expenses, and financial assistance of relatives of deceased members. Its membership covered the whole spectrum of black groups, both local and foreign, in Luderitz.[79]

Two members of the UNIA executive are mentioned recurrently in the administration's files. Fritz Headley, the president, was clearly the dominant figure in the organisation, and John de Clue was a prominent member of both the UNIA and the ICU. Both men were describd as West Indians. John de Clue was the owner of a cafe in the black township, while Headley was chief stevedore at the Luderitz docks and earned a daily salary of seven shillings plus rations.[80] According to a summary of wages drawn up by Native Affairs Department of Luderitz from labour contracts approved by the Department the average daily wage for blacks ranged between one shilling and 2/6.[81] When members of the UNIA and ICU in Luderitz broke away from these two organisations to form the SWA African National Congress, the reason given was that the two organisations were dominated by West Africans and South African blacks respectively.

The issues taken up by the Luderitz branch of UNIA were also indicative of the distinctive interests of its leadership. Although the organisation called for a unity and freedom from colonial oppression on behalf of all blacks, these appeals were characteristically couched in the vaguest of terms. On the other hand, where the Luderitz branch expressed more concrete grievances, it was representing the interests of a small and privileged minority, a distinctive and largely foreign black petty bourgeoisie. This is clearly illustrated by a letter written by Headley, as president of the Luderitz branch, to the <u>Negro</u>

World in 1921.[82] Headley begins his letter with a protest against the "tyrannical system of serfdom and injustice" applied in Luderitz and other parts of Namibia. Towards the end of the letter he criticises the inadequate medical facilities provided for blacks in Luderitz. However, sandwiched between this show of altruism, and taking up the larger part of the letter, is a clearly spelt out appeal on behalf of black traders in Luderitz. This marginal trading class established four small businesses in the black township, but were being threatened by white-owned stores operating on the periphery of the township. The question of black trading rights in Luderitz was a leading issue for both UNIA and the ICU. When black delegations representing these organisations petitioned the magistrate of Luderitz in 1921 and the Native Commissioner in March 1922, black trading rights were a central grievance.[83] This issue also came up in correspondence between the Luderitz branch of the ICU and Kadalie.[84] In this regard it is perhaps significant that at least one of the owners of the four black businesses in Luderitz, John de Clue, was a prominent member of both the UNIA and ICU.

However, once the movement spread beyond Luderitz, its composition and activities underwent fundamental changes. In particular, the Windhoek branch of the organisation assumed a character markedly different from that of the Luderitz branch, although the initiative for its formation had come from Luderitz and it was initially run by West Africans.[85] By January 1922 when the Windhoek branch applied to the local municipality for permission to erect a hall for the organisation, the executive of the branch had already come under the control of local black leaders. Herero leaders, in particular, were prominent in the organisation. These included Hosea Kutako, who was later to emerge as the dominant figure in Herero politics and one of the most powerful Namibian leaders until the formation of the nationalist organisations in the late 1950s, Aaron (John) Mungunda the brother of Kutako, Traugott Maherero, the Herero leader of Okahandja and Nikanor Hoveka, another prominent Herero leader and later headman of the Epukiro Reserve. Although the Hereros appeared to be the dominant force in the Windhoek branch, the leaders of other groups were also represented on the executive. The Damara leaders, Alpheus Harasemab and Franz Hoisemab, were both on the executive.[86] During 1922 the president of the Windhoek Branch was Aaron Mungunda, although the administration suspected, with some justification, that his brother, Hosea Kutako, was "the controlling spirit". The chairman was Solomon Monguya, a Xhosa employed by the Railways, and the secretary Clements Kapuuo, the father of Clements Kapuuo who was to become leader of the powerful Herero tribal grouping after the death of Kutako.[87]

The UNIA spread rapidly in Windhoek and it surrounding areas. According to the leaders of the Zwartboois, a Nama grouping which was opposed to the organisation, "almost all the natives of Windhoek and also of the farms of the districts" had joined the organisation by the end of 1922. These included both "black" (Herero, Damara, etc.) and "yellow" (Nama) people.[88] In November 1922 the Department of Native Affairs inspected the books of the organisation and found that 871 members had paid the required 3/3 entrance fee. The membership of the organisation was probably much larger than indicated by the subscription figures because the office bearers were unable to account for all the money in its bank account, and subscriptions were also "very much in arrears". Membership of the organisation was open to all blacks in the territory, and Windhoek office-holders stated that they "intended establishing branches in Okahandja, Karibib and Usakos, and in the course of time throughout the protectorate".[89] Although the Department of Native Affairs, Windhoek, found it "significant" that control of the Windhoek branch had shifted from its West African founders to local groups,[90] West Africans continued to play a role in the Windhoek organisation. Two Liberians, for example, accompanied the delegation which met Native Affairs official Harry Drew in November 1922. There are indications, however, of tensions between the West African and local members of the Windhoek branch. Drew remarked that at the conclusion of his meeting with the UNIA leaders, representatives of the two groups of leaders (i.e. Liberians and Hereros) asked for private interviews with him.[91] The relationship between the Windhoek and Luderitz branches was also ambiguous. The petition of the Windhoek branch to establish a hall for the organisation was, for example, supported by a letter from Headley, the president of the Luderitz branch. It appears also that at this early stage (February 1922) Headley was recognised as president of the Windhoek branch. However, subsequently the two branches attempted to expand into other parts of the territory independently of one another. Headley made use of West African and West Indian contacts in attempting to establish branches of the organisation in Swakopmund and Usakos, while the indigenous UNIA leaders relied on more indigenous channels and structures.[92]

While the administration saw the suspicion between the foreign and local components of UNIA as a product of ethnic hostilities or of the opportunism and dishonesty of the foreign element, more fundamental differences divided the two groups. The foreign group was not only materially privileged in relation to the indigenous population, but was also self-conscious of its advantage in terms of Western education. Headley, for example, maintained that illiterates should not be office-holders in UNIA "for nowdays a man who cannot read and write for himself is nothing else but a fool to this movement ..."[93] Investigation by administrative officials of the Windhoek branch of UNIA disclosed that the predominantly local leaders of the organisation "are hampered by want of education in regard to which they seem ambitious".[94]

Headley and the other UNIA leaders in Luderitz also appeared to be unable to understand conditions in other parts of the territory. Besides the specific class interests of many of the Luderitz leaders, the UNIA executive was hampered by the isolation of Luderitz and the special circumstances that existed there. Even today, the town of Luderitz is cut off from its hinterland by the Namib. The nearest permanent settlement is at Aus, more than 100 kms away. The desert terrain surrounding the town is of little or no use for agriculture, and Luderitz has therefore relied almost exclusively on the diamond mines and fishing industry. Furthermore, in the 1920s the labour force consisted largely of foreign and migrant workers. Coloured and African labourers from South Africa and further afield were accorded special privileges, while Ovambo migrants were isolated from the town by strict control of the compounds. Given these circumstances, it is understandable that the UNIA executive in Luderitz was incapable of comprehending the tensions that existed in other parts of the territory, and which in 1922/3 had brought blacks and whites to the brink of a state of war. In 1922, for example, Joseph Hailand, a UNIA member in Usakos, had written to Headley asking what could be done to alleviate the oppression of government and farmers, and expressing alarm about the way in which local whites were arming themselves. Headley replied that he did not "know of any war between white and blacks".

> We are living in a peaceful state down this way in Luderitz, both white and blacks, alike, and I dosn't (sic) see the cause of anybody arming themselves. One thing that I will ask all of my people is to obey the laws of the Government, and abide by the Constitution of the Protectorate, and I am sure that the Government, or the Farmers, cannot molest you ...[95]

The attitude adopted by Headley and other literate or semi-literate West Indians and West Africans to the overwhelmingly illiterate indigenous population was often blatantly paternal. In a letter to a local newspaper in March 1924, for example, Headley described the objects of the UNIA in the following terms:

> To establish a universal Confraternity among the race: to promote the spirit of pride and love; to reclaim the fallen; to administer to and assist the needy; to assist in civilising the backward Tribes of Africa; to assist in the development of independent Negro Nations and Communities or Agencies in the principal countries and Cities of the World; for the representation and protection of all Negroes irrespective of nationality; to promote conscientious worship among the natives of Africa; to establish Universities, Colleges, Academies and schools for the racial Education and Culture of the people; to conduct a world wide Commercial and Industrial Intercourse for the good of the people;[96] to work for better conditions in all Negro Communities.

Even if one overlooks the inherent paternalism and vague, high-flown terminology of this passage (which was clearly aimed at the white readers of the newspaper), the aims outlined by Headley were hopelessly remote from the pressing needs and interests of the local population, struggling for survival in the rural areas. In the same letter, the UNIA president went on to argue that

> ... the Negroe's that are domociled in the Protectorate (SWA), has as much interest at stake into the Financial and Industrial development of the Republic of Liberia, as he has at the present time, if any, in the Windhoek Native Location ...

Local leaders of the Windhoek branch approached the administration in July 1922 to obtain permission for some of their leaders to travel to New York, where Garvey had his headquarters. The three leaders who were to make the trip included the Windhoek president, Aaron Mungunda, and two others, one a Nama and the other a Herero. The plan was squashed by the Native Commissioner who "suggested various difficulties in the way even if permission were granted".[97]

Windhoek leaders thus concentrated their attention on propagating the aims of their organisation in other parts of the territory. In October and November 1922 Mungunda and Theodore Hanbanue, a Damara, visited Karibib, Usakos and Okahandja in order to hold meetings with the local black population. It is clear from the response they received that the ideas of the UNIA had already penetrated the areas beyond Windhoek and generated considerable interest. According to the report of a police spy at Usakos, Mungunda urged "the black men to pull together and to unite as one and then they will get their liberty as this is their land". He explained the strength of the whites in terms of their unity. Blacks should do the same and assist one another, no matter if they were Hereros, Damaras or Ovambos. At Karibib Mungunda was reported to have told a meeting that their organisation was working in conjunction with Americans and that they wanted to establish their own administration.[98]

The UNIA envoys seemed to have aroused the most interest in Okhandja, at the time a major centre of the Hereros. Four meetings were held there, and the report of the local police spy on these meetings clearly illustrates the extent to which Garveyism had already become associated with millenarian expectations. At the first meeting Mungunda explained that the object of the organisation was to unite blacks. He urged his audience to listen carefully to what he had to say as he had already been wrongly reported in other districts. At the next meeting Mungunda complained that what he had said at the first meeting had been misunderstood, because all the young men and women had been asking him "when the Americans were coming to release them".

> If I told you that the American Negroes were coming to release you, I think you would be satisfied, but it would be a lie. I know nothing about America. The society has been formed through American ideas, but Americans only explained it but did not do the work - we must do that. It is no use holding out false hopes about America, because I do not believe that they will ever be able to come here to help you.[99]

The police spy who attended the meeting, concluded his report by stating that although he did not think the Okahandja blacks would rebel, talk that the Americans were coming to free the country had spread throughout the district.

The millenarianism that became associated with Garveyism in the Namibian countryside, took a number of different forms, all of which were grounded on the basic premise that help could come from the "Americans" or some other external source. According to some versions, the Americans would arrive in ships or aircraft, in other versions soldiers would issue from the ground. The Rhenish missionary in Omaruru reported that a rumour had spread in the district that certain people had landed at Cape Cross and that the government should find out whether they were not American soldiers.[100]

Almost everywhere in the Police Zone, Garveyism created an air of expectancy which, combined with the disillusionment of blacks and the underlying tensions of the society, produced a general attitude of defiance and persistent reports of an approaching revolt. For example, a police spy operating in the Okahandja district was told "that three days beyond Gobabis there are a lot of natives including Hereros, Bushmen and American negroes waiting for the white people to come there to start a fight. There are altogether about three hundred natives there with rifles, and some without rifles. They still want more arms. A Herero came from there to get recruits." From what he had heard during his tour of the district, the spy gained

> the impression that the natives intend to rise and that the action is being engineered by American negroes. The trouble if it arises will begin on the eastern border of the district when the rain starts. One of the causes of discontent is the sheep inspection and the branding law. Vaccination has also caused a great deal of discontent. The American negroes have advised them not to brand their stock, refuse to allow their sheep to be inspected, and refuse to be vaccinated.[101]

These impressions were supported by another police informer who toured the same district a few weeks later. He reported that a number of people had joined UNIA, had collected money for the organisation and were waiting for badges.[102] Yet another informer reported that at Okasise he had been told that "the Herero people want to fight but have no rifles".

> At Okamatero I met some Hereros who said they were waiting for the Americans, then they would start ... At Okambahe I found a Herero who said that the American People had written on the stone at Karibib. He said that the Americans had built houses at Windhoek, where they can come together ... At Waldau the Hereros spoke of the Americans giving a button, to keep until the time is come ... I think the American negroes are at the bottom of all the unrest, and that the Hereros, except for the American influence, would never think of fighting again, having once fought the Germans. The Hereros are very eager and anxious for the Americans to come.[103]

While millenarian movements have often been described as essentially irrational and backward looking, as Keller points out, they also represent "an attempt to cope with the present, to change it, and to create a more promising future".[104] Michael Barkun has argued that many millenarian movements can be seen as a response to disaster.

> Men cleave to hopes of imminent worldly salvation only when the hammerblows of disaster destroy the world they have known and render them susceptible to ideas which they would earlier have cast aside.[105]

Robert Edgar has used Barkun's framework to illustrate the context that gave rise to Wellington Butelezi's brand of Garveyism in the Transkei[106] - a form of Garveyism which shared many characterisitcs with that of the Namibian countryside. The situation in Namibia in the early twenties provides some confirmation of the disaster hypothesis. Pre-colonial Namibian societies had been subjected to a series of traumas and disasters, including colonial conquest, the rinderpest epidemic of 1897, near annihilation and an unusually harsh form of forced labour. In the early 1920s disaster had culminated in the cruel shattering of the hopes created by the defeat of the Germans. That the millenarian tendencies of Garveyism should have taken root most firmly among the Hereros, also lends some credibility to the disaster hypothesis.

However, there are aspects of millenarianism other than the response to disaster which need to be considered. What is particularly striking about the Namibian situation in the 1920s is not merely the destructive (and disastrous) impact of colonialism on Namibian societies, but also the essential powerlessness of the colonised in the face of the organisational and military capabilities of the colonial state. It is clear that even those who had placed their faith in the "Americans" were aware that the colonial state could only be dislodged by military force, but it was equally apparent that indigenous communities did not on their own possess the means to take on the military power of the colonial state. For the most part Namibians did not passively regard the "Americans" as liberators, but rather as a catalyst which would help to bring about a general rising of the Namibians themselves. Seen against this background, the millenarian beliefs expressed by Namibian Garveyites appear less absurd or irrational. It may be argued that the political and military assertion of the Namibian people only became a practical possibility when external developments helped to balance the disproportionate power of the colonial state. That South African military forces had been able to dispose of the German colonial regime raised the possibility that a third external power - especially one perceived as being black - might be able to sweep away the new oppressors.

Another important aspect of millenarianism in Namibia is that it not only served as a means of boosting the morale of the colonised (and thus providing ideological support for active defiance of the administration and settlers), but also helped to undermine the morale and confidence of the settler and colonial state. While settlers and colonial officials scoffed at the absurdity of the beliefs that the "Americans" would come to the aid of black Namibians, there was a distinct uneasiness in their reception of these reports. There appears to be a certain relish in the way in which black Namibians divulged to white employers, police informers or colonial officials reports of imminent rebellions or "American" activities. There is something of a taunt in the example mentioned earlier that certain unknown people had landed at Cape Cross, and that the government "should see whether these were not Americans". The millenarian content of Namibian Garveyism may thus also be seen as a specific form of political struggle, or even as a means of extending the long tradition of military resistance in Namibia. George Balandier has argued that in certain contexts, religion may become "a smokescreen for politics".[107] In Namibia, millenarian assertions seem sometimes to approach a form of "psychological warfare".

During 1922-23 white fears of a general rising reached unprecedented heights. Reports of impending rebellions reached the administration from nearly all districts. Settlers maintained that conditions in 1922-23 were similar to those that preceded the rebellion of 1904 "when the former German Government made light of everything, even answering with threats, until eventually the memorable days of January 1904, broke upon us".[108] In February 1922 the magistrate of Keetmanshoop appealed to the administration to supply the town with 300 rifles. He maintained that he was "satisfied there is mischief brewing - and if the Police were in a position to protect the public or even the public in a position to protect themselves, I would have delayed writing to you".[109] In the latter half of the same year, following the circulation of a letter calling for the unity of Ovambos, Namas, Damaras, Hereros and San, the management of the OMEG copper mine asked the administration for "at least two machine guns".[110]

Although the colonial authorities went out of their way to squash and discourage rumours or reports of impending rebellions, they were at times also infected by the alarm and insecurity that pervaded the country. The apparently panic-stricken response of the administration to the Bondelswart Rebellion is only one example of the tenuousness of the confident image the administration attempted to project.[111] In October 1922 Native Commissioner Manning was doubtful that a general rising would occur but foresaw the possibility of small "outbreaks" in isolated parts of the country after the rains set in.

> As submitted in previous Memoranda, the question of settled conditions in parts where no strong tribal control exists largely depends upon a sufficient number of Police and outposts for regular patrols strong enough to carry out the law and - in the absence of a small mobile force which seems very desirable - rifle associations in every district ... I would respectively venture the opinion that the means of enforcing all laws or promptly dealing with possible outbreaks in this large Territory are not adequate at the present time.[112]

During the same month the Secretary for South West Africa sent a coded telegramme to the magistrate of Okahandja requesting him to employ spies to ascertain the extent to which blacks in the districts were armed. It would be "bad policy" to open small stations and have men and equipment captured, he advised. Forces should be concentrated.

In a situation of this sort, the fine dividing line between the intention to create fear and insecurity among whites and the more active intention to encourage or bring about an actual rebellion is blurred. That between 1922 and 1925 there were two large-scale rebellions and a number of other smaller incidents of resistance and defiance, is on its own an indication that rumours of a general rising went beyond the mere attempt to frighten the settlers and the administration. The dilemma this posed for settlers and administration is expressed by the Rhenish missionary A Kuhlmann:

> If there was a question of an armed rising we would hardly find it out, for as long as the people talk big, there is no direct danger, but if the hidden spark of hostility contin-

ues to smoulder on there is no saying when it may burst into flames.[113]

Indications of rebellion were apparent even before the Bondelswart revolt erupted in May 1922. The Bondelswarts had come close to an active rebellion in 1917, and thereafter there were frequent reports of unrest in the district of Warmbad. More important, there were indications that the Bondelswarts may have expected their rebellion to develop into a general rising. According to a police informer, talk of a general rising in the Herero stronghold of Okahandja had begun in 1921.[114] In February 1922 the magistrate of Keetmanshoop appealed to the administration for military assistance to meet what he termed his "strong suspicion of native unrest in this town and District". Although he was reproached by the Secretary for SWA for exaggerating the situation, the magistrate refused to back down, asserting that there was indeed a "restlessness among the Natives". To back up his claim, the magistrate stated that only a few days before there had been a "big meeting" in the Warmbad district (the district of the Bondelswarts). "Even the Hottentots from this district were notified to attend and their masters were unable to hold them back."[115]

In March 1922 the magistrate of Rehoboth also reported "unrest amongst the Hottentots in this country". A Baster field cornet had been told that the Namas were preparing for war. The Baster captain, Cornelius van Wyk, told the magistrate that "since the New Year he had noticed strange Hottentots in his area and that letters are passing between Hottentots here and others outside the District". A patrol sent out to investigate had found the suspected Namas in possession of Garveyist propaganda.[116] In his own account of the Bondelswart rebellion, the administrator, Gysbert Hofmeyr, maintained that fear of a general rebellion had prompted the administration into bombing this small and poorly armed community into submission. He claimed that after the outbreak of the revolt he received information which convinced him "of the possibility if not probability, of the whole country going ablaze and the history of German times being repeated unless a peaceful settlement was quickly announced ... or a decisive blow was quickly struck".[117] Further evidence to support this emerged after the rebellion. The Keetmanshoop police reported in October 1922, for example, that during the rebellion, Jan Hendriks, leader of the Veldskoendraers, had convened a meeting of Nama and Herero leaders in his area "with the object of assisting the Bondelswarts". It was also reported that another meeting had been held in the Berseba reserve where the Isaacs faction and the younger people had decided to help the Bondelswarts. It was only through the intervention of the collaborative Chief Goliath that they had been prevented from doing so.[118] According to evidence presented to the Bondelswarts Commission, the Bondelswart leader, Jacobus Christian, wielded considerable influence not only over his own people in the Warmbad area, but also over Namas at Berseba and Keetmanshoop. Shortly before the military campaign against the Bondelswarts, the Keetmanshoop Nama captain, Manasse, wrote to Christian asking what could be done about the pass laws.[119]

During the rebellion a Basuto who was employed by the municipality as a foreman of the Keetmanshoop black township addressed a meeting urging the people to attack the town and sieze arms and ammunition. In July a police patrol which had been sent out to arrest Jan Hendriks, captain of the Veldskoendraers, and six others for failing to pay the dog tax, was fired upon. Hendriks was later sentenced to six years imprisonment for attempted murder.[120]

In the same month the magistrate of Gobabis was killed by a poisoned arrow during a skirmish between the police and a large group of San. The conflict with the San had begun in June 1922 when a police patrol was sent from Gobabis to investigate stock thefts on an isolated farm and was ambushed by a large group of San. In July the Gobabis magistrate set out with an armed patrol to locate the San and "negotiate" with them. At Epukiro the magistrate received information to the effect that the San under Zameko were going to fight and that they had collected large quantities of dried meat as provisions for the kriegsleute (soldiers). "They say straight out that they are going to make war." A missionary from Epukiro who had gone out to investigate the theft of some stock was compelled to beat a hasty retreat when he came under fire from the San. A few days later the magistrate and his patrol located the San and in the ensuing battle the magistrate was killed by a poisoned arrow.[121] After this incident the administration received information which connected the San revolt with a more general rising of blacks in the territory. According to one informant, two representatives of Samuel Maherero had entered the territory from Bechuanaland, and had toured the country, in order to discuss the strategy for a future rebellion. The tactics of 1904 had been inadequate because the Hereros had first attacked the farms, giving the whites in the towns the opportunity to mobilise. The mobility of the Hereros had also been restricted by their large herds of cattle. In preparation for the coming war, blacks should therefore sell their cattle and buy horses and donkeys, and when the time came they should attack the towns first. The messengers had also stated that the Damaras and Bushmen (San) would also be involved in the war.[122] Although this report may have been fabricated by the farmers of the district, who had long been agitating for police reinforcements, other information that emerged during this period lends some credibility to the report. For example, a missionary at Epukiro reported in the same month that the San were going to make war. In June 1922 the magistrate of Rehoboth reported that the Hereros were buying horses on a "large scale". This and other information led him to believe that the Hereros were preparing to rebel.[123] In September and October there were persistent reports linking a general rising to the eastern frontier, and including the San among the rebels. For example, one informant stated that Hereros, San and "American Negroes" had gathered on the eastern frontier to prepare for a war.[124] Another referred to the killing of the Gobabis magistrate adding that

> (t)hose were native people who did that, and all natives are the same. We can easily get rifles ...[125]

As the rainy season approached, talk of an impending rebellion became more persistent. In Omaruru, for example, a police informer stated that

> (t)he talk is that if there is any trouble here, they, the Hereros, are to let Samuel Maherero know; they also state that they can get guns and ammunition in a day. This talk

> is general in the location among Hereros including men and women.

The informer went on to say that he had heard "a little while back" that Herero emissaries had been sent from Windhoek into the area occupied by the Bondelswarts.

> The Hereros, the Rehoboth Bastards and the Bondelswarts are on friendly terms. The Hereros say that the Bastards have declined to give up their arms to the whites and that the Hereros would stand by the Bastards in trouble.[126]

Another informant from the same district stated that meetings had taken place from the Okahandja district in the centre of the country to the Grootfontein district in the far north. Whenever the Hereros met on the farms, "their first and general conversation" was about the rising.[127]

However, the general rising which had been so widely anticipated in 1922-23, failed to materialise. The spirit of insurrection instead spent itself in more limited acts of defiance and resistance which only served to impress on the people the preponderant power of the state. In various parts of the country blacks defied colonial regulations relating to branding, sheep inspection and compulsory vaccination.[128] In the Rehoboth district a group of Namas who had not been allocated a reserve simply moved onto private farms with their stock, and threatened to "kill any policeman who was sent to turn them off".[129] By 1924 the optimism and militancy of 1922-23 was already giving way to resignation and passivity. At the beginning of 1924 the administrator was able to report that "(n)o rumours of Herero or other native risings have been circulated as has been the case in practically every preceding year".[130] Acts of resistance still occurred, but these were more sporadic and isolated.

None of the other organisations established in Namibia during this period were able to match the influence and popular appeal of the UNIA, and all failed to spread beyond the small, and relatively privileged, populations of the towns. The ICU, first launched in Luderitz in December 1920, was from the start dominated by South African immigrants, who, like the West Africans, formed a distinctive segment of the Namibian population and received preferential treatment from the authorities. In terms of an administration circular sent out to municipal authorities in 1922, for example, it was pointed out that "Cape Coloured persons and people of that class" did not fall under the pass laws, the curfew regulations, and the municipal by-laws which required blacks to keep off the side walks of certain Namibian towns. With the exception of the prohibition against their obtaining liquor, "these people are entitled to be placed on an equal footing with Europeans in so far as the law is concerned".[131] The circular also suggested that "wherever possible separate areas should be reserved for coloured persons at some distance from the ordinary locations". In general a "liberal and progressive attitude" was advised in regard to all blacks in urban areas. That these perceptions of differential status were shared by the leaders of the ICU and UNIA in Luderitz is made explicit in a report by the Native Commissioner for SWA on a meeting with ICU and UNIA leaders in March 1922.

> It was noticed that although this deputation seemed concerned about the welfare of visitors - presumably natives as a rule - they said they thought their class should not have to live in proximity to raw natives.[132]

The ICU in Luderitz never got much beyond attempts to maintain the organisation and the occasional articulation of grievances of the privileged urban groups. As such, it did not represent a great threat to the authorities, whose major anxiety was that it might spread to the contract labourers on the mines or to farm labourers.[133] Measures were therefore taken to isolate the ICU from labourers beyond the townships, and office holders were warned to restrict their activities to the "educated class".[134] The organisation was also contained by restricting the movement of organisers within the territory, and isolating the two Namibian branches from headquarters in South Africa.[135] Another major tactic of the administration was to encourage splits in these organisations. Here it was clearly aided by the suspicion that developed among local blacks of the foreign origins and privileged status of expatriate blacks in both the ICU and the UNIA. The clearest example of this strategy was the formation of the South West African National Congress (SWANC) in Luderitz in the latter half of 1922.

The major catalyst for the establishment of the SWANC in Luderitz was S M Bennett Ncwana, a rather strange figure who flits in and out of black politics in the Cape and SWA.[136] Ncwana visited Luderitz in the latter half of 1922 in order to launch the organisation and held the position of "chief organiser". According to the Luderitz Native Affairs Department which had interrogated members of the new organisation, the SWANC "was the outcome of dissatisfaction on the part of SA and SWA natives with the IC Union (chiefly dominated by Capeboys) and the UNIA Association (introduced and directed by West Indian and West Coast natives) which is continually calling for funds for American propaganda".

> The local natives have apparently realised that they were being made use of by the others and now wish to look after their own interests. It is difficult to ascertain what their aims in this direction were except that they were desirous of helping one another.[137]

According to Ncwana, the major grievances of Namibian blacks were the "unsympathetic administration, no outlet for discussing native grievances, unreasonable taxation considering the absence of profitable work, and the absence of native educational facilities". Ncwana was apparently also "emphatic in his professions of being desirous to work in harmony with the authorities".

> "I have been a moving spirit" he said, "in the native movement, but never an agitator. I did adopt an aggressive policy in my paper, but I found that it was not judicious. I dropped the paper and tried to start afresh on the lines of educating European opinion."[138]

Although the SWANC planned to adopt the constitution of the SANNC, it was intended that the Namibian congress would be an entirely separate body and not a branch of the South African organisation.[139]

The administration was not slow to realise the potential usefulness of an organisation like the SWANC to its attempts to curb organised black resistance in the territory. In a letter informing the administration in Windhoek of the formation of SWANC, the officer in charge of Native Affairs in Luderitz clearly outlined the strategy which the administration was to follow with considerable success.

> In the absence of any law forbidding the formation of native unions the most this department can possibly do to minimize the danger which may arise from such unions is to endeavour to split the membership into different factions - as has been done here - but there is little doubt that determined efforts will be made by one of the older bodies to eventually bring them under the same banner again ...
>
> It is probable that a purely native Congress can be handled more easily than the UNIA or the ICU - especially with a few Union natives, with an ingrained respect for the white man's authority at the head of affairs - and, if the Congress were taken under the wing of the Government, at its formation, with some unobtrusive, but effectual, provisions for Government supervision it might be a good policy.[140]

These views were strongly endorsed by both the Secretary of the Protectorate and the Native Commissioner. The latter observed that "under official guidance this new association ... might prove very useful in upsetting dangerous, irresponsible foreign doctrines". He added that the "combination of native races in SWA" had been "unknown in former years" and that this was causing alarm among white residents of the territory.[141]

Although documentation of this period of the ICU in Namibia is at best sketchy, it would appear that the Luderitz branch did not survive the various problems it experienced in 1923-24. As for the Keetmanshoop branch, there is no evidence that it existed in anything but name. UNIA experienced similar difficulties. The Native Affairs Department reported in September 1923 that local blacks had withdrawn from the UNIA branch in Windhoek and that no meetings had been held "for some time". The conviction of Marcus Garvey in New York on a charge of fraud may have contributed to the decline of the association, it was suggested.[142] The Luderitz branch was experiencing similar difficulties, and in 1924 the administrator reported that the Luderitz branches of both UNIA and ICU had "practically died out and it is only the South-West Africa National Congress which still has some adherents and occasionally holds meetings".[143] It is not known how long the SWANC survived, but it appears to have made no significant contribution, and is unlikely to have lasted beyond 1925.

The defiance and militancy which reached a peak in the 1922-23 period may have died down completely if it had not been for the Rehoboth rebellion of 1925. Although this rebellion revolved around the essentially "internal" issue of local autonomy for the Baster community at Rehoboth, it once again helped to provide a focus for the more generalised and dispersed resistance of other communities - and in particular for the Hereros. It further involved issues which transcended the interests and concerns of the immediate community.[144] As a semi-autonomous community, the Rehoboth Gebiet represented the last refuge for black stock-owners from the labour extractive system that was taking shape in Namibia during the early 1920s. Because the Rehoboth community was itself undergoing a process of impoverishment, the renting of pasturage to black stock-owners provided an important source of income to the Basters.[145] Proclamation 11 of 1922, which made squatting illegal, was not applied to Rehoboth, and it was not until the Baster Agreement of 1923 that the authorities obtained the legal means to control squatting within the Gebiet. However, the resistance of Baster rebels who opposed the agreement prevented the administration from taking action against squatters, and it was only after the suppression of the Rehoboth rebellion in 1925 that African tenants of the Basters were prosecuted within the Gebiet. The magistrate of Rehoboth pointed out after the rebellion that the prosecutions of squatters

> which was hardly possible under the old system of control by the Raad, has certainly had the effect of stimulating the labour supply and driving out loafers as well as preventing the Gebied from becoming a refuge for deserters.[146]

It was clearly in the interests of black squatters in Rehoboth to exert every available influence towards retaining or extending Baster autonomy. In terms of size of population and stock-ownership alone, the Africans in Rehoboth formed a significant group. In 1925 the population of the Gebiet numbered 3,500 Basters, 2,500 Africans and about thirty whites. Between 1925 and 1928, 230 Herero families were removed from Rehoboth, taking with them 8,000 head of large stock and 25,000 head of small stock.[147]

For the Hereros outside Rehoboth, the Basters rebels also offered potential allies against the colonial regime - particularly as the Rehoboth Burghers had retained most of their arms. Already in 1922 there were reports that the Herero leaders in Windhoek had established contact with the Basters.

> The Hereros say that the Bastards have declined to give up their arms to the whites and that the Hereros should stand by the Bastards in trouble.[148]

These shared interests between Hereros and Basters became particularly important during the Rehoboth rebellion because the rebellion coincided with the administration's attempts to remove the Hereros from the "temporary" reserves in the central districts of the territory to the newly established reserves in the Sandveld. The Herero leaders had strongly resisted the move, arguing, with some justification, that the allocated area could support neither them nor their stock, that it was "a country only good for wild beasts".[149]

By all accounts Africans, and particularly the Hereros, in the Gebiet responded enthusiastically to the cause of the Baster rebels. It is significant, for example, that more non-Basters than Basters were arrested, and finally prosecuted, during the culmination of the rebellion. Of the 632 people so arrested, 289 were Basters, 218 Hereros, seventy five Namas and fifty Damaras.[150] In his annual report, the administrator expressed concern about the role of non-Basters in the rebellion.

> The most serious aspect of the attitude of the opposition in Rehoboth, not only in this instance, but during the past eighteen months, has been the effect on the natives who have apparently come to regard the Gebiet as a sort of haven where no law exits ... the attitude of natives incited by the opposition section was openly hostile ... It follows that the natives do not wish to see our laws enforced in the Gebiet.[151]

The Rehoboth magistrate reported that he had received information to the effect that the Hereros were in favour of attacking the police several days before the South African forces moved into Rehoboth.[152] Some months before the Rehoboth rebellion reached a head, the administration feared that a general rebellion might break out in the territory. In December 1925 the Administrator's Office sent an urgent communique to all magistrates in the territory warning them that "the administration has received reports of native unrest which has been accentuated by the attitude of the Rehoboth Community as a result of Proclamation No. 31 of 1924". It was believed that "native emissaries" had been sent from one district to another and that "secret communications" were being exchanged. While the administration cautioned against alarm, the magistrates were instructed to keep a close watch on all "native movements" and to submit a weekly report on developments in each district. The magistrates were also urged to establish "intelligence systems" to facilitate the removal of whites from isolated rural areas should a rising occur.[153]

Towards the end of March 1925 the head of the military forces in the territory urged the Union Government to proclaim martial law in the Rehoboth district, arguing that if resistance in the Gebiet was "not immediately checked by extreme and drastic measures, conflagration may rapidly spread over the whole country and place us in position to face a serious situation which under present adverse conditions will be difficult to cope with".[154] A few days after the suppression of the rebellion, reports continued to reach the administration of a possible rising of the Hereros. The magistrate reported on 7 April that he had received information that the Hereros intended to rise. He had been unable to ascertain the date of this rising, but "gathered that it would be in about three weeks time."[155]

Perhaps the clearest evidence of the administration's fear of a general uprising were the measures adopted by the military in other parts of the territory after the suppression of the Rehoboth rebellion. Herero witnesses maintained that the aircraft used to intimidate Rehoboth rebels, not only flew over Rehoboth but also over the Herero reserves of Orumba.[156] Following the suppression of the Rehoboth rising, the administration pressed the Union government to sanction "bombing demonstrations" in selected areas throughout the territory including Ovamboland. The proposal was at first vetoed by the Minister of Defence, probably because of the international outcry that followed the bombing of the Bondelswarts in 1922. The administrator continued to insist on the importance of these "demonstrations" and permission was finally granted.[157] The aim of these "bombing demonstrations" was to impress upon potential rebels the great power of the state, and thus avert a possible general rising. The "bombing demonstrations" were used, for example, to impress upon leaders of the Orumba "temporary reserve" the consequences of continuing to resist the move to their new reserve in the Kalahari sandveld.[158] They also appear to have served their purpose in other areas. The magistrate of Keetmanshoop, for example, reported that he had taken "advantage of the presence of the Hereros in Tses Reserve at Kl. Vaalgras on the occasion of the Bombing demonstration, to address them on the question of branding and am glad to say that they all without exception are having their cattle branded."[159]

CONCLUSION

Essentially there were three major sets of factors which accounted for the failure of this first phase of popular resistance in Namibia: the fragmented nature of the Namibian social formation, the composition and nature of political organisations established during this period, and the preponderant power of the colonial state.

Largely on account of ecological conditions, Namibia has a relatively small population scattered over an area which is two-thirds that of South Africa. The vast distances and scattered population have provided a major obstacle to national organisation throughout Namibian history. However, in the early 1920s the Namibian population was still in the process of recovering from the shattering impact of the colonial wars and repression of indigenous institutions of the early twentieth century. Although they were largely dispossessed, the people of the Police Zone lacked the social integration to constitute a proletariat. The larger part of the population was scattered among the various farms and in small and badly organised rural communities. The urban population was small even in relation to the total population, and tightly controlled by the colonial state. A foreign component of the black population, with distinct interests of its own, played a dominant role in the urban areas and added further diversity (and disunity) to the Namibian social formation.

The division of the territory into the Police Zone and northern area placed additional obstacles in the way of national organisation, and effectively excluded the more densely populated northern areas from the political movement that developed in the Police Zone. Similarly, migrant workers from the northern areas were effectively isolated from the rest of the population by the contract labour and compound systems. However, despite the isolation of the north and cooption of tribal leaders into a system of indirect rule, there are indications that some of the Ovambos were also influenced by the spirit of rebellion that permeated the southern and central regions. During the period of intense resistance towards the end of 1922 and the beginning of 1923, Ipumbu, king of the Ukuambi Ovambos, issued ammunition to his people and ordered them to guard the Onolongo and Ondangua routes into his country in order to prevent whites from entering or passing through his territory. There were also reports that the Ukuambi were selling stock to obtain ammunition and gun powder. In December 1922 an Ukuambi headman who had quarrelled with Ipumbu informed the administration that the Ukuambi king had been sending agents into the Police Zone in order to acquire both arms and information.

> They (Ipumbu's agents) invariably go without passes and are clever in evading the police. They are all after buying rifles and ammunition. He does not send a few at a time, twenty to thirty are always away south. They bring him stupid information such as "this Government is finished, we hear all over that the Americans are coming to take this country."[160]

Early in 1923 the Portuguese representative at Namakunde on the border with Angola stated that he had received reports "that natives in Damaraland were making preparations with Ovambos and natives in our territory to rise against our and your Governments".[161] Earlier there had been a rumour in the Outjo district that the Hereros were obtaining arms from Ovamboland.[162]

In spite of these and other, earlier-mentioned signs of co-operation, the anti-colonial movement in the territory never achieved the degree of coordination necessary to pose a serious threat to the colonial state. On each occasion the authorities were able to isolate and deal swiftly with manifestations of resistance, thus preventing further outbreaks elsewhere in the territory.

The structures in Namibian political organisations during this period were also unsuited to the task of leading effective and unified resistance to the colonial state. Both the UNIA and ICU were externally-based organisations, and this allowed the authorities to isolate the Namibian branches from their headquarters in Cape Town and New York. Furthermore, the millenarian content of Garveyism tended to deflect Namibian resistance away from internal organisation towards a hopeless dream of external intervention. Most damaging, however, was the class basis of the leaders of both organisations. Garvey's organisation essentially represented the interests of the Negro petty bourgeoisie, and it was therefore to be expected that his economic nationalism would attract members of a similar class in Namibia. Comparable difficulties were associated with the leadership of the ICU.[163] Like their counterparts in South Africa and the United States, the Luderitz leaders of UNIA and the ICU occupied a relatively privileged, if somewhat marginal (and therefore ambivalent), position within the Namibian social formation. That these leaders were also predominantly foreign made their privileged position in the community particularly visible and helped to generate resentment among the local population. Even more important, where this embryonic class secured control over one of the organisations, it ensured that its own interests would be given precedence. Finally, internal cleavages within both organisations provided the administration with an ideal opportunity to drive a wedge between their different factions.

In the final analysis, however, it was the disproportionate military and organisational resources of the state that brought about the abandonment of this phase of resistance in Namibia. In particular the aeroplane changed the whole complexion of guerrilla warfare in the territory and provided a powerful symbol of colonial supremacy with which to intimidate the colonised. Aircraft had been used not only to effect the swift suppression of the Bondelswart rebellion and to intimidate the Rehoboth rebels, but also to impress upon other indigenous communities the military power of the colonial state. While military technology may under most circumstances be less important than political and ideological means of control,[164] the analysis in the first part of this paper suggested that between 1915 and 1925 the colonial state was still in the process of consolidating its hold over the indigenous communities of Namibia. It was only after 1925, with the establishment of reserves, the co-option of indigenous and urban elites, and the further elaboration of the legal superstructure, that the colonial state was able to exercise effective control over the colonised population. Given the circumstances of the early 1920s, the colonial state was forced to rely more heavily on its "instruments of violence". The introduction of aircraft was therefore crucial in preventing localised outbreaks of rebellion from spreading to other parts of the territory. It may be argued that although the circumstances and consciousness of most of the black population favoured a general rising, it lacked the organisational structures necessary to plan and coordinate such a rising. This meant that a general rising would only be possible if a specific community took the initiative in leading the rebellion and was able to hold out long enough for other communities to join it in the struggle. The administration clearly realised this, and therefore acted swiftly and brutally to suppress both the Bondelswart and Rehoboth rebellions.

Without the resources to challenge the enormous power of the colonial state, overt resistance ceased to be a practical or rational alternative, and the colonised could do little but wait for some development to change the balance of power in their favour. For the next twenty years of Namibian history, resistance in the police zone took largely covert and symbolic forms.

NOTES

(Except where indicated, all archival sources used are from the State Archives, Windhoek).

1. See, for example, G L M Lewis, The Bondelswarts rebellion of 1922. MA thesis, Rhodes University, 1977; G M Cockram, South West African mandate. Cape Town: Juta, 1976; R Freislich, The last tribal war. Cape Town: C Struik, 1964; P Pearson, 'The Rehoboth rebellion', in P Bonner (ed.) Working Papers in Southern African Studies, Vol. two. Johannesburg: Ravan Press, 1981.

2. Z Ngavirue, Political parties and interest groups in South West Africa: a study of a plural society. Ph.D. thesis, Oxford University, 1973; SWAPO, To be born a nation: the liberation struggle for Namibia. London: Zed Press, 1981.

3. "Truppenspieler" movements, such as the Herero Otjiserandu or "Red Band" organisation, were particularly active during the inter-war period. Sharing many of the characterisitcs of the Beni societies of east and central Africa, the Namibian "Truppenspielers" combined features of pre-colonial and colonial societies in para-military organisations which provided an outlet for both protest and recreation by the assumption of military ranks, uniforms and drilling. See, for example Ngavirue, op. cit.

4. J S Coleman, 'Nationalism in tropical Africa'. American Political Science Review, 48, 2, 1954, pp. 404-426, for example, used an explicitly "modernisation" perspective in this early discussion of "primary" and "secondary" resistance. The relationship between the primary/secondary distinction and the "tradition-modernity" dichotomy is particularly evident in this article.

5. B Davidson, Africa in modern history. Harmondsworth: Penguin, 1978, pp. 150-153.

6. T Hodgkin, Nationalism in colonial Africa. New York: New York UP, 1957, pp. 113-114.

7. E Kedourie, Nationalism in Asia and Africa. London: Frank Cass, 1971, p. 106.

8. P Worsley, The trumpet shall sound. London: MacGibbon & Kee, 1968.

9. E Hobsbawm, Primitive rebels. Manchester: Manchester UP, 1959.

10. A Isaacson, 'Social banditry in Zimbabwe (Rhodesia) and Mozambique, 1894-1907: an expression of early peasant protest.' Journal of Southern African Studies, 4, 1977/78, pp. 1-30.

11. C van Onselen, Studies in the social and economic history of the Witwatersrand 1886-1914, Vol. two: New Nineveh. Johannesburg: Ravan Press, 1982, pp. 171-201.

12. S Cross, *World War I and social movements in East and Central Africa*. Paper delivered at conference on Africa and World War I, School of Oriental and African Studies, London, March 1977.

13. For example, S J Schoeman, *Suidwes-Afrika onder Militêre Bestuur 1915-1920*, MA thesis, UNISA, 1975; I Goldblatt, *History of South West Africa*. Cape Town: Juta and Company, 1971, pp 206-209. While Schoeman's study is the most comprehensive, it is essentially descriptive and fails to provide an adequate analysis of the transition process.

14. See, for example, D Innes, 'Imperialism and the national struggle in Namibia.' *Review of African Political Economy*, No. 9, 1978.

15. South West African People's Organisation, *To be born a nation*. London: Zed Press, 1981, p. 20.

16. M Scott, *In face of fear*. Johannesburg: M Scott, 1948, p. 37.

17. H Drechsler, *Let us die fighting*. London: Zed Press, 1980, p. 248.

18. R Moorsom, *Colonisation and proletarianisation*. University of Sussex, MA thesis, 1973, p. 74. Most of these studies provide little, if any, evidence to back up their claims: an indication that the proposition is regarded as self-evident.

19. Rathbone, 'World War I and Africa: Introduction', *Journal of African History*, 19, 1, 1978, p. 4. See also R W Imishue, *South West Africa: an international problem*. Institute of Race Relations, 1965, pp. 2-5.

20. M H Swanson, 'South West Africa in Trust, 1915-1939', in Gifford, P and Louis, W R (eds.) *Britain and Germany in Africa*. New Haven: Yale UP, pp. 643-647.

21. University of Witwatersrand Library, J C Smuts papers, Gorges - Botha, 21/1/18.

22. See for example, E H L Gorges, *Report on the Natives of South West Africa and their treatment by Germany*. London: HMSO, CD 9146, 1918, p. 6.

23. Imishue, *op. cit.*, p. 15.

24. This is clearly illustrated by the Administration's quandary in 1916 when it decided to send a military expedition against the defiant Ovambo King, Mandume. Fears that the German settlers in the south of the territory might rebel while a large contingent of SA troops was engaged in the north prompted military administrator Gorges to telegraph Smuts for reinforcements from the Union.

25. Report on the Natives of SWA, op. cit., p. 158-159. See also H Bley, South West Africa under German Rule. London Heinemann, 1967 and H Drechsler, Let us die fighting. London: 2nd ed. Press, 1980.
26. SWA, Native Affairs Memorandum, 1916.

27. Ibid., p. 8.

28. Ibid., p. 10.

29. UG 22-17, Papers relating to certain cases dealt with by the Special Criminal Court, 1917.

30. ADM 567/2. For example the Verband der Verwertungs Vereiningungen of Windhoek complained (to the Secretary, 7/1/20) that some farmers lived more than 200 kms from the nearest magistracy and might be compelled to spend 8-14 days away from their farms.

31. ADM 567-2, Magistrate, Malthohe - Secretary, 23/6/20; Deputy-Commissioner - Secretary, 7/5/20.

32. ADM 567-2, Deputy-Commissioner - Secretary, 7/5/20; SWA Police Warmbad - Magistrate, Warmbad, 26/7/20; Magistrate, Maltahohe - Secretary 23/6/20.

33. ADM 567/2, Magistrate, Gibeon - Secretary, 3/1/20; See also Magistrate, Windhoek - Secretary, 21/8/20.

34. Native Affairs Memorandum 1916, op. cit., 1916; Administrator's reports, 1924 and 1925; ADM 263/3.

35. ADM 567/2 eg. Verband der Verwertungs Vereiningungen - Secretary, 7/1/20; Agricultural Society, Karibib - Magistrate, 30/4/16.

36. ADM 567/2, Administrator - Acting Prime Minister, 8/4/19; ADM 567/6 Magistrate, Okahandja - Secretary, 18/11/17.

37. ADM 567/2, Magistrate, Outjo - Secretary, 30/6/20.

38. ADM 567/2, Magistrate, Okahandja - Secretary, 9/3/20.

39. State Archives, Pretoria, PM 214/8/1916, Administrator's report for 1915-16; ADM 13/23.

40. ADM 567/2, Magistrate, Otjiwarongo - Secretary, 9/6/20.

41. ADM 567/2, Deputy Commissioner - Secretary, 7/5/20; Magistrate, Maltahohe - Secretary, 23/6/20.

42. ADM 567/2.

43. ADM 567/2, Magistrate, Otjiwarongo - Secretary, 9/6/20.

44. ADM 567/2, Secretary - Acting Prime Minister, undated.

45. Testimony of Fridoline Kazombiaze, M Scott, *op. cit.*, pp. 37-38.

46. About half of the German population of Namibia, consisting mainly of administrative and military officials, was repatriated in 1919. The remaining Germans were incorporated into the settler population and provision made for them to assume South African citizenship. (See, for example, Union of South Africa, Administrator's report 1939, UG 30-40, 1949, pp. 14-16). In 1926 the SWA Legislative Assembly adopted a resolution to the effect that Copies of the 1918 Imperial Blue book, *Report on the Natives of South West Africa and their treatment by Germany* should be removed from official files and libraries and destroyed. This proposal was later implemented (H Drechsler, *Let us die fighting*. London: Zed Press, 1980, pp. 10-11).

47. See, R H Davies, *Captial, state and white labour in South Africa 1900-1960*. Brighton: Harvester Press, 1979; D O'Meara, *Volkskapitalisme*. Johannesburg: Ravan, 1983.

48. Both, Karibib - J Smuts, 2/6/15; W K Hancock and J van der Poel (eds.), *Selections from the Smuts Papers*. London: Cambridge University Press, 1966, p. 639.

49. University of the Witwatersrand Library Smuts Papers, A 842/B1, Ballot, D W F E, Memorandum, 20/7/1935.

50. See, for example, Administrator's reports, 1920 and 1921.

51. See, for example, Administrator's report, 1921, p. 5.

52. See Ballot memorandum, *op. cit*.

53. SWA Administration, *Report of the Land Settlement Commission*, Windhoek 1935. See also A312, Item 25, 'Land Settlement in SWA'.

54. ADM 2163/3 (1), Native Affairs, Windhoek - Deputy Secretary, 10/7/16.

55. Administrator's report, 1921f f. 14.

56. Administrator's report, 1925, f. 59.

57. Administrator's report, 1922, UG 1923, p. 13 and Administrator's report, 1923, UG 21-24, 1924, p. 13.

58. Administrator's report, 1924, UG 1925, p. 24 and Administrator's report, 1925, UG 26-26. 1926, p. 29.

59. Administrator's report, 1924, UG 33-25, 1925, p. 24.

60. Administrator's report, 1924, p. 21.

61. SWA, Report of the Native Reserves Commissioner, LA 2-28, Windhoek, 1928.

62. Administrator's report, 1924, p. 21.

63. See, for example, Administrator's report, 1922, pp. 16-18.

64. ADM 599, Native Affairs, Keetmanshoop - Native Commissioner, 22/9/15.

65. ADM 599, Native Affairs, Keetmanshoop - Native Commissioner, 25/11/15.

66. ADM 567/2, Magistrate, Warmbad - Secretary, 9/6/20.

67. Administrator's report, 1922, p. 21.

68. Union of South Africa, Bondelswarts Commission Report, 1923, p. 8.

69. Lewis, op. cit., p. 50.

70. ADM 599/2, Magistrate, Warmbad - Secretary, 30/8/17.

71. Lewis, op. cit., pp. 28, 164-165.

72. See footnote 1, above.

73. SWAA A492/2, Memo. to Native Affairs, Luderitz, 15/4/19; Native Affairs, Luderitz - Secretary, 16/11/20.

74. SWAA A492/2, vols. 1 and 2.

75. SWAA A492/2, Magistrate, Luderitz - Secretary, 26/4/20.

76. SWAA A492/2, SWA Police, Windhoek - Secretary, 29/9/20; SWA A492/2, Native Commissioner - Secretary, 6/5/22.

77. T Martin, Race First. London: Greenwood Press, 1976, p. 45.

78. Ibid., 45-46. See also, R L Okonkwo, 'The Garvey movement in British West Africa'. Journal of African History, 21, 1980, p. 108.

79. Union of South Africa, Administrator's report, 1925, UG 26-26, p. 21; SWAA A50/31/1, Native Affairs, Windhoek - Secretary, 21/12/21; ADM C248, Native Affairs, Luderitz - Secretary, 7/9/22.

80. SWAA A50/31/1, Magistrate, Luderitz - Secretary, 20/3/22.

81. ADM 3823/3. Wages in Luderitz compared favourably with those in other parts of the territory. According to the administrator's report for 1922, black labourers employed by the mines, railways and industry earned "9 d. rising to 1/3 d. and more per shift", while farm labourers on average earned between "10/- and 15/- to 20/- per month, with food and occasional clothing". Union of South Africa, Administrator's report, 1922, UG 21-23, p. 21.

82. SWAA A50/31/1, cutting from Negro World, 8/10/21.

83. SWAA A50/31/1, Magistrate, Luderitz - Town Clerk, Luderitz, 19/11/21; ADM C248, "Coloured and Native People, Luderitz: Alleged Grievances", 24/4/22.

84. See, for example, ADM 152/C248, W Andrianse - C Kadalie, 26/1/22.

85. SWAA A50/30/1, Native Affairs, Windhoek - Secretary, 22/11/22; Liebig's Co. - Secretary, 20/1/22.

86. A312, Item 77, Executive, UNIA, Windhoek - Major, Windhoek, 2/1/22.

87. SWAA A50/31/1, Native Affairs, Windhoek - Secretary, 22/11/22. It was men like Kutako, Mungunda and Kapuuo who provided the links between the first phase of populist resistance in the 1920s and the creation of a mass-based nationalist movement in the late 1950s.

88. SWAA A50/31/1, David Zwartbooi et al. - "The Government", undated. (Date of translation, 30/11/22).

89. SWAA A50/31/1, H Drew, Windhoek - Secretary, 10/11/22.

90. SWAA A50/31/1, Native Affairs, Windhoek - Secretary, 22/11/22.

91. SWAA A50/31/1, H Drew, Windhoek - Secretary, 10/11/22.

92. A 312, Item 77, Headley, Luderitz - G R Hofmeyr, Windhoek, 6/2/22; Executive, UNIA, Windhoek - G R Hofmeyr, 17/2/22; SWAA A50/31/1, Headley, Luderitz - Abraham, Swakopmund, 25/3/22; Headley, Luderitz - Hailand, Usakos, 14/11/22.

93. SWAA A50/3/1, Headley, Luderitz - William Abraham, Swakopmund, 23/5/22.

94. SWAA A50/31/1, H Drew, Windhoek - Secretary, 10/11/22.

95. SWAA A50/31/1, Headley, Luderitz - J Hailand, Usakos, 14/11/22.

96. Algemeine Zeitung, 9/3/24, cited by Z Ngavirue, Political parties and interest groups in South West Africa: a study of a plural society. Ph.D. thesis, Oxford University, 1972, p. 256. Headley was quoting here from the "General Objectives" of the UNIA constitution.

97. SWAA A50/30/1, Native Commissioner - Secretary, 11/7/22.

98. SWAA A50/31/1, SWA Police, Usakos - Magistrate, Karibib, 26/10/22; SWA Police, Karibib, 19/10/22.

99. SWAA A396/4, "Report of Native Corporal Jacob", 6/11/22.

100. H Vedder, 'The Herero', in C Hahn, H Vedder and L Fourie, The Native Tribes of South West Africa. Cape Town: Cape Times, 1928, p. 163; SWAA A396/13, Statement by A Kuhlmann, Omaruru, 11/10/22.

101. SWAA A396/4, Statement by David Ngxibi, 3/10/22.

102. SWAA A396/4, "Report of Native Corporal Jacob", 27/10/22.

103. SWAA A396/4, Statement by John Retsang, 31/10/22.

104. B B Keller, 'Millenarianism and resistance: the Xhosa cattle-killing'. Journal of Asia and African Studies, 13, 1-2, 1978, p. 96.

105. M Barkun, Disaster and the millenium. New Haven: Yale University Press, 1974, p. 1.

106. R Edgar, 'Garveyism in Africa: Dr Wellington and the American movement in the Transkei.' Ufahamu, 6, 3, 1976, pp. 31-57.

107. Quoted by Keller, op. cit. p. 97.

108. SWAA A396/4, Letter to editor, Lander-Zeitung, 11/10/22. See also SWAA A396/13, Statement by A Kuhlmann, 11/10/22.

109. SWAA A396/10, Magistrate, Keetmanshoop - Secretary, 2/2/22.

110. SWAA A396/4, Native Commissioner - Acting Secretary, 12/10/22.

111. See, Bondelswarts rebellion report, op. cit.

112. SWAA A396/4, Secretary - Magistrate, Okahandja, 13/10/22.

113. SWAA A396/13, Statement by A Kuhlmann, 11/10/22.

114. SWAA A396/13, Statement by David Kobase/Gowaseb, 17/10/22.

115. SWAA A396/10, Magistrate, Keetmanshoop - Secretary, 2/2/22 and 10/2/22; W Theron - A J Waters, 21/2/22. The misgivings of the Keetmanshoop magistrate were justified when only two months later the Bondelswarts actively rebelled against the administration.

116. SWAA A396/6, Magistrate, Rehoboth - Secretary, 14/3/22 and 18/3/22.

117. Union of South Africa, Report of the Administrator on the Bondelswarts rising, 1922. UG 30-22, pp. 4-5.

118. SWAA A396/10, SWA Police, Keetmanshoop - SWA Police, Windhoek, 30/11/22.

119. G L M Lewis, op. cit., p. 196.

120. Union of South Afria, Administrator's report, 1922, UG 21-23, p. 25; SWAA A396/10, SWA Police, Keetmanshoop - SWA Police, Windhoek, 27/7/22; Magistrate, Keetmanshoop - Secretary, 25/7/22.

121. SWAA A50/25, Acting Magistrate, Gobabis: 'Report on the Bushmen trouble in the Gobabis district', 17/9/22; SWA A50/25, Van Reyneveld, Epukiro - Karalowa, 12/7/22.

122. SWAA A50/25, Statement by Max Hallmann, Gobabis, 17/8/22.

123. SWAA A50/25, Magistrate, Gobabis - Secretary, 17/8/22; SWAA A396/6, Magistrate, Rehoboth - Secretary, 29/6/22.

124. SWAA A396/A, Statement by David Ngxibi, Okahandja, 3/10/22.

125. SWAA A396/4, Magistrate, Okahandja - Secretary, 1/9/22. Hunter - gatherers like the San have generally received little attention in the history of southern Africa. For example, W G Clarence-Smith, in his study of southern Angola, maintains that hunter-gatherers were "of negligible historical importance". (Slaves, peasants and capitalists in southern Angola 1840-1926. London: Cambridge University Press, 1979, p. 72.)

126. SWAA A396/13, Statement by William Kaapnaar, Omaruru, 16/10/22.

127. SWAA A396/13, Statement by David Kobase/Gowaseb, Omaruru, 17/10/22.

128. See, for example, SWAA A219/2; A219/6; A219/12; A396/4; A396/13.

129. SWAA A396/6, Magistrate, Rehoboth-Secretary, 7/12/22 and 6/1/23.

130. Union of South Africa, Administrator's report, 1923, UG 21-24, p. 12.

131. ADM C248, Circular to all municipalities: "Control of Natives and Coloured Persons in Urban Areas", 20/7/22. Initially, the administration regard the ICU as an organisation representing Cape Coloureds, and early documents even referred to it as the "Industrial Coloured Worker's Union".

132. ADM C248, "Coloured and Native People, Luderitz: Alleged grievances", 24/4/22.

133. ADM C248, CID, Windhoek - Secretary, 29/12/20; Magistrate, Luderitz - Secretary, 5/1/20 (letter misdated, should be 1921); Native Affairs, Luderitz - Secretary, 25/5/21.

134. ADM C248, Natives Luderitz - Protsec, 31/12/20.

135. Clements Kadalie, for example, was repeatedly refused permission to enter the territory.

136. Ncwana was an early and fairly prominent member of the ICU, who moved periodically between the ICU and its rival ICWU. After defecting from the ICWU, Ncwana joined the ICU for a short period before deserting this organisation in 1921 and launching a bitter attack on it in his newspaper, The Black Man. Later he again joined the ICWU and helped found the African Land Settlement Scheme with the object "to assist the Government by inducing natives living in towns to settle on the land". At other times Ncwana also acted as the general organiser of the Cape Native Voters Association which mobilized black voters for the South African party, and according to Kadalie helped write the election literature for the Nationalist candidate Professor Schoeman who defeated Maragaret Ballinger in 1949.

137. ADM C248, Native Affairs, Luderitz - Secretary, 7/9/22.

138. SWAA A50/13/1, undated report from Windhoek Advertiser (see fn 65, above).

139. ADM C248, Native Affairs, Luderitz - Secretary, 19/9/22.

140. ADM C248, Native Affairs, Luderitz - Secretary, 7/9/22.

141. ADM C248, Internal Memo., C N M - Secretary, 14/9/22; Secretary - Native Affairs, Luderitz, 29/9/22.

142. SWAA A396/5, Memorandum, Native Affairs, Windhoek, 28/9/23.

143. Administrator's report, 1924, pp. 27-28.

144. For further information about the Rehoboth Gebiet and the dispute that led up to the rebellion, see P Pearson, op. cit.; J D Viall, The History of the Rehoboth Basters. Memeo, 27/10/59.

145. Pearson, op. cit., pp. 33-44.

146. SWAA A50/6, Magistrate, Rehoboth - Native Commissioner, 3/9/26.

147. Vial, op. cit., p. 46.

148. SWAA A396/13, Statement by William Kaapnaar, 16/10/22.

149. Scott, op. cit., p. 59.

150. Administrator's report, 1924, p. 13.

151. Ibid., p. 12.

152. A312, Item 79, Manning, Rehoboth - Administrator, 11/4/25.

153. A312, Item 79, Administrator'S Office - All magistrates, 20/12/24.

154. A312, Item 79, Secretary - Hoofd., Cape Town, 30/3/25.

155. A312, Item 79, Magistrate, Grootfontein - Secretary, 7/4/25.

156. Scott, op. cit., p. 62.

157. A312, Item 79, Administrator - Minister of Defence, Cape Town, undated; Secretary, Windhoek - Hoofd., Gibeon, 9/4/25; Hoofd., Cape Town - Administrator, 11/4/25.

158. Scott, op. cit., p. 63.

159. SWAA A219/2 (2) Magistrate, Keetmanshoop - Native Commissioner, 25/4/25.

160. A312, Item 39, Statement by Ukuambi refugee headman, Festus, Ondonga, 28/12/22.

161. SWAA A396/15, Portuguese Representative, Namakunde - Union Government representative, 19/1/23.

162. SWAA A396/11, Magistrate, Outjo - Secretary, 20/3/22.

163. Philip Bonner has argued that one of the fatal flaws of the ICU in South Africa was its petty bourgeois leadership. P Bonner, 'The decline and fall of the ICU - a case of self-destruction?' in E Webster (ed.), Essays in Southern African labour history. Johannesburg: Ravan Press, 1978, pp. 114-120.

164. See, for example, Barrington Moore, Jr., Injustice: the social bases of obedience and revolt. London: MacMillan, 1979, p. 85; Claude Welch, Jr., 'Continuity and discontinuity in African Military organisation', Journal of Modern African Studies, 13, 2, 1975, pp. 236-237.

*Class Contradictions and Class Alliances: The Social Nature of ICU Leadership, 1924-1929**

Helen Bradford

> '(The ICU) differed from the ANC in one other important respect: Its leaders were not drawn from the "respectable classes". They had come straight from the ranks of the workers themselves, and they had a ruggedness and militancy that men accustomed to making obeisances before authority found outrageous.'[1]
>
> 'Whereas in European trade unionism, trade union leadership had developed organically from the working class, in the ICU movement had been created and a leadership imposed more or less from the outside. From the outset, therefore, the movement was characterised by the cult of personality and by contradictory bourgeois aims.'[2]

Startling though the contradictions between these two quotes are, there are three reasons for utilising both of them to identify the social origins of Industrial and Commercial Workers' Union (ICU) leadership. Firstly, the class nature of Union leadership changed markedly over time. Between 1919 and 1924, the ICU was, as Ngubane suggests, largely led by men who were themselves wage-earners, or had spent years working as unskilled labourers, or had as little education as most ordinary workers. Epitomizing organizers of this period was James la Guma, a branch secretary from 1920, and assistant general secretary from 1923 to 1926. Of French-Malagasy origin, la Guma was eight years old when apprenticed as a leather worker; ten when he participated in his first workers' demonstration; in his teens when labouring on the diamond diggings near Luderitz; and in his early twenties when he led a diamond miners' strike and pass resistance there in 1918-1919.[3]

After the Pact electoral victory of 1924, however, petty bourgeois Africans began to replace working class 'Coloureds' as organizers. Top leadership positions were filled by men like Allison Wessels George Champion: president of the Transvaal Native Clerks Association, landowner, and 'immediate future leader of the rising Native Middle Class'.[4] Middle leadership became the province of men like Samuel Dunn, proud possessor of a 100 acre allotment in Dunn's Reserve.[5] And the branch positions were eagerly taken up by scores of teachers, traders, clerks and craftsmen - a veritable army, as Bonner indicates, of middle class reformers.

The distinction between levels of the Union suggests the second reason for retaining the notion that organizers had varied class backgrounds. Commonly, paid positions (from branch secretary upwards) were from the mid-1920s filled by middle class blacks. Sometimes these organizers were chosen on the basis of political criteria, such as recommendations by African National Congress leaders or prominence in certain organizations. More commonly, appointees fulfilled considerably less stringent criteria, such as membership of kinship, service-

*As this stands, the very structure of the paper intensifies the contradictions it attempts to tease out. A substantially revised version has been published in the *Journal of African History*, 25, 3, 1984.

mens' or old boys' networks. As one disgruntled member expressed it, ICU policy was one of 'Jobs for friends of pals'[6] - and the friends tended to have similar social backgrounds to their middle class pals.

At a local level, however, a considerably more democratic procedure operated in selecting members of the eleven-person executive, of whom only the branch and assistant branch secretaries were paid. Since officials were sensitive to the need to create a sense of popular control, most local leaders (sometimes including the secretary) were elected at the first or second Union meeting. Consequently, social groups other than the black middle class were represented on branch committees. Strong grass roots pressure in favour of those with prestige in pre-colonial society often manifested itself, and occasionally - like the chief who became chairman in Bethal - members of the traditional elite braved the wrath of officialdom to become Union leaders. Far more frequently, wage-earners were elected to the committee. Thus in Estcourt, the branch executive included road workers as well as a shop assistant chosen for his prowess in the soccer club. In Middelburg, the first chairman in 1926 was a water-cart driver employed by the municipality, while the same position was filled in Pietermaritzburg in 1929 by a domestic servant. Some executives may even have fulfilled their constitutional obligation of representing all sectors of labour by including farm workers. Whether they did or not, it is clear that minor officials were often - in the words of a contemporary opponent of the Union- 'half-educated or raw natives'.[7]

Not that petty bourgeois blacks were excluded from branch positions: indeed, they almost certainly predominated on committees established in small country towns. In part, this was because ICU officials who arrived in a village tended to gravitate towards members of the elite for organizational assistance - and hence bathed such men in the aura of the Union.[8] In part too, it was because many members of the intermediate strata were already viewed by the masses as having political skills, and as being capable of challenging the white man successfully. In addition, as will be indicated below, middle class blacks often had their own reasons for flocking to take up branch positions.

This brings us to the third - and for the purposes of this paper, the most important - reason for the co-existence of conflicting accounts of the social origins of ICU leadership. This is the contradictory nature of the petty bourgeoisie itself. In capitalist society, the middle strata stand 'between the dominant relations of production of capitalism - that is to say the capital/labour relation - and as such (are) pulled two ways'.[9] By juxtaposing the inconsistent claims that ICU officials originated in the working/capitalist classes, it is possible to capture some of the ambiguities of their petty bourgeois nature.

Unfortunately, however, few commentators on ICU leaders have examined the extent to which they arose from the under classes. Instead, many liberal and radical scholars have tackled the problem of ICU organizers' alleged failure of the masses in terms of the leadership's elitist/bourgeois nature. Thus the former have perceived Union officials as lagging behind the masses largely because they had passed through the appropriate ideological institutions. Christian blacks of this period, they have argued, were prone to constitutional methods of struggle. Schooling reinforced this: 'a policy of insistent, but respectful moderation ... suited the inclinations and experiences of the leaders of the ICU, many of whom had been educated by white missionaries and shared some of their assumptions about the possibilities for gradual expansion of African opportunities in South Africa.'[10] And since they were immersed in the 'Cape tradition' they naturally associated with white liberals, which further distanced them from the restive masses.[11]

Radical intellectuals on the other hand have explained leadership defects in terms of class, rather than such superstructural phenomena as mission schools and Victorian virtues. Why did officials - who unfortunately had not the faintest idea of theory and tactics - rush around the countryside enrolling pre-determined losers rather than organizing the proletariat? 'The reason for this negligence can be traced to their elite or petit-bourgeois background.'[12] Wherein lies the explanation for leaders' personal ambition and lack of commitment to the struggle? In the fact that they were not members of the working class. Why were they so susceptible to moderate forms of protest? Because teachers, clerks and the like 'had won sufficient stake within the existing system to identify themselves with certain tenets of liberal ideology ... (and) were not by nature socially radical'.[13] From all shades of left-wing opinion emerges a litany for the masses: trust not the petty bourgeoisie, for the stench of their privileged backgrounds rises from the graves of their class suicides.[14]

Interestingly enough, both liberal and radical accounts of ICU leadership assert the existence of a strong relation between the social origins of organizers and the ideology they articulated. Indeed, too strong: there was not, as liberals claim, a one-to-one relationship between organizers' passage through certain institutions and the beliefs they espoused. Nor were political and ideological orientations as class-specific as the revisionists argue: membership of the petty bourgeoisie cannot account for practices ranging from disorganized thinking to dissolute living. Furthermore, the ICU's message was also crucially dependent on the nature of the organization into which they were incorporated, and on the kind of constituency into which they were integrated.

Nonetheless, it is undeniably true that the social nature of the leadership affected the content and form of the Union's discourse. In particular, the background of rural organizers crucially influenced the way in which the ICU operated in the countryside, which became a major arena for Union activities at precisely the same time as the class nature of leadership was changing. And it is only by focusing on plebeian as well as elitist aspects in the make-up of these officials of the latter twenties that it is possible to resolve a contradiction permeating so much of the historiography of Union leadership. Namely: that members of the much denounced petty bourgeoisie headed one of the largest organizations ever to operate in Africa, and mobilized rural blacks in a way no South African movement has accomplished before or since.

The consensus amongst radical historians that (paid) ICU organizers of the later 1920s had not developed organically out of the working class is fairly accurate. In a society in which some 66 per cent of Africans were non-Christian, about 80 per cent were labourers or rural cultivators, nearly 90 per cent were illiterate, and almost 100 per cent had no voice in parliament,[15] ICU officials were predominantly Christian, educated males, drawn from the middle strata, and including amongst themselves a good sprinkling of voters. There is clearly some justification for terming them part of the elite, and it is these aspects of their backgrounds that will be examined first. Since the great bulk of the Union's support was drawn from Natal,[16] it is organizers in this province who will receive the most attention.

In many and probably most cases, ICU officials were the children of the privileged. Some obtained their preferential access to resources through being related to pre-colonial ruling groups. More frequently, they were the sons of professionals such as ministers or teachers. To a significant degree, they were also drawn from a rural elite: from relatively wealthy families based on freehold property, on mission reserves, on locations and even on farms. Prosperous rural cultivators were being slowly strangled from the late nineteenth century, but many - especially those in the eastern Cape and Natal - survived long enough to direct their children to alternative paths of privilege.[17]

In so doing, they took good care to name their offspring in a way symbolizing acceptance of the cultural superiority of their white rulers. While the overwhelming majority of Union leaders had English (often Biblical) names, some - like Cecil Rhodes Mama and Conan Doyle Modiakgotla - bore even more overt signs of originating in households which approved of the civilizing mission of the imperialists. Acquiring an identity as a child of God, a reader of books and a citizen of the Empire was an integral part of the childhood of numerous ICU organizers. So too was emulating the lifestyles of wealthier whites, with some leaders having fathers 'who insisted upon us living and behaving as respective (sic) Europeans'.[18]

In consolidating a group of black 'AmaRespectables', church had been crucial for the parent generation. By the 1920s, Christianity had diffused outwards to win over one third of the African population, and education rather than spiritual beliefs characterised the new elite. Even so, most ICU leaders were immersed in the religion of missionaries at both home and school. They were spared the sermon on the eighth commandment given Lovedale students in 1929, in which pupils were told of the sanctity of property and the sinfulness of Communism. But most members of the black elite were subjected to equally crude religious practices, designed to inculcate a faith in which obedience to God was inextricably tied to subordination to white capital and to class differentiation.

If religous instruction was important in separating the sheep from the goats, then secular education was at least as powerful. The very form of tuition taught students to revere individual achievement, to bow to authority, and to emulate the lifestyles of their conquerors. Similarly, content was directed at teaching pupils to equate civilisation with colonial expansion and barbarism with tribal Africa. Thus English was far and away the most important subject, while geography syllabuses usually revolved around the characteristic features of British colonies. Often arithmetic was taught in terms of purchasing consumer goods, while history examinations in Natal crudely emphasised the facts of conquests with questions like: 'What took place on December 16, 1838?'[19]

So in ways ranging from teaching the secrets that distinguish mental from manual labour, through to encouraging the singing of 'Rule

Britannia', mission schools devoted much effort to nurturing a black middle class imbued with the values of Cape liberalism. Their success - together with that of other institutions - was reflected in the fact that some 25% of Africans enlisting for overseas duty in World War I were drawn from the educated elite, mainly from the teaching profession. Amongst the many future ICU organizers who demonstrated loyalty to the Empire in this way was the well-schooled Jason Jingoes, who joined up partly because 'I, as a member of the British Commonwealth, felt deeply involved'.[20]

Yet if education was one pathway to liberal values and the middle strata, it was a straight and narrow one. In 1924, only 702 African pupils were in grades higher than Standard 6, while eight years later merely 5% of school-age children were in classes above Standard 2. In such a society, paid Union organizers of the later 1920s were intellectual giants. Almost certainly, the great majority had passed Standard 2. A considerable number - including at least one third of the 1927 National Council - had obtained their Standard 6. Many had attended teacher-training institutions, while not a few had actually completed the three year, post-Standard 6 course which qualified them as instructors. Nor was all this force-feeding on mission school diet restricted to head office leaders. Of the seven branch organizers whose educational histories are known, all had passed Standard 6. Three had qualified as teachers, and four - in a country where only about 100 Africans held Junior Certificates - had their JC's. Strange bedfellows though they may be, right-wing 'dominees' and left-wing historians are at least accurate in complaining that the ICU of this period was run by 'geleerde Kaffers'.[21]

Most 'educated Kaffirs' of this period did all they could to avoid the harsh conditions and low wages of unskilled labourers. Many, probably most ICU paid officials, had previously been white collar employees. As such, they had helped reproduce the subordination of blacks to white employers, white authority and white culture. James Dippa, one of the numerous ICU organizers who had been a mine compound clerk, had participated in waking workers at 4 a.m. and sjambokking them into line. Albert Nzula, one of the many state employees who subsequently became ICU organizers, had translated magisterial pronouncements to those convicted under the pass laws. And Gilbert Coka, who like the majority of Union branch secretaries had been a teacher, had been actively involved in instilling the inferiority of manual to mental labour and of black to white lifestyles. Understandably, such employees evoked a volatile mixture of admiration and anger from ordinary blacks. As Es'kia Mphahlele succinctly expressed it when writing of Marabastad life in the 1930s, other women felt 'at once jealous, envious, annoyed and humble' when Ma-Lebona repeatedly stressed that she had once been a school mistress.[22]

At this point, it is necessary to note that ICU organizers were not always male. There were female delegates to conferences, female branch leaders, and - at least in the eastern Transvaal and Natal - female officials who organized for a separate Women's Section of the ICU. But black women, subordinate to men in almost every sphere and isolated from most political activity, were hardly obvious leadership material for a male dominated protest movement. Hence they were always in a tiny minority among Union officials, and at least some appear to have reached these positions through their relationships with male officials. (As Elijah Ngcobo recalled, the minimum duty of the wife of an organizer was to join the Union, otherwise 'the members of the ICU would ask the leader where his wife was'.)[23] Moreover, it appears to have been middle class women - like the nurse Miss C B Ntombela - who most easily broke through the web of constraints inhibiting female participation. As with their male counterparts, such women often had interests which were opposed to those of ordinary blacks.

If both male and female white collar employees were often antagonistically placed vis-a-vis the masses, so too were middle strata blacks able to earn an entirely or partially independent living. In the context of the ICU, this was particularly evident when organizers retained an interest in property. Johannes Mogorosi, the Kroonstad branch chairman who simultaneously ran an eating house and rented three stands in the location, was wary about risking his investment by prolonging Union protest over municipal rates.[24] Sam Dunn, who was probably using outside labour to produce sugar cane on his allotment, was noticeably antagonistic to the advocacy of strikes. Then there was Champion, whose world view was profoundly shaped by his inheriting an interest in his father's holdings in 1921; his ownership of an Inanda plot worth £210; and his investment of ICU funds in Durban property held in his own name. According to him, the Communists wanted a system in which 'men like myself who hold landed property should be dispossessed of them and these properties should be given to other people who have less than I have ... That is where I disagree with Communism'.[25] Prone to such delightfully unambiguous statements, Champion is deservedly the darling of radical historians of the ICU's petty bourgeois leadership.

In addition to Champion and Dunn, there were a number of other ICU organizers who retained an interest in land, including Abel Ngcobo and Richard Mdima who rented mission reserve plots in Natal. In this period, it was still possible to consolidate privilege by channelling salaries or profits into the rural areas. Thus there were ministers - including the father of ICU organizer Selby Msimang - who saved thousands of pounds for farms, as well as teachers, traders and lawyers who were simultaneously progressive farmers and landowners. Moreover, it was becoming increasingly lucrative to rent out such land, given the ongoing squeeze on both market- and subsistence-oriented rural blacks. Between 1915 and 1936, the population on African-owned farms in Natal actually doubled, and the rack-renting, land-grabbing proclivities of kholwa landowners certainly earned them the hatred of many poorer Africans.[26]

If the economic interests of middle strata Africans were often opposed to those of the masses, then their political concerns also tended to set them at a tangent to the popular classes. Many members of the intermediate strata were able to escape some of the worst forms of political coercion to which most blacks were subject. Like numerous Natal ICU officials, some were allowed to join the 'izemtiti': those exempt from customary law and from various pass regulations. Or they might be excluded from forced relocation in segregated townships, or from 'native' taxation, or from some of the other myriad laws that repressed blacks and made the world safe for white capital. Even the vote was possible, since the values of Cape liberalism were still entrenched in the qualified franchise. By 1927, 16,481 male Africans, including some ICU officials, had been adjudged sufficiently alienated from workers and poor peasants to be politically incorporated into the state.[27]

Culturally too, middle strata blacks were often differentiated from the masses, insofar as many had both the income and the inclination to participate in the 'civilization' of the white dominant groups. Apart from being distinguished by their religion and education, they also tended to be disproportionately represented amongst those whose diets excluded mealie meal, or who played tennis in clubs like the Daffodils, or who danced to the strains of swing orchestras in swallow tails and ties. There could have been few rural Africans in the Kranskop district who owned, as did the ICU branch secretary James Ngcobo, three suits, three ties, a Stetson hat, and the entire gamut of equipment deemed necessary by motor cycle fanatics. Such status symbols, representing as they did social distinctions and the extent to which middle class Africans had accepted the world of white capitalists, could evoke considerable antagonism from the under classes. Blacks were certainly aware of the slick style of many ICU officials, and some bitterly resented Union organizers' attempts to ape the white man culturally.[28]

The various differences between the black middle classes and the masses tended to be reflected in separate organizations. Champion for instance was a founder member of both the Roodepoort Progressive Society and the Exempted Natives' Association of South Africa. In the early 1920s, like ICU officials Selby Msimang and Alexander Jabavu, he was also involved in various Chamber of Mines financed institutions, established to regain the allegiance of the black elite after the post-war explosion of protest. These included the Johannesburg Joint Council, which provided an arena for members of the African middle classes to voice their grievances, and the Bantu Mens' Social Centre, where the African elite was expected to while away leisure hours in respectable activities. Finally, Champion was by 1927 also prominent in a black businessmen's organization - the United National Association of Commerce and Industry Ltd - and in the late 1920s he succeeded Kadalie as Minister of Labour in the African National Congress.[29]

All such associations, together with those like Native Advisory Boards, provided organizational experience for innumerable ICU officials. Apart from fostering a self conscious elitist identity, they also often promoted ideals and tactics overtly opposed to those of 'irresponsible agitators'. Indeed, this was the initial aim of Congress, which was the body in which numerous ICU organizers served their political apprenticeship. More than two thirds of the delegates to a 1927 Union conference belonged to the ANC, and they were undoubtedly influenced by its programme of equal opportunity for progressive individuals and its tactics of constitutional suasion. To an ever-increasing extent, they were also affected by the projects of white liberals. In early 1929, Kadalie claimed with considerable accuracy that Union business was being 'delegated to a coterie of Europeans and natives who assembled in the Bantu Mens' Social Centre'.[30]

Also of significance in the development of bourgeois aspirations amongst ICU leaders was the Garveyist movement. 'Africa for the Africans' was a slogan that greatly appealed to many actual and aspirant middle class blacks, not least because of the class character of its nationalism. In the United States, the Universal Negro Improvement Association placed enormous stress on creating a worldwide network of

Negro businessmen through a six million dollar self help fund. Inspired by this example of mobilizing funds on a nationalist ticket, the ICU's first business venture was 'The Black Man' company, promoted in 1920 by such ICU-cum-UNIA members as Kadalie. The aims of the undertaking included the establishment of co-operative stores, the publication of a journal '<u>The Black Man</u>', and the organization of African workers 'by means of establishing a Branch ... of the Company in various centres deemed necessary by the Directors'.[31] In attempting to create a trade union wing of their economic self-help movement, members of the African petty bourgeoisie preceded their Afrikaner counterparts by more than a decade.

ICU efforts to harness the masses behind the creation of an elite independent of wage labour continued throughout the 1920s. Perhaps the most striking example of this was provided by Henry Tyamzashe, who in 1927 told readers of the Union's newpaper that:

> 'Carpentry, shoemaking, cabinet-making, co-operative societies, wholesale stores, banks, schools, religious work, and a thousand and one other business ventures are all avenues which the Native could exploit independently and with success ... A six million shilling fund will produce £300,000. This is enough money to start one thousand £300 ventures all over the country ... This will sound the death-knell of all those bad laws and Ordinances.
>
> Thus we advise an industrial policy that will make the Native scratch for himself. When it is discovered that the South African black man is determined to fend for himself, those who look upon him now as if he were a child of three years will only be too glad to come forward and share the profits and privileges of the country with him.'[32]

Encouraging the African labourer to 'scratch for himself' - or more accurately, to scratch for his leaders - was hardly the most worker-oriented industrial programme. Like innumerable other facets of the ICU - ranging from organizers' obsession with electoral politics through to their addiction to fast living - it was rooted in the bourgeois aspirations of Union officials. As liberal and radical historians have stressed, most leaders of the 1920s were drawn from an elite objectively and subjectively opposed to the black masses along certain economic, political and cultural lines. This, together with their simultaneous support for many of the interests of the white dominant groups, was to infuse the very fabric of ICU ideology and organization in the countryside.

Yet ICU activities in the rural areas were never unidimensional. In precisely the same year that Tyamzashe penned the above, Union organizers in Kroonstad distributed a red pamphlet which urged:

> 'Now is the time to consolidate and strengthen the LABOUR MOVEMENT in preparation for the next SOCIALIST COMMONWEALTH ... WORKERS OF THE WORLD UNITE, YOU HAVE NOTHING TO LOSE BUT YOUR CHAINS.'[33]

Far from having being 'completely bought off' as has been alleged,[34] the petty bourgeoisie of the 1920s clearly had some life in it yet. To understand how middle class organizers came to be traipsing around the countryside calling for the overthrow of capitalism, it is necessary to examine other - distinctly plebeian - aspects of their background.

Of cardinal importance is the fact that the black middle strata of this period were being brutally undermined. From the late nineteenth centry, economic weight and political dominance were shifting from merchants and landowners to mining capitalists, manufacturers and commercial farmers. In the process, an African labour force was created on a scale and with a speed that left little room for 'black Englishmen'. From the 1890s, the peasantry and the mercantile-missionary-liberal axis that supported it were under vicious attack. By the turn of the century, all African chiefdoms were being radically reshaped under the twin impact of colonial conquest and the burgeoning mining industry. And by Union, black allies were being sought amongst illiterate chiefs and headmen rather than enfranchised peasants and professionals, while the policy of segregation was permeating all the fissures of South African society.[35]

As already noted with regard to the Joint Councils, attempts were made to halt this process of erosion when the black middle classes became involved in the post-war upsurge of popular protest. As well as the private initiatives of white liberals and the Chamber of Mines, there occurred a hydra-headed attempt by the state to co-opt the African intermediate strata. Various political safety valves were created, in the form of Native Advisory Boards, Local Councils and 'native' conferences. Simultaneously, draft bills eased the impact of pass laws on the middle strata, and offered urban freehold rights and better housing conditions to 'more advanced natives'.[36]

But these were the solutions of large mining capitalists, and they were strongly opposed by many struggling farmers, white wage-earners and members of the white petty bourgeoisie. As black resistance subsided during the 1920-1923 depression, and as white wage-earners' opposition to African advancement intensified and culminated in the Rand Revolt, so the costs to monopoly capital of consolidating a black middle class were re-evaluated. The South African Party government itself abandoned the abovementioned draft legislation, spurred on by the ongoing flood of 'poor whites' into the towns and the fact a weak national bourgeoisie was seeking allies against imperial interests. And when the National Party-Labour Party coalition government came to power in 1924, it extended all measures hampering the development of the black middle strata. Thus within three years the political representatives of national capitalists and white wage-earners had introduced the Native Bills (which threatened to strip the African elite of the vote and to confine them to 13% of the land); they had passed the Native Administration Act (which reinforced the subordination of educated blacks to chiefs and headmen); and they had done all in their power to encourage the movement of whites rather than blacks into skilled positions. As a disillusioned Kadalie argued in 1926, the government had not lived up to its promise of redistributing the goods previously reserved for big finance amongst all South Africans. Instead, it had given 'the (black) child stones in the form of the

Colour Bar Bill, enforcement of Pass Laws ... (and) the retrenchment of Natives from state undertakings ...'[37]

It is in the light of these attempts to crush the African elite that the emphasis by many radical historians on the bourgeois nature of the petty bourgeoisie is particularly misplaced. In all capitalist societies, the middle strata are pulled in two directions by the contradictory forces of capital and labour. Because of the racial nature of South African capitalism, the traction of the subordinate classes on the black petty bourgeoisie is especially powerful. And in the context of the class levelling policy of the state and capital in the 1920s, as well as the enormous impact on the intermediate groups of struggles in the wider society, it is impossible to assume that the elite automatically identified upwards rather than downwards.

Instead, the potential for downward identification by the sub-elite who predominated in ICU leadership positions was present almost from the moment of their birth. Nearly all of them were born after 1886 - indeed, many were conceived after 1900 - and their lives were intimately affected by the tightening of the noose around the middle strata. Gilbert Coka, for instance, was born in 1910 as the son of relatively prosperous Vryheid 'squatters'. Two years later, the landlord demanded the labour services of Gilbert's elder brother, and his parents were forced to leave for town to safeguard their children's education. But like so many other ICU organizers, Gilbert was a junior son, disadvantaged as regards life chances in comparison to his elder siblings. By the time he was ready for secondary education, his father could no longer scrape together the required £10 - £20 p.a. Consequently Gilbert spent part of 1923 herding cattle, and it was only through teaching for a year that he was able to clamber into secondary school.[38]

Partly because pupils like Coka were often intimately acquainted with the struggles of the under classes, these mission schools were less successful than liberals have claimed in instilling moderate methods of protest. On the contrary: Champion was in fact expelled for organizing students against the missionaries' disciplinary regime, while innumerable ICU officials must have been affected by the 1920 conflict at Lovedale, their alma mater. In the midst of countrywide popular struggles linked to soaring inflation, the students here refused to eat the cheaper bread foisted on them. About 300 of them hoisted the Red Flag and marched on the school, where they gutted the grain store, wrecked the electric power house, smashed every window in the church, and stoned the principal.[39] The theory that mission education inculcated submission is clearly somewhat threadbare.

So too is the belief that ICU officials were once-and-for-all imbued with liberal ideas at these institutions. Firstly, ICU leaders - unlike many of the older Congress officials - were taught at a time when schools were being wrenched into line with the policy of segregation. To an ever increasing extent, mission education of the 1910s and 1920s was directed at preparing pupils for lives of obedient subordination rather than equal opportunity - and as such was bitterly resented. Secondly, the world views of the dominant groups are transformed as well as absorbed by those to whom they are imparted. Thus ICU leaders who had spent years learning of the British Empire told their audiences the English were savage cannibals before they were conquered by the Romans, while Thomas Mbeki told farm labourers 'of the rise and fall of the Kingdoms starting with the Roman Empire right up to the republic of America. He said, "the writing is on the wall"'.[40]

If schools were not particularly successful in instilling beliefs in eternal British superiority, neither was immersion in the so-called Cape tradition. Especially after Union, English 'friends of the natives' were at best largely impotent and at worst amongst those who brutally suppressed black aspirations and protest. Disillusioned by ruling class responses to their wartime sacrifices, inspired by world-wide struggles against colonialism, and wooed by Afrikaner nationalists, the African elite of this period grew increasingly sceptical of their British inheritance. By 1920, even Congress leaders were denouncing the imperialist government for having betrayed them, while the Nationalist Party had the support of all major black organizations - including the ICU - in the 1924 elections.[41]

Equally problematic is the notion that religious indoctrination by white missionaries automatically helped reconcile Union leaders to the rule of white capital. For one thing, Christian ideology was often at odds with the daily reality of life in a racially oppressive society, and was therefore explicitly rejected by some organizers. For another, members of the sub-elite were in this period transferring their allegiance to Ethiopian churches. Not only did they learn techniques of mass organization here, but they were also immersed in Biblical tales of deliverance from bondage and in sermons which promised black ascendancy over whites. Militant nationalism, rather subservience to white rule, was the overwhelming message imparted by these separatist bodies.

It was from these churches that were drawn most of the ministers and lay preachers who became ICU organizers. (One such enterprising man was Lucas Sethabela of Lindley, who had for years been attempting to sue the Brethren Mission Church for expelling him as their preacher. His ultimate solution was to win chairmanship of the local ICU, to establish the *Union* Brethren Mission Church, and to continue 'the quarrel for he trust the money of the ICU'.)[42] And almost certainly, it was to these churches that the majority of Union organizers who adhered to Christianity belonged.[43] Small wonder that the religious idiom that infused the Union's discourse was hardly that of apologists for white bourgeois rule. As Alex Maduna told his Graaff-Reinet audience in 1927 (before repairing to a separatist church to enrol members):

> 'The white man tells you of a great man living in the sky beyond the clouds and his teaching is peace on earth and good will to men, but the white man means suppression and suppression means revolution. Furthermore, the white man tells you there is a hell, a big fire waiting for you. The only hell the black man has is this suppression under which we all live.'[44]

It was precisely because Maduna could claim that *all* blacks experienced hell on earth that an alliance between the middle strata and the masses was possible. If being Christian, educated and a voter did not necessarily distance a Union organizer from the masses as much as liberals have assumed, neither did membership of the petty bourgeoisie.

In particular, for a substantial section of the middle strata, the all-encompassing grievance of racial discrimination incorporated the three major plaints of the masses: low wages, pass restrictions and lack of land.[45]

Self-employed blacks certainly had an indirect interest in a general increase in wages of their overwhelmingly black clientele. But it was for those forced into the servitude of the salariat that the issue of pay was of the essence. Most received pitifully inadequate salaries, a tiny fraction of what was earned by whites in equivalent jobs. (As Reverend Dube stated sourly in 1931, 'It does not matter how much a Native has improved or qualified himself, he is only "A Kaffer"; that is the ordinary white man's view, "He is only 'A Kaffer' and ought to get a Kaffer's wage".')[46] Moreover, the pay of those at the lower levels of the salariat - such as most mine clerks and teachers - was often at best only marginally greater than that of labourers. Even amongst those salaried employees who secured higher earnings than workers, greater impoverishment was often experienced: either because they were fully proletarianized, or because they were frantically trying to maintain 'civilized' standards.[47]

Impelled by economic necessity, and inspired by the example of the white salariat and black labourers, there was consequently a post-war surge of collective organization amongst white collar Africans. This was especially noticeable amongst teachers, a profession into which many blacks moved reluctantly and from which they escaped with relief. Even state officials commented on the 'lean and hungry look' of black school staff in 1919,[48] and shortly afterwards a national African Teacher's Union was formed to fight the miserably low salaries. With little success: throughout the 1920s, teachers continued to receive £2 - £5 a month, irregularly paid at long intervals. Since, in 1928, 79 per cent of the Natal staff and 70 per cent of those in the Free State were unqualified, a large proportion of teachers were in fact concentrated at the lower end of this salary scale, and struggling to make ends meet. Small wonder that the ICU's branch secretaryship - at £4 a month - was attractive to these men, many of whom were so disillusioned with their posts that they were entering the job market every three months.[49]

Passes were another grievance shared by both the masses and the middle strata. Understandably, the sub-elite was especially hostile to these controls: exemption was not for example applicable to unqualified teachers in the Free State, to ministers in most independent churches, or to hawkers. Moreover, it was becoming ever more difficult to join the 'izemtiti'. After the draft bill easing the burden of passes for the elite was abandoned in 1923, a South African Agricultural Union resolution - 'That exemptions be more restricted' - was given legislative force in 1927. Almost simultaneously, Kadalie's application for exemption was rejected, and like so many other ICU officials, he was harassed by pass laws throughout his period in the Union.[50]

Not that the 'izemtiti' escaped the drag-net of pass control. They still had to carry their exemption certificates and remained subject to police harassment. Furthermore, letters of exemption were only applicable in the province of issue, and at least one member of the 'izemtiti' found himself once again subject to the full battery of pass legislation when transferred as Union organizer from Natal to the

Transvaal. In addition, even exempted blacks continued to be forced through a veritable thicket of municipal pass laws - which, to the horror of the Cape elite, was extended countrywide in 1923. In the Free State, such local controls which affected Union organizers included visitors' passes, residential passes and stand permits, as well as seeking work passes, employment registration certificates, work-on-own-behalf certificates and entertainment permits.[51]

If the issues of wages and passes could serve as the foundation for a class alliance, so too could that of land. The most notorious turn of the screw preventing middle strata Africans from acquiring land was of course the 1913 Land Act. Under its repressive provisions, only forty two applications by Africans to buy land in the three northern provinces were approved between 1919 and 1928. And although there was another rash of administrative and legislative action in the 1920s, the difficulties faced by blacks in obtaining credit, and their meagre incomes, were steadily making legal restrictions redundant. Thus in 1922, a government report referred to the 'gradual but certain elimination of the Native landowner'.[52] By 1926, African owned holdings were less in area than ten years previously, and Champion was in the process of selling the plots he had inherited from his father. Little wonder that prominent members of the black middle classes felt it pointless to identify areas where Africans would be allowed to purchase farms, since '(t)he Native had no money and his earnings capacity was being kept down by the Colour Bar Act'.[53] Indeed, a number of struggling landowners and less well established members of the middle strata had by the 1920s abandoned their faith in the capitalist land market, and were simply arguing that land should be <u>given</u> to blacks.[54]

If the African sub-elite was able to unite with the masses on a number of key issues, this was also partly because they too were being battered by the forces of proletarianization. Most obviously, this was evident with regards to land. Not only landowners but also those who had invested in cattle and crops in the urban areas, or had access to plots in the countryside, were deriving ever less support from their rural base. According to a spokesman for a Natal mission station in 1918, 'there is nearly always a famine there. The natives have not got enough gardens to work'.[55] As Sam Dunn discovered, even a 100 acre allotment was inadequate to make an independent living and he was amongst those ICU organizers impelled off the land into the urban labour market.[56]

White collar employees were also subject to the forces of proletarianization. During World War I, it was noted with concern that 'the openings for merely book-learned Native men and women are few. The tendency to close all clerical occupations to Natives makes teaching almost the only non-manual vocation open to them'.[57] By 1921, less than one per cent of African males could find work as professionals, interpreters, shop assistants or clerks, and the large majority of Congress members were educated blacks unable to find jobs suited to their qualifications. After the Rand Revolt, and more especially after the election of the Pact government, 'Colour Bar' measures heightened the barriers to middle strata advancement. Simultaneously, the teaching conduit began to prove incapable of absorbing those emerging from mission schools. Although the number of African staff in Natal and Transvaal schools swelled by 50 per cent between 1925 and 1930 - itself a poignant indication of desperation amongst educated Africans - this was often at the expense of qualified teachers (thrown into unemployment because untrained instructors were cheaper) or married women. And by the end of the decade, teachers, clerks and artisans were all in oversupply, while state functionaries were anxiously intoning that job opportunities for educated Africans were 'everywhere deplorably limited'.[58]

Educated blacks of this period, then, were frequently forced into unemployment, into living on their wits, and into becoming ordinary labourers. This was especially common amongst schooled foreign-born blacks, unable to speak the vernacular, and hence unable to serve as transmission belts between white capitalists and black workers. Amongst the significant number of alien blacks in ICU leadership, many had suffered this fate. West Indian-born J G Gumbs, for instance, was a qualified chemist reduced to serving as a rigger on the docks during his presidency of the Union. Similarly Nyasaland-born Kadalie, although he had held a succession of white collar jobs in colonies to the north, was forced to work almost exclusively as a packer, messenger and parcel 'boy' for three years after he moved to South Africa in 1918.[59]

Self-employment tended to be equally insecure and frustrating, and in 1921 less than 0,1 per cent of the African male population were traders, hawkers or artisans. Whether carpenters or card-sharps, most independent operators faced the problems of fierce competition, lack of funds and dependence on penurious consumers. Their development was rigidly restricted by the state: particularly in rural towns, municipal authorities tended to be extrememly sensitive to the interests of the white petty bourgeoisie and to farmers' fears of a labour shortage. Thus Peter Malepe, ICU organizer in Parys from 1927, was in 1928 allowed to hawk wood in the location, but was on principle refused permission to run an eating house. African traders were in fact prohibited in the Free State, and here as elsewhere, burdensome licence fees, exorbitant rents for stands, and a myriad petty restrictions stifled most other forms of accumulation.[60]

Consequently, even if the scramble into self-employment was achieved, the probability of being extruded as a proletarian was considerably greater than that of emerging as a capitalist. 'I am not making a living, I am making only a little bit of a living'[61] complained a butcher in 1931, doubtless expressing the feelings of the various butchers who were prominent in ICU branch structures. Like Doyle Modiakgotla, a building contractor with no fixed job when he became an ICU official, such Africans were constantly being forced into the ranks of the lumpen-proletariat or the working class. Independent black shoemakers - those 'typical working class intellectuals'[62] as conspicuous in ICU branch leadership as in the East Anglican rural uprising of 1816 and Paris in the Year II - were amongst the numerous small-scale operators being squeezed out of their trade. Many if not most mission trained craftsmen were in fact unable to subsist through working for themselves. It is likely that James Ngcobo - 'a bricklayer and carpenter by trade, and an architect by profession' - was economically insecure as well as professionally frustrated before becoming branch secretary in Kranskop.[63]

Thus it was that numerous supposedly 'petty bourgeois' ICU leaders had at one time or another spent considerable lengths of time in the ranks of the working class. Some had previously worked as underground miners, experiencing to the full the horrors of compound life, low wages and vicious white overseers. Like the educated and exempted Thomas Mbeki who became Transvaal Provincial Secretary, others actually joined the Union as labourers. One J Malaza, previously a farm worker, was appropriately enough the district secretary for Bethal, and captured the attention of audiences in this area by relating how his baas had nearly thrashed him to death in his youth.[64]

Of course, it was possible for middle strata Africans to fall further than the law-abiding working class or the unemployed. Before joining the ICU, numerous organizers were no strangers to such everyday features of black existence as acquiring aliases or being jailed for offences against racially oppressive laws. A significant proportion, however, had a shadier past than this. Stealing from white employers was a favourite way of closing the gap between middle class incomes and the cost of living, and prominent organizers such as Alex Maduna and Sam Dunn both had such thefts in their backgrounds. Not atypical was the criminal record of Simon Elias, an important Free State leader who appears to have been an independent legal agent before becoming a Union official in 1925. In 1907, after three years of working for a pittance for a Bloemfontein commercial firm, Elias was instantaneously sacked when he asked for a rise. He decided then and there that 'I could not work for a white man unless he considered I was a human being'. But the following eighteen years of self-employment were difficult ones, and in 1910 Elias spent a month in jail for theft. Five years later, his repertoire had expanded to housebreaking and theft, for which he earned three months hard labour or a £15 fine. Apparently, the sentences neither served as a deterrent nor taught him to conceal his tracks;[65] in 1925 he spent three months in prison for stealing from the ICU.

Bluntly claiming, then, that ICU officials had a 'petty bourgeois background', is a singularly inadequate way of capturing the divisions within and dynamics of this grouping. 'Petty bourgeois' Congress officials, for example, differed markedly from their ICU counterparts. A significantly higher proportion of Congress leaders appear to have been relatively economically secure, often with independent sources of income, and - judging by the number of overseas degrees that studded their ranks - considerably better educated. (According to ICU leaders, Congress men were the 'Old Brigade', or 'the upper stratum of the native bourgeois', or the 'good boys' who graced the Chamber of Mines clubs.)[66] ICU leaders on the other hand were drawn largely from the frustrated sub-elite - the penurious salariat and those losing access to independent livelihoods - from whose ranks men were constantly disappearing into the proletariat or more marginalized groups. As Congress intellectuals sourly perceived the situation, their ICU counterparts were half-educated, lower class youths, with a penchant for separatist churches and Communism.[67]

It was indeed true that numerous educated blacks of this period were open to ideas with a socialist content, partly because of their closeness to the under classes, and partly because of their own intimate knowledge of capitalist exploitation. Amongst them was Herbert Msane, who, a decade before becoming ICU branch secretary in Greytown, was a mine labourer involved in the Industrial Workers of Africa, a union established by white socialists. As one of the considerable number of future Union organizers involved in the post-war protest against passes and low wages, Msane wrote a pamphlet denouncing the exploitation of black workers by white capitalists. Another IWA veteran who became an ICU leader was William Thibedi, a teacher who also spent years in the Communist Party (CP). Especially after 1924 when it resolved to concentrate on the black proletariat, the CP had a profound influence on the development of ICU intellectuals. The first Union branch in the Transvaal was in fact established by white Communists and their African recruits, who included Thomas Mbeki. By 1926 five members of the ICU's National Executive were Party members, and even after their expulsion in this year, passionate denunciations of capitalism remained regular features of ICU meetings. Tactically and theoretically, black Communists were often more sophisticated than other African organizers, and the CP certainly concentrated the minds of some middle class ICU organizers on the aspirations of workers and peasants.[68]

Not that exposure to socialist ideas was essential for this identification. In 1921, Tyamzashe claimed bitterly that most trained craftsmen were unable to find work, and hence lived 'riotous degraded lives, associating with the lowest class, and even with criminals'.[69] Given the policy of class suppression and racial oppression associated with segregation, such fraternisation was almost inevitable even for those who were neither unemployed nor labourers. Lower middle class Africans, living cheek by jowl with other blacks in overcrowded townships, meeting them at soccer, church or dancing hall, and often forced by starvation incomes into illicit beer brewing, were repeatedly being hurled back into the milieu of workers and the marginalized.[70]

This occurred to an even greater extent in the countryside, where penurious middle class blacks tended to be drawn relentlessly into the way of life of the under classes. As principal of a ramshackle school in a Natal reserve, Gilbert Coka for the first time in his life lived in a hut and subsisted largely on mealie meal. Through daily visits to pupils' homesteads, he also gained an intimate knowledge of the hardships of families of migrant labourers. Most rural teachers were similarly impelled into living near and with the people - to overcome their own isolation, to maintain school attendance, and to win favour with local notables who generally had considerable power over their posts. For ICU leaders like Jacob Nhlapo, who taught for two years at a Reitz farm school before becoming a Union branch secretary there, such linkages with influential families and parents were of crucial importance in ICU penetration of the countryside.[71]

As Coka discovered, ethnically-based cultural events were also of help in integrating him into the community. Even when middle class blacks were drawn from households which had partially dissociated themselves from chiefdoms, they generally grew up speaking the language of a particular ethnic group, participating in some of its political and cultural practices, and acquiring a pantheon of its heroes who had resisted white conquest. Thus in addition to racial oppression, ethnic traditions could be used to elide class differences. Champion, for instance, put the fact that he was, 'of course, a pure-blooded Zulu' to good effect in Durban, where his Xhosa-speaking predecessor had won little support from the overwhelmingly Zulu migrant population.[72]

Another way in which organizers and schooled blacks were drawn into communities was through their role as elaborators and disseminators of ideas. As the only fairly well educated people available, they also often served as mediators between local Africans and white authority. In the countryside, for instance, rural blacks often sought out the teacher 'for help and advice in their own difficulties of various kinds; he often occupies a position of authority and respect, and by virtue of the education he has acquired he is frequently interpreter to them of the European civilisation'.[73]

Understandably, such middle strata blacks did not necessarily interpret that civilization or offer the advice their white superiors would have preferred. Self-interest alone usually necessitated some sensitivity to the needs of the community: if self-employed Africans dependent on black clients could rarely afford to become known as 'Enemy of the Natives', neither could those like teachers whose position depended largely on good relations with the local people. Furthermore, the servile position of middle strata Africans with regard to white capital and the state considerably inhibited their desire - or ability - to act as collaborators. Consequently, educated blacks could well come to identify with those against whom they were expected to represent white authority, but whose daily struggles and hardships closely paralleled their own.[74] And when rural Africans elected such men to ICU branch committees, it was frequently in recognition of the fact that they had served not as petty bourgeois henchmen of the white dominant groups, but as organic intellectuals of the black under classes.

There was always the possibility, however, that middle class ICU organizers could act in either of these roles. On the one hand, as we have seen, they were derived from social groups which were economically, politically and culturally distinct from - and often opposed to - the masses. It is on these bourgeois aspects of their background that both liberal and radical historians have focused, thereby considerably enlarging our knowledge of how leaders' elitist origins influenced the Union's ideology and organization in the countryside.

On the other hand, a central argument of this paper has been that the bourgeois nature of the ICU's petty bourgeois leadership has been overemphasized by these scholars. Firstly, institutions such as school, church and parliament were less important in moulding liberal world views than has been suggested. Secondly, the ICU leadership was able to identify with the black under classes on the key issues of wages, passes and land - and this meant that the class content of their liberatory message was of considerably more relevance than that of Congress. As Charles Kumalo neatly expressed it, 'The ICU fought for freedom. Those of the Congress also fought for freedom, but didn't talk about money.'[75] Thirdly, this identification was possible partly because the ICU's leadership was mainly drawn from a sub-elite, which had established organic links with workers, peasants and the marginalized, into whose ranks these struggling middle class men were continually being drawn.

The contradictory nature of the leadership was reflected in the ICU's discourse, where socialist demands jostled with those of bourgeois nationalists, and where contempt for the illiterate heathen coexisted with adulation of the black worker. To move beyond those liberal scholars who have dismissed this as confusion, it is necessary to root these inconsistencies partly in the very nature of the intermediate strata, pulled in different directions by antagonistic social forces. And to move beyond radicals who have swept away contradictions by focusing almost exclusively on the bourgeois aspects of the ICU message, it is essential to grasp that sections of the middle strata were linked to, shared the interests of, and were being thrown back into the under classes. Otherwise, it becomes impossible to comprehend how 'petty bourgeois' leaders could adopt the following preamble to their constitution in 1925:

> Whereas the interests of workers and those of the employers are opposed to each other, the former living by selling their labour, receiving for it only part of the wealth they produce; and the latter living by exploiting the labour of the workers; depriving the workers of a part of the product of their labour in the form of profit, no peace can be between the two classes. A struggle must always obtain about the division of the products of human labour, until the workers through their industrial organisations take from the capitalist class the means of production, to be owned and controlled by the workers for benefit of all, instead of for the profit of a few ... This is the goal for which the ICU strives along with all other organized workers throughout the world.'[76]

NOTES

1. J Ngubane, An African Explains Apartheid (London 1963), 87.

2. P Bonner, 'The Decline and Fall of the ICU - a case of Self-Destruction?' in E Webster, ed., Essays in Southern African Labour History (Johannesburg, 1978), 117.

3. T Karis and G Carter, From Protest to Challenge, Vol. 4, (Stanford, 1977), 53; H and R Simons, Class and Colour in South Africa 1850-1950, (Harmondsworth, 1971), 266-267.

4. Church of the Province of South Africa (CPSA), University of the Witwatersrand (UW), Industrial and Commercial Workers' Union Records, A924, File 3, W Ballinger to W Holtby, 2 September 1930.

5. Pietermaritzburg Archives Depot (PAD), Chief Native Commissioner (CNC), 39/4, N2/8/3(27), Part I, Sam Dunn to CNC, 8 October 1929.

6. University of Cape Town (UCT), Forman Collection (FC), B2.59, 'The ICU Funds' by G Lenono.

7. Star 25/8/27. Information in this paragraph is drawn from J Jingoes, A Chief is a Chief by the People (London, 1975), 100-105; The Workers' Herald (WH) 18 March 1927; UW, African Studies Institute (ASI), Oral History Project (OHP), interview with C Kumalo by V Nkumane (VN) and Helen Bradford (HB) at Mooi River 28 November 1981; Central Archives Depot (CAD), Middelburg Municipal Correspondence (MMC), 4 January 1920, T Ramonti to Sub-Native Commissioner (SNC), 10 April 1926 (thanks to Rob Morrel for archival and press information relating to Middelburg); UW, W Ballinger Collection (BC), A410/C2(g), File 4, L Greene to W Ballinger 1 March 1929.

8. The Middelburg Observer (MO) 15 May 1926; G Coka, 'The story of Gilbert Coka of the Zulu tribe of Natal, South Africa' in M Perham, ed., Ten Africans (London, 1936), 296-297.

9. P Bonner, 'The Transvaal Native Congress 1917-1920' in R Rathbone and S Marks, eds., Industrialisation and Social Change in South Africa (Harlow, 1982), 271.

10. S Johns, 'Trade Union, Political Pressure Group, or Mass Movement?' in R Rotberg and A Mazrui, eds., Protest and Power in Black Africa (Oxford, 1970), 707-708.

11. Accounts from which these remarks are drawn include Johns, 'Trade Union'; P Walshe, The Rise of African Nationalism in South Africa (London, 1970); M Benson, The Struggle for a Birthright (New York, 1966). And although it is difficult to classify them as 'liberals', see also Simons and Simons, Class and Colour.

12. Bonner, 'The Decline and Fall', 118.

13. T Lodge, 'Black Opposition: a historical perspective', The Black Sash, (February, 1979), 16-17.

14. Other accounts from which these remarks are drawn include D du Toit, Capital and Labour in South Africa (London, 1981); K Luckardt and B Wall, Organise or Starve! (London, 1980).

15. 1921 Census Report, UG 37 - '24, 240, 243, 244; Walshe, Rise of African Nationalism, 240.

16. In 1927, over 60 per cent of Head Office finance was derived from Natal, and membership here in this period was more than double that of any other province.

17. Sam Dunn and Clements Kadalie were amongst those related to chiefs, while Henry Tyamzashe, Abe Phoofolo and Selby Msimang were amongst those who were the sons of professionals. Organizers with rural connections included Champion, Abel Ngcobo and Gilbert Coka. Cf. C Bundy, The Rise and Fall of the South African Peasantry (London, 1979), 140. Organizers possibly connected to the Mfengu peasantry were Ethelbert Maliza, born in Fort Peddie, qualified as a teacher, and in favour of extending Land Bank facilities to Africans, and Absolem Geduka, described as a 'Fingo of 28' in 1928.

18. PAD, CNC 39/4, N2/8/3(27), Part I, Secretary of Native Affairs (SNA) to CNC, 25 August 1928, enclosing petition from the Dunns. See also CAD, Department of Native Affairs (NTS) 49/328, A Champion to Prime Minister 28 September 1931, where Champion refers to enjoying 'a European standard of living since my birth'.

19. C Loram, The Education of the South African Native (London, 1917), 318.

20. Jingoes, A Chief is a Chief, 74. Information about the war is drawn from A Grundlingh, Die Suid-Afrikaanse Gekleurdes en die Eerste Wêreldoorlog, D. Litt. en Phil., Unisa, 1981, 207-208. ICU leaders who enlisted included Sam Dunn, Doyle Modiakgotla, Jason Jingoes, S Bennett Ncwana and J H London.

21. Notule van die Vyf-en-Vyftigste Algemene Vergadering van die Nederduitse Ger. Kerk van Natal, April 1928, p57. Educational statistics: see Walshe, African Nationalism, 77; Report of the Native Economic Commission, UG 22 - '34, 90. Standard 6 graduates included Kadalie, Champion, J Kokozela, W Makgothu, A Jabavu, and H Tyamzashe. The branch organizers referred to are J Mancoe, E Maliza, and A Nzula, all of whom had qualified as teachers; N Tantsi, E Maliza, J Nhlapo and G Coka, all of whom had their JC's; and J Jingoes, who had at least Standard 6.

22. E Mphahlele, Down Second Avenue (London, 1973), 60. Cf. also A Gramsci, Selections from Prison Notebooks (London, 1978), 14. Other information drawn from WH 15 May 1926; R Cohen, 'Albert Nzula: the Road from Rouxville to Russia', in B Bozzoli, ed., Labour, Townships and Protest (Johannesburg, 1978); Coka, 'The story of Gilbert Coka', 285; C Kadalie, My Life and the ICU: The autobiography of a black Trade Unionist in South Africa (London, 1970), 222.

23. UW, ASI, OHP, interview with E Ngcobo at Bulwer by VN and HB, 3 December 1981. Other information drawn from WH 15 December 1926, WH 15 June 1927, Star 31 May 1927, P Wickins, The Industrial and Commercial Workers' Union of Africa, Ph.D., University of Cape Town, 1973, 272. Women organizers included Mrs Elias, Mrs Lande, Miss Mildred Ngcayiya, Bertha Mkize, Mrs Pearse, Mrs Busakwe, Magdalena Mashalane and Miss Maggie Maguga. Mrs Siluma and Mrs L Mkwanazi were respectively Chairlady and Secretary of the Womens' Section which was organizing female workers in the Eastern Transvaal in late 1926.

24. Bloemfontein Archives Depot (BAD), Supreme Court, Free State Division (HG) 4/1/2/253, Case No. 101 of 1927, J Mogorosi vs Rex.

25. CAD, NTS 7665, Minutes of Evidence of Native Riots Commission, 337-338.

26. PAD, CNC 36/7, N2/2/2(28), CNC to Rev. Jessop 1/6/27, R Mdima to Inspector of Locations 30 May 1927; S Marks, 'John Dube and the Ambiguities of Nationalism', Conference on 'South Africa and the Comparative Study of Class, Race and Nationalism', New York, September 1982, 4, 16-17.

27. Walshe, African Nationalism, 240. Those who were exempted included Champion, Zondoni Hlubi, Kenneth Makanya and Thomas Mbeki, while voters included Kadalie and S Masabalala.

28. PAD, Kranskop Criminal Records, Case No. 158 of 1928, Rex. vs. J Nel and others; Mphahlele, Second Avenue, 64; Ons Vaderland (OV) 12 October 1928, WH 15 June 1927.

29. Wickins, ICU., 265-266; S Trapido, 'A Preliminary Study of the Development of African Political Opinion 1884-1955', B.A. Hons., UW, 1959, 28.

30. Star 25 January 1929. See also Star 7 January 1928.

31. CAD, Department of Police (SAP) Conf. 6/698/19, Abridged Prospectus of 'The Black Man' Company. See also Walshe, African Nationalism, 168.

32. WH 15 October 1927.

33. BAD, Bloemfontein Municipality Files (MBL) 4/6/4/46, enclosed in Town Clerk Kroonstad to Town Clerk Bloemfontein 11 June 1927.

34. P Bonner, 'The 1920 Black Mine Workers' Strike: a preliminary account', in Bozzoli, Labour, Townships, 289.

35. M Legassick, 'The Making of South African "Native Policy", 1903-1923: The Origins of Segregation', Institute of Commonwealth Studies (ICS) seminar, 15 February 1972.

36. R Davenport, 'The beginning of urban segregation in South Africa: the Natives (Urban Areas) Act of 1923 and its background, Occasional Paper No. 15, Institute of Social and Economic Research, Rhodes University, 1971.

37. Wickins, ICU., 241. See also J Wells, 'The Exclusion of African Women from the pass laws: the Native Urban Areas Act, 1923-1945', paper given at University of Natal 29 April 1980; R Bloch, 'The State in the townships: state, popular struggle and urban crisis in South Africa 1970-1980', mimeo.

38. Coka, 'The story of Gilbert Coka', 274-288.

39. R Shepherd, Lovedale (Lovedale, 1940), 338; Star 27 April 1920.

40. WH 18 March 1927. See also M Legassick, 'The Rise of Modern South African Liberalism: its Assumptions and Social Base', ICS Seminar paper 1 March 1972; Report of the Superintendent of Education for the year 1929, NP 3, 1930, 12.

41. Walshe, African Nationalism, 71, 90, 104; Kadalie, My Life, 60; S Neame, 'The ICU and British Imperialism', ICS Vol. 1, 1970.

42. BAD, Lindley Municipal Files (LLI) 2/1, N9/10/2, B Moshanyana to Magistrate Lindley 26 April 1928.

43. D Jabavu, 'Christianity and the Bantu' in M Stauffer, ed., Thinking with Africa (London, 1928), 121.

44. Star 24 June 1927.

45. Report of the Native Economic Commission 1930-1932, (NEC) UG 22-'34, 100.

46. UW, CPSA, Evidence to the Native Economic Commission, (ENEC), Box 6, 6262.

47. In 1920, mine clerks were averaging some £3-£5 a month, which was no more than the earnings of many underground miners. See also M Wilson, 'The growth of peasant communities' in M Wilson and L Thompson, eds., The Oxford History of South Africa, Vol. 2, 59.

48. Report of the Interdepartmental Committee on Native Education, UG 29 - '36, 16.

49. R Peteni, Towards Tomorrow, (Morges, 1979), 22; Report of Committee on Native Education, 39-40, 109; P Cook, The Native Student Teacher (Pretoria, 1940), 11.

50. Report of the Native Affairs Commission for the year 1923, UG 47 - '23; E Brookes, The Colour Problems of South Africa (Lovedale, 1934), 11; Kadalie, My life, 91, 146.

51. UCT, FC, B3.102, J Kunene to A Champion 24 September 1927; Star 27 May 1927; Report of the Interdepartmental Committee on the Native Pass Laws 1920, UG 41-'22.

52. Report of the Native Affairs Commission for the year 1922, UG 36 -'23, 11. See also M Lacey, Working for Boroko (Johannesburg, 1981), 389.

53. Report of the Native Affairs Commission for the years 1925-1926, UG 17-127, 72.

54. Minutes of Evidence of the Natal Natives Land Committee, UG 35-18, 181.

55. Ibid., 105.

56. PAD, CNC 39/4, N2/8/3(27), Part II, Minutes of meetings with 57 members of the Dunn family 14 September 1931.

57. Loram, Education of the Native, 149.

58. UW, CPSA, ENEC, evidence of the Kranskop magistrate 14-15. See also 1921 Census 244; Report on Native Pass Laws 5; Report of Committee on Native Education, 27; Peteni, Towards Tomorrow 19-20; Report of the Superintendent of Education for the year 1929, 66; NEC 88-89.

59. Kadalie, My Life, 33-37.

60. 1921 Census, 244; Bonner, 'Transvaal Native Congress', 286-87; BAD, Parys Municipality (MP) 1/1/7, Minutes of Town Council meeting 26/1/28.

61. UW, CPSA, ENEC, evidence of C Mbolekwe, 8518.

62. A Peacock, Bread or Blood (London, 1965), 49-50. See also E Thompson, The Making of the English Working Class (Harmondsworth, 1977), 172; BAD, Kroonstad Municipality (MKR) 1/3/8/1, Native Affairs Committee meeting 9 July 1931. Bootmaker organizers include Alphabet Caluza of Weenen, Stephen Nkosi of Vryheid and Joseph Bhengu of Empangeni.

63. PAD, Kranskop Criminal Records, Case No. 158 of 1928, Rex. vs. J Nel and others. See also A Dodd, Native Vocational Training (Lovedale, 1938), 44, 106; H Tyamzashe, 'Why have you educated me?' in F Wilson and D Perrot, eds., Outlook on a Century (Lovedale, 1973), 210.

64. Jason Jingoes and Herbert Msane had both worked as miners, and the former had served as a domestic servant in his youth. See OV 23 December 1927 for Malaza.

65. Wickins, ICU, 87, 497, 667; UW, CPSA, BC, File 3, P Seme to A Champion 9 November 1928; BAD, MBL 4/8/1/81, Minutes of a meeting of a municipal Wages Commission (for Elias' work experiences); BAD, HG 4/1/2/240, Case 124 of 1926, Rex. vs. S Elias. Elias Kuzwayo, a Natal secretary, had an even worse record than Elias. He was convicted for theft in 1918, for housebreaking and theft in 1920, for theft again in 1924, and was dismissed from the ICU for theft.

66. WH 15 December 1926; CAD, Department of Justice (JUS) 289, 3/1064/18, T Mbeki to G Hardy 25 June 1926.

67. Star 21 January 1928; Jabavu, 'Christianity and the Bantu', 121.

68. F. Johnstone, 'The IWA on the Rand: Socialist Organising among Black Workers on the Rand, 1917-1918', in Bozzoli, Labour, Townships, 255-265; Bonner, 'Transvaal Native Congress', 294; E Roux, S P Bunting (Johannesburg, 1944), 70-72. CP members who were ICU leaders included J la Guma, E Khaile, T Mbeki, J Nkosi, A Nzula, S Silwana, J Gomas and R de Norman. TWK 'Mote was among those who did not join the CP but was considerably influenced by it ideologically, while A Maduna was a renegade CP member by the end of 1926.

69. Tyamzashe, 'Why have you educated me?', 210.

70. Bonner, 'Transvaal Native Congress', 278.

71. Coka, 'The story of Gilbert Coka', 284-287; Peteni, Towards Tomorrow, 71.

72. CAD, NTS 7665, Minutes of Evidence to Native Riots Commission, 342.

73. I Schapera, 'The Teacher and his Community' in H Dumbrell, ed., Letters to African Teachers (London, 1935).

74. Kadalie, for example, claimed that 'it was the systematic torture of the African people in Southern Rhodesia that kindled the spirit of revolt in me' - Kadalie, My Life, 78.

75. UW, ASI, OHP, interview with C Kumalo.

76. 'Preamble to the 1925 Revised Constitution', in <u>South African Labour Bulletin</u>, 1,6,(1974), 21.

'The Simplicity of the Native Mind': Black Passengers on the South African Railways in the Early Twentieth Century

Ronald Ellsworth

The proletarianisation of Africans in the evolving capitalist economies of southern Africa has received much attention recently. Numerous studies detailing the breakdown of African peasant societies, the emergence and rapid growth of labour migration, the development of worker consciousness among proletarianized Africans, and other aspects of this disruptive process have appeared. This literature highlights a number of interrelated themes which illuminate the life experiences of African societies and individuals during a period of rapid economic and social change.

This paper is intended to add, if only slightly, to our understanding of this process of proletarianization. The paper gives attention to a subject which has received little sustained study: transport. In a system of labour mobilisation organised around the principle of migrancy, transport would appear to be a factor of some importance. Drawing the bulk of its labour from rural areas located long distances from the centres of production, capital developed a clear interest in cheap and rapid transport for migratory labour. For permanently urbanized Africans, as well as their employers, transport again assumed a position of prominence. The urban segregation movement which gathered force early in this century displaced thousands of Africans from the city centres, forcibly resettling them in "native locations" situated on or beyond the outskirts of the urban areas. This physical removal of urban African workers from the vicinity of the work place enhanced the importance of urban transport.

Hence there is reason to believe that the study of passenger transport in early twentieth century South Africa can contribute to our knowlege of African proletarianization. This paper represents only a small first step in this direction. A paper of this length necessarily must be selective in terms of the material it presents. The emphasis is therefore on one (albeit crucial) aspect of proletarianisation: African responses to this traumatic experience. An examination of black passengers on the South African Railways is illustrative in this respect.

The managers and staff of South Africa's state-owned railways frequently discussed the "irregularities" of the African passenger traffic. African passengers often missed trains for which they held tickets or travelled on trains with invalid tickets. Some were caught travelling without tickets. African passengers would detrain at the wrong stations, either leaving the train before it reached the appropriate station or "overrunning" their tickets.

In their lucid moments railway officers and employees realised that these "irregularities" could be explained, in part, by factors beyond the control of Africans. African passengers themselves, as well as some white observers, complained loudly and often that blacks were given little help or information by white railway employees.[1] Not all of the frustrations suffered by African passengers could be blamed on the railway staff, however. While management periodically admonished the staff to show special consideration to African passengers,[2] these top officials seem to have acted only gradually and sporadically to improve the conditions under which Africans travelled by rail. Africans complained recurrently over the shortage of non-European coach accommodation, for example. This caused serious overcrowding of coaches. Thousands of Africans must have missed trains because when the "Native Special" steamed in its coaches were already packed to overflowing.[3]

Railway officers acknowledged that these and other practical factors helped account for the "irregularities" of the African passenger traffic. But when discussing these "irregularities" they at times adopted a different mode of explanation, one derived from and reflecting the racist assumptions of white South Africa's dominant ideology. Hence one occasionally finds references to the supposed working of the "native mind" and its bearing on the African passenger traffic.

In November 1922 a South African Railways (SAR) Assistant Manager commented on the psychology of African passengers. He remarked that Africans held only 'vague ideas' about train schedules and therefore hung about stations for long periods. Moreover many Africans travelling on Reef trains were in the habit of "overrunning" their tickets, apparently out of an inability to grasp the passenger ticket regulations. In any event, it was claimed, such passengers usually reacted badly when conductors demanded the payment of an excess fare, because 'The native mind cannot understand this action on the part of the "white" man and it may be accepted that the course followed by ticket examiners in such circumstances is viewed by the native with the greatest suspicion.'[4]

Another "irregularity" frequently discussed by the railway authorities was the tendency of Africans to travel on trains for which their tickets were technically invalid. This applied particularly to migratory labourers travelling by rail. In order to help mining and agriculture attract labour, migrants were permitted to travel at concessionary fares. In theory, these "special native fares" were available only to migrants travelling by goods train or "recognised native train". For a variety of practical reasons this regulation could not be enforced, but in 1933 SAR General Manager T H Watermeyer claimed that the root of the problem went considerably deeper:

> The chief difficulty is, however, the simplicity of the native mind, and the probability that natives would be quite unable to understand and observe restrictions based upon an elaborate schedule of "permitted" or "non-permitted" trains ...[5]

Opinions of this nature about African railway passengers reflected more general European attitudes about the adjustment of tribal Africans to the modern industrial world. Perhaps the two most common characteristics attributed to Africans who had been drawn into the world of industrial capitalism were those of irrationality and stupidity. Thus it was not uncharacteristic for the Director of the Government Native Labour Bureau to conclude that when booking clerks issued migratory labourers tickets to the wrong stations 'These mistakes may be due to the Booking Clerk's ignorance of a native language but more probably to the stupidity of the natives themselves'.[6] Recent studies of the southern African labour market have already done much to identify and demolish these standard stereotypes formulated by white South Africans. These studies show that Africans responded rationally and intelligently to the pressures and demands of industrial capitalism.[7] This paper will offer further evidence to support this interpretation by examining the behaviour of African railway passengers. The balance of the paper will consist of two sections and a short conclusion. In the first section some of the "irregularities" of the African passenger traffic will be subjected to closer scrutiny. It will become apparent that such "irregularities" were at least partially a result of deliberate petty frauds perpetrated on a wide scale by African passengers. Secondly, the paper will survey evidence pertaining to the relationship between transport costs and labour recruitment. It will be argued that potential migrants displayed a keen sensitivity to transport costs which could act as a hindrance to recruitment.

Acts of petty fraud committed by Africans travelling on the railways were common. How characteristic such behaviour was of African passengers as a whole it is impossible to say. Fraud is difficult to detect, especially when successful, and any attempt at qualification is obviously out of the question. But some of the varieties of petty fraud practiced by African passengers can be identified and fraudulent acts can be shown to have been widespread.

For example, Africans incessantly travelled on trains for which their tickets were technically invalid. The railway administrations' inability to enforce its own regulations greatly improved an African passenger's chances of successfully ignoring them. The regulation applicable to the "special native fares" is a case in point. As noted, Africans purchasing such tickets were supposed to travel by goods train or "recognised native train". No serious attempt was made to enforce this regulation, however. Enquiries launched by General Manager W W Hoy in 1917 revealed a lack of uniformity in the conveyance of Africans travelling at the reduced fares. While most of the divisional officers urged that henceforth the regulation be enforced strictly, headquarters concluded this was 'impracticable'.[8] So it remained into the 1930s.

In the absence of a firm policy to regulate the African passenger traffic in this respect, Africans took advantage of the situation. 'Natives who hold native fare tickets frequently and deliberately miss a particular train for the purpose of travelling by the ordinary train', it was reported in 1933, 'and up to the present it has not been possible to cope with such cases owing to the lack of any deliberate instruction or hard and fast rule.'[9] Evidently Africans had some incentive to avoid riding on the "recognised native trains" and in "native coaches" attached to goods trains. Atrocious travelling conditions seem to have provided this incentive.

The typical form of coach accommodation supplied for the conveyance of Africans travelling by goods or "recognised native" train was known as the "Bombella" coach. These coaches were former livestock trucks which had been converted into rough passenger coaches.[10] In 1910 S M Pritchard, Director of the Government Native Labour Bureau, described the typical Bombella used to carry migratory labourers from East London to Johannesburg, at that time a journey of two and a half days by goods train.

> At present the average available Native compartment is a converted cattle truck, measuring about 30 feet by 7 feet, in which I have seen huddled as many as 40 to 45 Natives. They are fitted with a narrow seat round the inside some 12 inches wide, and a bench down the centre of about double that width. The result is that not only are the trucks dreadfully overcrowded, but the Natives have practically no rest whatsoever, - being compelled, during the long journey, to sit and sleep bolt upright.[11]

Pritchard persuaded the railway administration to effect changes calculated to provide Transkeian migrants with a quicker and more comfortable journey to and from the Rand.[12] For the majority of Africans travelling by goods or "recognised native" tain, however, it appears that travelling conditions improved only slowly. The Bombellas were gradually retired from service and replaced by relatively more comfortable coaches, but in the meantime many Africans travelled in these converted livestock trucks.[13]

While agreeable to improving the "special native fare" coach accommodation to the extent that traffic priorities and finances permitted, the railway authorities held that standards should not be improved beyond a certain point. Since Africans taking advantage of the concessionary fares travelled more cheaply than other passengers (including Africans who paid third class fares), the administration insisted that they should not be provided with equally comfortable accommodation. For this reason the General Manager disapproved when he learned in 1930 that "special native fare" ticket holders regularly travelled in third class coaches on the Orange Free State lines.[14] But the SAR's inability to confine "special native fare" ticket holders to goods and "recognised native" trains meant they likewise could not be prevented from riding in third class non-European coaches, which were attached to most passenger trains. Several ticket examiners drew attention to this use of third class coaches by Africans who were 'not by any means the best type'.[15]

While railway officials might consider it 'invidious' for different classes of passengers to ride together in the same coaches,[15] the better standards of comfort available in third class coaches induced large numbers of "special native fare" passengers to avoid the Bombellas. Moreover Africans had at least one further strong reason to travel by ordinary passenger train whenever possible: more rapid transit to their destination.[17] Aside from the sheer inconvenience of delays in transit, the rigours of the pass laws "encouraged" Africans to travel quickly, as an observer noted:

> They argue that under the Pass Laws their position demands, they should get home, on a particular date, and at a particular time ... and that if they are refused permission to board a particular train, through no fault of their own ... they are subject to arrest, and punishment. To say they must always be in good time will not help them ... the train may be full before it arrives at the station at which they are waiting. Time, under such circumstances, is everything to a native ...[18]

If Africans tried to avoid travelling by goods train and "recognised native train", however, they displayed no such reluctance about taking advantage of the cheaper fares restricted, in theory, to Africans travelling in this way. A memorandum written in 1918 observed that practically no male Africans travelling by rail purchased third class tickets, while in 1933 an official wrote that male African passengers could be divided into two groups: those who knew enough to ask for "special native fare" tickets, and those who did not. It disturbed these officials that Africans who travelled third class with "special native fare" tickets were depriving the administration of 'legitimate revenue'.[19] This brings us to a second form of sharp practice employed by African passengers: petty monetary fraud. As General Manager Hoy remarked in 1914, 'there is a marked disposition amongst the natives to evade the payment of legitimate charges and ... difficulty is sometimes experienced in collecting same'.[20]

Take the case of Johannesburg's Zulu washermen. Charles van Onselen has shown how the flourishing laundry trade built up by these urbanised Africans in the 1890s declined after 1900 as a result of restrictive measures imposed by the state and the rapid development of commercial laundry services on the Reef. Van Onselen also portrays the efforts of the washermen to resist proletarianization.[21] The methods of resistance chosen by the washermen included organised fraud directed against the railway administration. In 1906 the Transvaal state forced the washermen to abandon their traditional washing places near the white residential areas and relocated them at the newly proclaimed Klipspruit location, thirteen miles southwest of Johannesburg. The cost of transporting laundry by rail between Klipspruit and Johannesburg added to the financial constraints already threatening the viability of the laundry trade. Responding to complaints by the washermen and subsequent representations submitted by the Johannesburg municipal authorities, the (then) Central South African Railways agreed in April 1907 to halve the rate charged for the conveyance of laundry between certain Reef stations and Klipspruit. Henceforth bundles of laundry could be transported between these points at a charge of 6d. per bundle, with a weight limit of 200 lbs. per bundle. Bundles exceeding the weight limit were to be assessed an additional 6d. charge.[22]

A 'serious irregularity' soon came to light and was brought to the attention of W W Hoy, then Chief Traffic manager of the CSAR. An investigation of the laundry traffic conducted by the station master of Nancefield station (located about a mile from Klipspruit) revealed that many bundles conveyed by the washermen exceeded the weight limit, though only one 6d. ticket had been purchased for each of these bundles. An inspection of the overweight bundles revealed the reason for their excessive weight: The washermen were banding together and amalgamating two or more small bundles into one large bundle. Indeed, one giant bundle weighing 513 lbs. contained eleven separate bundles of laundry. Hoy drew the appropriate conclusion:

> The concession fixed was that the boys should be charged 6d. for their bundles provided the weight did not exceed 200 lbs.; now it seems the boys are combining - one case no less than eleven boys pooled their bundles - in order to escape the carriage.[23]

Having uncovered this "irregularity", the railway authorities now had to decide how to deal with it. The Nancefield station master had taken the line of forcing washermen to pay extra charges of overweight bundles. The washermen had responded by means of an organised protest at the office of Klipspruit's location superintendent. This episode upset the Johannesburg municipal authorities, who were anxious that 'nothing should occur which might tend to make the natives leave the location ...'[24] Respecting the wishes of the municipality, Hoy settled for a compromise arrangement. He considered it 'not unreasonable' for extra charges to be imposed on combined bundles which exceeded the weight limit since the original concession had been intended to apply to individual bundles only. However, Hoy instructed the staff to exercise tact when handling the laundry traffic. While excess charges were to be imposed for noticeably overweight bundles, servants were to avoid harassing washermen whose bundles exceeded the weight limit by only a few pounds. Moreover one 6d. ticket was to be accepted as payment for such bundles 'without too close a scrutiny being made as to whether more than one boy's washing is in the bundle or not'.[25] As a consequence of this decision 'to make conditions as easy as possible for the natives consistent with business', along with the difficulty of supervising the laundry traffic properly at busy Reef stations, the washermen continued to work their racket.[26]

In fact, the fraudulent propensities of African passengers caused endless headaches for Nancefield's station master, who complained that 'the Natives beat by far the White people in endeavouring to do the Department down, at least the Natives of Klipspruit who are an advanced set.'[27] This remark was occasioned by the fraudulent activities of African women conveying packages and bundles of laundry with them on the Nancefield trains. This matter came under consideration in 1912 after some women complained they had been compelled to pay railage for laundry they felt entitled to transport free of charge. Indicating that the individuals in question were only 'girls' and no 'Zulu wash boys', the municipal Superintendent of Locations urged that the women be permitted to convey small bundles of laundry without payment; otherwise 'All the natives will be up in arms, meetings will be held and delegates sent from here to the Native Affairs Department, and no end of trouble will be the ultimate result'.[28] The railway authorities then decided that bundles weighing up to 25 lbs. could be conveyed free so long as the women travelled by "native train", while bundles weighing more than 25 lbs. would be assessed a 6d. charge.[29]

Nancefield's station master had warned that this kind of arrangement would lend itself to fraud,[30] and he was proven correct. African women found it easy to slip substantial packages 'containing almost anything' past the station staff:

> Unfortunately the Natives are not looked after sharp enough and many packages get through weighing far above the amount allowed. The packages being put under the seats or in any out of the way place that might escape the Examiner's eye.[31]

More direct methods of evasion could be employed when necessary. One Saturday in August 1916 the station master personally confronted six or seven women who had refused to buy tickets for laundry they intended to carry with them on a train which had not been accorded "native" status. Two of these women immediately 'sought shelter in the female lavatory and when the train came in rushed out amongst the crowd and escaped payment'.[32]

The concessionary fares which these women were abusing had been introduced to help "popularise" location life, but they also derived from a recognition of Africans' limited earning power. With the urban segregation movement gathering force, the increased (or, in many cases, new) expense of commuting between home and work placed additional pressure on the finances of poorly paid black workers. The SAR devised and implemented a plethora of "native location fares" in tandem with this mass resettlement of Africans. Besides inaugurating economical single and return fares, the railway also offered the "Native Location Season Ticket" - available on a weekly or monthly basis - to urban African commuters.[33] The General manager of Railways explained in 1933 that these concessionary fares had been introduced 'Primarily for the purpose of facilitating the policy of concentrating urban native workers at convenient locations and to provide a fare to and from work in keeping with their earning power'.[34] In effect, then, the location fares served a twofold purpose and acted to resolve a potential contradiction inherent to the urban segregation movement. Cheap transport for urban African commuters assisted the segregation drive while shielding employers against having to bear its costs, in the form, for example, of demands for higher wages by black workers.

Predictably enough, petty fraud became an endemic feature of the location passenger traffic. In 1917, for instance, Africans travelling on the Canada-Nancefield-Klipspruit run quickly took advantage of a breakdown in the ticket examining routine. The "location" return fare between Canada and Nancefield came to 5d., while Africans travelling between Canada and Klipspruit paid 6d. This extra 1d. charge proved to be somewhat theoretical, howeer, since 'a large number' of Africans purchased tickets to Nancefield only and travelled the extra distance to Klipspruit, a little over a mile, free of charge. A railway servant could find no explanation for this practice except 'the saving of 1d. on each ticket and a slight risk of detection'.[35] Holders of weekly and monthly season tickets likewise defrauded the railway administration with impunity. In 1927 it was reported that 'on Saturday afternoons the native trains are full of piccanins travelling with weeklys (sic), presumably given to them by natives who have had a full week's travelling on same'.[36] Though the tickets were stamped "not transferable", it was almost impossible to prevent ticket holders from loaning or giving their tickets to friends and relatives, or to detect this when it happened:

> At Nancefield over 400 Season tickets are issued every Monday, the majority bearing the names of "George" or "Jim" and the regulation regarding non-transferance of the tickets is therefore a dead letter.[37]

Moreover some ticket holders retained their expired tickets and tried to use them for a second week or month of commuting. This was difficult to deter because of the lack of a colour-coding system and the overcrowding conditions of the location trains, which made ticket examination an awkward task.[38]

Clearly the African residents of Klipspruit location showed great resourcefulness in devising tricks and stratagems designed to illegally deprive the SAR of "legitimate revenue".[39] An intense exposure to industrial society and especially to railway travel undoubtedly accounts in part for their well-honed ability to defraud the railway administration. But indirect evidence suggests that many "raw natives" as well quickly learned to exploit larcenous opportunities. In the half-decade after Union the railway authorities engaged in a recurring dispute with the Witwatersrand Native Labour Association (WNLA) over ticket arrangements on the labour trains carrying Mozambiquan migratory labourers between Komatipoort and the Rand. An arrangement concluded by the CSAR and WNLA in 1909 required the latter organisation to supply conductors for this long-distance service. The work performed by these WNLA employees failed to impress W W Hoy, however. Persistent "irregularities" which afflicted this service raised the suspicion that "unattached" Africans surreptitiously joined WNLA gangs (whose fares had been paid in advance by the labour recruitment association) and rode the railways free of charge. Though WNLA Secretary F Perry denied this, Hoy remained unconvinced and insisted that improved ticket distribution and inspection arrangements be introduced and maintained.[40] That the labour trains offered ample scope for suspicious "irregularities" to arise regardless of the methods chosen to issue and inspect tickets is indicated by the experience of a railway ticket examiner who joined a train of Mozambiquan migrants being railed from Pretoria to Johannesburg:

> There were over 900 natives on this train and I had great difficulty in examining it owing to the condition of the rolling stock, filth, smell and heat. I am compelled to pass through lavatories the floors and seats covered in human filth. The trouble is I could not pass through them owing to the handles of the door in the inside being broken off and lying on the floor in the filth and even after getting it fixed up and cleaned and tried in the door to find it would not open. I then had to wait until the train stopped at the next station. The side doors would be locked from the outside and I could not get out without going back through two or three coaches looking for a door that opened from the inside.

At least Ticket Inspector Watson's day was not a total disaster. Despite these terrible working conditions he managed to apprehend "Bob" and "Nikkis", a pair of Mozambiquans who were travelling on the train without tickets.[41]

Like "Bob" and "Nikkis", many other Africans were caught while travelling on the railways in an "irregular" fashion under somewhat suspicious circumstances.[42] It is of course impossible to estimate even approximately the number of Africans who tried to defraud South African Railways in the early twentieth century, let alone those who succeeded. But the absence of quantitative exactitude should not scare us away from the conclusion that acts of petty fraud were common indeed. Moreover the fraudulent acts of African passengers can be traced to quite obvious and rational motives. Africans avoided the Bombella coaches and "recognised native trains" because of the grossly uncomfortable conditions characteristic of this mode of transport and the desire or need to travel at their own pace instead of that determined by the railway administration. The petty monetary frauds committed by African passengers are best understood when placed in the context of South Africa's labour-repressive, low wage political economy. In these circumstances, in fact, it would have been surprising if many Africans had not resorted to fraud as a basic tool of survival. A remark by S M Pritchard, though appearing in a different context, is apposite here. Honest Africans would 'merely contribute more of their somewhat meagre earnings to railway revenue'.[43]

A study of African passenger transport in early twentieth century South Africa therefore must acknowledge the position of increasing numbers of Africans as a subjugated labour force in a colonial political economy. The temptation to apply moral strictures condemnatory of the petty frauds committed by Africans travelling on the railways should be tempered by a recognition of the callous exploitation of African workers perpetrated by capital and sponsored by the state. The physical need of impoverished Africans to conserve scarce financial resources in South Africa's developing capitalist economy compelled them to devise various means of reducing their transport costs. One of these methods was fraud. Another was the adoption of a highly cost-conscious approach to travel.

If there is one feature of migratory labour systems which distinguish them from other systems of labour supply, that feature is movement. By its nature an economic system organised around the institution of migratory labour demands a steady flow of labourers between their places of residence and the centres of production. In South Africa large-scale labour migration derived from two interrelated developments: capitalist industrialisation and rural immiseration. Capitalist industrialisation in this specific environment created an insatiable demand for cheap, unskilled labour. The coincidental subjugation of African societies and demolition of African peasant economies compelled countless Africans to join the growing army of migrants trooping to and from the areas of industrial employment. Labour migration on any substantial scale in southern Africa can be traced to the opening of the Griqualand West diamond fields in the 1870s. But the scale of these early migrations pales in comparison to the enormous expansion of the system subsequent to the Witwatersrand gold discoveries of the mid-1880s. With its voracious appetite for masses of cheap, unskilled labour, the Rand gold mining industry drew its labour supplies from a human hinterland stretching from the south coast to the heart of central Africa.[44] By the time of Union in 1910 the migratory system had become entrenched as the dominant mode of labour mobilisation and exploitation in southern Africa.

African migrants usually travelled on foot during the early years of large-scale labour migration, but the railway construction boom which accompanied mining industrialisation diverted much of this human traffic to the rails. Railing migratory labourers offered clear advantages to employers. Migrants travelling by rail would reach the place of employment more quickly and probably in a healthier condition as well. Improved speed and efficiency was matched by tightened security. Required migrants travelling by rail escaped the clutches of labour-hungry farmers, who regularly intercepted and impressed migrants who traversed their farms on foot. The "stealing" of labour from the original contractor by rival labour agents working for different capitalists could be alleviated to some extent. Finally, railed migrants found less time and fewer opportunities available for desertion, that particular bane of capitalists throughout southern Africa.

For migratory labourers the balance between advantage and disadvantage would appear to have been more uncertain. On the positive side, migrants travelling by rail avoided exhausting and potentially hazardous journeys on foot. Those travelling to the mines escaped arrest for "trespassing" on white-owned farms and subsequent sentences of labour servitude to white farmers, who found it difficult to attract "voluntary" labour because of the low wages they could afford to pay. On the negative side, however, the more rapid journey to work and the closer supervision exercised over migrants travelling in this way undoubtedly reduced the chances of successful desertion for those so inclined. A second disadvantage of rail travel for migratory labourers is particularly relevant to the theme of this paper. While capital needed to extract labour from the human hinterland of southern Africa and South Africa Railways co-operated by providing special facilities and concessionary fares for migrants, neither were prepared to foot the bill for these services. This meant that the expense of rail travel fell on those least capable of meeting it: the migratory labourers themselves. Under the "advance system", labour recruiters or employers paid the rail fares of recruited migrants in advance. Once a migrant began work on a farm or in a mine, the cost of his fare was docked from his pay. Obviously these transport costs had to be based on the principle of "what the traffic would bear". Or, put differently, they had to be slow enough not to actively discourage rural Africans from accepting work on farms or in mines located some distance from their homes.[45]

Prior to Union in 1910 several of the colonial railway administrations allowed farm and mine labourers to travel at special reduced fares. The Union railways rationalised and expanded these special fare facilities to the extent that male Africans could travel at the concessionary fares in most parts of the Union.[46] The incidence of these fares varied according to the distance travelled. In fact, for relatively short journeys of 100 or 115 miles migratory labourers paid fares generally equal to the third class passenger fares for these distances. At 100 or 115 miles the "special native fare" scale came into operation, and the further the distance travelled beyond these points the greater became the discrepancy between the "special native fare" scale and the third class passenger scale.[47]

On a per person per mile basis, the charges levied under both scales decreased as the distance of the journey increased. This was unexceptional and merely reflected a fundamental principle of railway economics: that cost of haulage per mile decreased as distance of haulage increased. For our purpose, the significant thing is the marked discrepancy between the "special native fare" scale and the third class passenger scale, especially over long distances. The former offered considerable savings over the latter. In setting these fares the interests of capital, rather than those of labour, most concerned the railway administration, however. During a period when employers suffered the effects of labour "shortages", stabilisation of labour supplies became a premier interest of capital. Capital as well as railway management perceived a definite relationship between transport costs and labour mobilisation. The recognition that high transport costs hindered labour recruitment underlaid the "special native fares" scheme.

One indication of capital's perception of a relationship between transport costs and labour mobilization is found in efforts by employers to secure an extension of the principle of concessionary fares so as to encompass white and coloured labour. Natal sugar planter L R Nightingale approached the SAR on this matter in 1925. Noting that sugar growers in his district faced a 'very serious shortage of native labour', Nightingale explained that he had discovered a potential labour supply in the Graaff Reinet district of Cape province, where the coloured population were 'starving'. Unfortunately, the cost of railing these labourers from Graaff Reinet to Natal - 'four per boy' - 'just kills the scheme'. Nightingale therefore requested that these labourers be transported to Natal for the "special native fare" applicable to this distance - £2.16s. per labourer.[48]

The railway department customarily turned down applications proposing concessionary fares for white and coloured labourers.[49] In particular, suggestions that such labourers should be permitted to travel for the "special native fares" were consistently discouraged. The General Manager had to inform more than one disappointed applicant that "special native fare" tickets could not be supplied to 'Cape Boys, Hottentots, native women or Asiatics nor, of course, to white labour'.[50] This determination to limit the extent of concession-giving is explained primarily by financial considerations. Clause 127 of the Act of Union compelled the state railways to keep revenue and expenditure in approximate balance and to meet working expenditure out of its earnings as a carrier. For this reason requests for reduced or concessionary tariffs were subjected to careful scrutiny as railway officials attempted to determine the probable effect of proposed tariff alterations on the administration's financial position. In the decades after Union, moreover, the SAR was bombarded with applications for reduced and concessionary tariffs continuously and from all sides. Only a relatively small proportion of these applications could be granted. As a leading business journal realistically commented, 'From the North and the South, from the East and the West, come demands for special facilities and special rates which if acceded to would speedily bankrupt the whole system ...'[51]

Hence the administration's refusal to respond favourably to L R Nightingale's application[52] should not be interpreted as representing a lack of concern for the interests of capital. The labour needs of Nightingale and others who wished to transport white or mixed-race labour at a cheaper cost had to be balanced against the financial position of the SAR and the claims for reduced tariffs advanced in favour of other classes and forms of traffic. As it was, the "special native fares" quoted by the railways represented a significant concession to employers of migratory labour. The success or otherwise of these cheap fares in actively encouraging labour migration would seem difficult, if not impossible, to judge. By attacking the question from a different angle, however, the purpose of the cheap fares can be further illustrated and, to return to the major theme of this paper, insight can be gained into African responses to proletarianisation. I will therefore take the approach of examining whether transport costs actively discouraged rural Africans from leaving their homes in order to work on South African farms and mines.

In 1921 a proposal to increase the "special native fares" came under consideration at railway headquarters. The Rates Office opposed this proposal for the following reasons:

> Throughout the last twenty years there has been a shortage of native labour ...; it must be taken into consideration that the fares of all natives are ultimately recovered from wages and while the proposed increase may not seriously affect recruiting operations there is every reason to assume that the higher the rail fare the greater will be the difficulty in persuading natives to leave their homes to work at industrial centres.[53]

The Vryheid (Natal) Railway Coal and Iron Company Limited learned the truth of this observation by experience. This company employed large numbers of migratory labourers to work its Hlobane colliery. Late in 1918 the state banned the company from recruiting labour in the northern Transvaal, traditionally its major source of supply. Faced with a sudden labour crisis, the company hired CA Hadley to recruit labour in the Transkei. Hadley's efforts on behalf of the company were unsuccessful, however. Transkeians refused to accept work at the colliery because of the high rail fares they would have to pay in order to travel between their homes and Hlobane via the long, roundabout route through Bloemfontein. 'Natives can easily obtain work at various parts of the Union where the average rail fare would be about £1 or a little over', Hadley explained, 'which is a little less than half the railway fares to Hlobane'. Even an offer by Hadley to pay ten shillings of the fare out of his own pocket failed to persuade Transkeians to accept work at the colliery.[54]

The difficulties of the Vryheid company suggest that unacceptably high transport costs (in relation to wages) hampered labour recruitment in the "native areas". Other pieces of evidence point to the same conclusion. In 1924, for example, the railways consented to a reduction of the "special native fares" after receiving strong representations from the Department of Native Affairs and the Rand mining industry to the effect that recruitment difficulties had arisen because 'many natives consider the fares too high'.[55] Africans already "in the pipeline" could react in a more militant fashion when the cost of rail travel exceeded the price they were willing to pay. In March 1931 the SAR suddenly increased the "special native fares" at very short notice. A WNLA spokesman explained in a subsequent letter of protest that this abrupt increase had led to trouble at the association's central labour compound:

> The sequel was that yesterday a large number of natives at our Compound, due for return home, showed a recalcitrant spirit in protesting against the increased fares, to the extent in some cases of refusing to accept them; and it is more than likely that other natives, assembled for repatriation, will cause similar trouble.[56]

When capitalists and labour recruiters complained about the "high" cost of rail travel for migratory labourers they were obfuscating the issue, however. As explained, under the advance system rail fares were ultimately deducted from the pay of migrants. It seems more pertinent to conclude that low wages rather than excessive transport costs caused recruitment problems. It is therefore not surprising to find the saddest tales of woe about the effect of "high" transport costs on labour recruitment emanating from the lowest wage sector of the South African economy: agriculture. The labour problems of the agricultural sector seem to have become particularly critical during World War 1. Besides having to compete for labour supplies with the higher wage mining and manufacturing sectors, farmers watched with frustration during these years as thousands of potential black farm workers joined the armed forces. As a spokesman for the South African farmer appealed to Minister of Railways and Harbours Henry Burton in 1917:

> It is obvious that if it were necessary to grant special rates before Union to Harvesters, that necessity still exists and, in my opinion, to a greater degree than at that time, because with the creation of new industries and the expansion of old industries and public works, which are more attractive to natives, and the shipment of thousands of natives overseas, the number of natives available for agricultural purposes, in view of the enormous expansion of the Agricultural Industry, is much less now than before Union. Farmers have to go far afield now to obtain labour, and compete in the price of labour with other industries which are not subject to the risks and vicissitudes of the Agricultural Industry, and which can therefore afford to outbid farmers. I think I am not unreasonable in urging that farmers should be placed on a more equal footing with other employers of labour, by being granted cheaper means of transporting their labour from a distance.[57]

I Gordon, attorney, auctioneer and deputy sheriff of Wolmaransstad, Transvaal described the plight of farmers in his district. Each farm worker received the 'exorbitant' wage of £2.10s. to £3 per month, and before a farmer could even 'get the boy' he had to pay £4.10s. to £5 in advance to cover the rail fare and capitation fee. "Getting the boy" at all could prove difficult, however, because:

> The position of the native is hardly more satisfactory from a financial point of view. The period of his contract is for six months. When, at the expiration of his term of service, he arrives at home he has about £3 for his six months labour.

No wonder that 'owing to the scarcity of labour our farmers are severely handicapped', a handicap which Gordon believed only a 'material reduction of railway fares' could remove.[58]

In order to alleviate this agricultural labour crisis, the railway administration introduced specially low fares for a particular type of African labour at the beginning of 1918. Farmers from the eastern

Transvaal district of Bethal had approached the administration with the request that concessionary fares be provided for male African adolescents who had been recruited to perform farm labour.[59] A M Mostert, whom the farmers had engaged to recruit such youngsters, remarked that 'the farmer does not want the physically strong big boy who expects to earn at least £3 a month, as the young boy at 25/- per month is able to do all the work they require'. While 'numbers of these youths' could be secured in the Transkei Territory', the cost of transporting them by rail to Bethal and back was so 'prohibitive' that 'it practically kills the scheme'. At the wage offered by the farmers, a youngster would be 'Practically working for his travelling expenses backward and forward'. The state's Acting Director of Native Labour supported these representations, indicating that 'there is at present little inducement to such natives to offer their services for agricultural employment'. After initially resisting this pressure, the administration relented and agreed to a reduced scale of fares applicable to male African adolescents fourteen to seventeen years of age who had been recruited to perform agricultural or industrial labour.[60]

These so-called "fares for native umfaans" undercut even the "Special native fares" for distances over 500 miles and were quite clearly intended to help farmers mobilize such labour at a considerable distance from the point of production. In fact, both the "special native fares" and the "umfaan fares" were introduced and maintained with the objective of easing the labour problems of farming and mining during a period of chronic labour "shortage". It is therefore worth repeating that low wages rather than high transport costs underlay these labour recruitment problems. The concessionary fares acted partially to offset the meagreness of the pay earned by migrants by permitting them to travel economically on the state railways. It will be seen that a familiar pattern has emerged. These concessionary fares represent only one small facet of a much larger process: the state's direct involvement in economy and society to promote capitalist development in South Africa. In this instance state assistance to capital took the form of cheap transport for migratory labourers, thereby helping to keep labour costs within the limits which capitalist farming and mining could afford to bear.

The existence of these cheap fares should not be attributed solely to the initiative of capital and the state, however. The cheap fares came into general prominence only because they were seen to be necessary by both parties. A full explanation as to why they were seen to be necessary must give some attention to the responses of African tribesmen thrust as migratory labourers into an evolving capitalist economy. According to the stereotype formulated by contemporary white society, Africans adjusted only slowly and awkwardly to this process of social and economic change. Black workers retained a noticeable patina of tribal "backwardness" and were prone to economically irrational conduct. Had this been the case it is doubtful whether "special native fares" would have been necessary to help draw migratory labourers to white-owned farms and mines. These fares must be seen in part as a tribute to the relative sophistication of Africans undergoing a process of transition from peasants to proletarians. When a moment of calculation revealed that transport costs would consume an inordinate proportion of the wages being offered by a prospective employer, Africans proved resistant to recruitment. Ultimately it was this manifestation of market intelligence that compelled the SAR to provide cheap transport for migratory labourers.

In the 1920s and 1930s Africans demonstrated the vitality of this market intelligence in an unmistakable fashion. These were the years in which mechanical road vehicles first began seriously to challenge the railway's virtual monopoly of goods and passenger transport. Between 1923 and 1928 alone the number of licensed motor cars and taxis operating on South African roads increased from 38,815 to 113,002; the figures for buses, vans and lorries show an increase of more than fivefold for the same period, rising form 1,989 vehicles in 1923 to 11,672 in 1928.[61] Relatively powerless to curtail this competition until the advent of restrictive legislation in the 1930s, the railway authorities watched with dismay as private road operators diverted "legitimate" rail traffic to the road.

Space precludes an extensive survey of the competition between road and rail transport for the patronage of African travellers. There is evidence, though, which indicates that Africans showed an extreme sensitivity to even slight variations in competitive road and rail fares. The willingness of private road carriers to undercut rail fares on competitive routes diverted significant numbers of African passengers to road transport. To cite several examples, it was reported in 1927 that 250 to 300 buses provided a regular service between Durban and Zululand, causing a 'severe loss' to the railways of approximately 100,000 passenger fares per annum;[62] and as of 10 June 1932 twenty-six long distance taxis operated a successful "native" service between Dundee, Natal and the Rand by undercutting the rail fares.[63] To regain traffic lost to private road transport the railways had to reduce their own fares to a competitive level. A particularly well documented case occurred in the Port Elizabeth area, where the SAR waged a three year fare-cutting war with private bus owners P M Engelbrecht and Mrs J R Slabbert for the African commuter traffic between Port Elizabeth and New Brighton location.[64]

This should surprise no one. Africans, after all, had every incentive to utilise the cheapest form of transportation available. Their rational and intelligent reaction to competitive transport conditions should dispel such notions such as "the simplicity of the native mind".

NOTES

1. In July 1920, for example, the Johannesburg Star severely criticised the staff at Reef stations for allegedly neglecting African passengers. According to the Star, Africans regularly missed trains because they had not been told at which end of the platform to wait and because booking clerks carried out their duties with undue slowness. Subsequent enquiries launched by S M Pritchard, Director of the Government Native Labour Bureau, tended to support this indictment. See Central Archives Depot (CAD), Pretoria, Government Native Labour Bureau (GNLB) 59 2239/12/20 (Accommodation and Treatment of Natives on Railways, General), Clipping from Johannesburg Star enclosed in Secretary for Native Affairs to Director of Native Labour, 17 July 1920; Director of Native Labour to Secretary for Native Affairs, 27 July 1920; Subsequent reports submitted by Inspectors of Native Labour, Reef area.

2. See, for example, CAD, Hoofbestuurder van die Suid-Afrikaanse Spoorwee (SAS) 1219 R4/4, Notice to all stations, Division 7, issued by Assistant General Manager, Johannesburg, 13 October 1920. This circular noted that the treatment of African passengers on the Western Transvaal division 'still leaves much to be desired'. Servants were instructed to afford 'better attention' to African passengers; those who ignored this order would be 'suitably dealt with'.

3. Some of Pritchard's inspectors commented critically about this shortage of non-European coach accommodation and consequent overcrowding of coaches. See, for example, GNLB 59 2234/12/ , Inspector of Native Labour, Johannesburg East to Director of Native Labour, 9 August 1920. This inspector stated that 'the general grievance (of African passengers) is the lack of third class accommodation'. (Note: This file number was left incomplete on the cover of the file.)

4. SAS 1219 R4/4, Assistant General Manager, Johannesburg to District Inspector, Johannesburg, 17 November 1922.

5. SAS 1219 R4/4, Acting General Manager to System Manager, Bloemfontein, 21 August 1933.

6. GNLB 59 2239/12/20 (Accommodation and Treatment of Natives on Railways, Germiston District), Director of Native Labour to General Manager, SAR., 10 April 1920.

7. Especially the work of Charles van Onselen and Ian Phimister. See Van Onselen's 'Worker Consciousness in Black Miners: Southern Rhodesia, 1900-1920', Journal of African History, 15, 2 (1974), 275-289, 'Black Workers in Central African Industry: A Critical Essay on the Historiography and Sociology of Southern Rhodesia', Journal of Southern African Studies, 1, 2, (1975), 228-246, and Chibaro: African Mine Labour in Southern Rhodesia 1900-1933 (London, 1976). Phimister's work includes 'The Shamva Mine Strike of

1927: An Emerging African Proletariat', Rhodesian History, 2 (1971), 65-88 and 'African Worker Consciousness: Origins and Aspects to 1953', South African Labour Bulletin.

8. SAS 1219 R4/4, General Manager to Assistant General Managers and Divisional Superintendents, 27 September 1917, 20 May, 1918; Divisional Superintendents, Durban to General Manager, 4 October 1917; Divisional Superintendent, Pretoria to Assistant General Manager, Johannesburg, 25 October 1917; Assistant General Manager, Cape Town to General Manager, 6 November 1917, 30 January 1918; Assistant General Manager, Bloemfontein to General Manager, 10 November 1917 and enclosed report from Divisional Superintendent, East London; Memo. by "Rates" on Native Fares, 11 February 1918; Memo. on Native Fares, initials illegible, 15 February 1918.

9. SAS 1219 R4/4, System Manager, Bloemfontein to General Manager, 22 June 1933.

10. According to Charles Villiers, Chairman of the Native Recruiting Corporation, unconverted cattle trucks were frequently used to convey migratory labourers in the early years of the "recognised native train" services. CAD k358, Native Grievances Enquiry of 1914, Minutes of Evidence, Box 1, Evidence of Charles Villiers, p 72. Reference supplied by Dr Alan Jeeves.

11. GNLB 8 523/10 (Main File: Correspondence with SNA, SAR), Director, GNLB to Acting Secretary for Native Affairs, 29 October 1910.

12. These changes are summarised in Pritchard's memorandum of October 29, 1910 (see note 11) and in the minutes of a meeting between Pritchard and the SAR's Assistant General Manager, Johannesburg. A copy of these minutes is enclosed in GNLB 8 523/10 (Main File: Correspondence with SNA, SAR), Assistant General Manager, SAR, Johannesburg to Acting Assistant Director, GNLB, 20 April 1911. The most important change was the inauguration of a "recognised native train" service to and from East London in order to speed up the journey and allow closer supervision of the passengers, who tended to desert while in transit to the Rand. The agreement also called on the SAR to provide more rolling stock for this traffic (so overcrowding of coaches could be alleviated), improve the coach accommodation and organise supplies of food and drink for the migrants.

13. In 1920, for example, an Inspector of Native Labour described the "native" coach accommodation available on one long-distance train. Two of the three coaches were crude Bombellas: 'The first two appear more like cattle or coal trucks, the seats run the full length of the coach, one on each side and one down the centre; for long distance travelling should say this mode of accommodation most uncomfortable, no privacy for the womenfolk and sleeping quarters "nil"'. GNLB 59 2239/12/20, Inspector, Native Affairs Department, Johannesburg to Director of Native Labour, 6 August 1920.

14. SAS 1219 R4/4, System Manager, Bloemfontein to General Manager, 9 July 1930; General Manager to System Manager, Bloemfontein, 28 July 1930.

15. SAS 1219 R4/4, Ticket Inspector, Bloemfontein to System Manager, Bloemfontein, 15 March 1932; Memo. by Ticket Inspector, East London enclosed in Acting System Manager, East London to Acting General Manager, 26 August 1933.

16. SAS 1219 R4/4, Memo. by General Manager's Rates Assistant, Natives Travelling by Alternative Route, 18 December 1928.

17. Migratory labourers travelling in Bombellas attached to goods trains ordinarily experienced long delays while in transit. The "recognised native train" services introduced on the Komatipoort-Johannesburg run in 1909 and the East London-Johannesburg run in 1911 had the objective of overcoming this problem in the case of migrants recruited to perform mine labour. The SAR only ran two or three trains per week in each direction, however, and if, for example, a migrant returning to the Transkei missed the Tuesday "down" train he would have to wait until Thursday to catch the next "recognised native train" travelling to East London.

18. GNLB 59 2239/12 , Inspector of Native Labour, Johannesburg East to Director of Native Labour, 9 August 1920.

19. SAS 1219 R4/4, Memo. by General Manager's Rates Assistant, Native Fares, 11 February 1918; System Manager, Bloemfontein to General Manager, 22 June 1933.

20. SAS 1260 R16/2/1/1, General Manager, SAR to Town Clerk, Johannesburg, 10 July 1914.

21. Charles van Onselen, 'AmaWasha: The Zulu washermens' guild of the Witwatersrand, 1890-1914', in van Onselen, Studies in the Social and Economic History of the Witwatersrand 1886-1914 (Johannesburg, 1982), Vol. 2, 74-110.

22. SAS 1260 R16/2/1/1, Memo. by CSAR Trains Section, Train Service - Klipspruit, 8 March 1907; Transvaal Railway Committee Minute 3883 (2), 5 April 1907.

23. SAS 1260 R16/2/1/1, Station Master, Nancefield to Chief Traffic Manager, 18 February 1908; Chief Traffic Manager to Inspector Murray, Braamfontein, 10 March 1908.

24. SAS 1260 R16/2/1/1, Town Clerk, Johannesburg to Chief Traffic Manager, CSAR, 22 February 1908.

25. SAS 1260 R16/2/1/1, Chief Traffic Manager to Inspector Murray, Braamfontein, 10 March 1908; Chief Traffic Manager, CSAR to Town Clerk, Johannesburg, 10 March 1908.

26. SAS 1260 R16/2/1/1, Station Master, Nancefield to Assistant General Manager, Johannesburg, 7 December 1912, 9 April 1914, 19 August 1916.

27. SAS 1260 R16/2/1/1, Station Master, Nancefield to Assistant General Manager, Johannesburg, 16 June 1915.

28. SAS 1260 R16/2/1/1, Superintendent of Locations, Johannesburg to Station Master, Nancefield, 1 March 1912.

29. SAS 1260 R16/2/1/1, General Manager, SAR to Town Clerk, Johannesburg, 30 September 1912.

30. SAS 1260 R16/2/1/1, Station Master, Nancefield to Assistant General Manager, Johannesburg, 1 September 1912.

31. SAS 1260 R16/2/1/1, Station Master, Nancefield to Assistant General Manager, Johannesburg, 16 June 1915.

32. SAS 1260 R16/2/1/1, Station Master, Nancefield to Assistant General Manager, Johannesburg, 28 August 1916.

33. On the Reef, for example, the CSAR introduced special weekly tickets when Klipspruit location was established in 1904. In 1906 the weekly tickets were supplemented by monthly tickets which could be purchased for 8s.6d. each, as compared to 2s.6d. for a weekly ticket and 6d. for an individual return ticket. The railway expanded these ticket facilities as the early locations became over-crowded and new locations were proclaimed. Hence when the Johannesburg municipality founded Orlando location in 1931 the location fares available to Klipspruit residents were extended, on a <u>pro rata</u> basis, to encompass Orlando residents. SAS 1221 R4/4/2, Chief Traffic Manager to Chief Traffic Inspector, 8 April 1904; General Manager, CSAR to Town Clerk, Johannesburg, 30 March 1906; SAS 1221 R4/0402, Acting System Manager, Johannesburg to General Manager, 2 July 1931; Memo. by General Manager, New Native Location: Canada-Klipspruit, 29 July 1931; Railway Board Minute 21,493, 6 August 1931.

34. SAS 1222 R4/4/8, Acting General Manager to System Manager, Port Elizabeth, 18 July 1933.

35. SAS 1221 R4/0402, untitled memo. initialled RWS, 30 November 1917.

36. SAS 1221 R4/0402, Memo. by Suggestions Committee, Third Class Weekly Tickets: Klipspruit to any Station to Jeppe, 25 October 1927.

37. SAS 1249 R12/13, Unsigned Memo. Issue of Tickets to Natives: Witwatersrand Area, 30 September 1920.

38. SAS 1221 R4/0402, Memo. by General Section, Surrender of Third Class Weekly and Monthly Tickets: Johannesburg-Klipspruit Sec-

tion, 17 June 1926; Memo. by suggestions Committee, Third Class Weekly Tickets: Klipspruit to any Station to Jeppe, 25 October 1927; Memo. by Rates Office, Third Class Weekly Tickets: Klipspruit Location, 31 October 1927.

39. So much so that the SAR had to take action to reduce the incidence of fraud. Early in 1928, for instance, the administration introduced an elaborate new kind of weekly ticket which included blank spaces on the right and left hand side of each ticket. Ticket examiners received instructions to nip each ticket in the appropriate space (on the right hand side of the ticket for each outward journey, and on the left hand side for each return journey), to ensure that passengers used their tickets for only one journey per day in each direction, to collect all the tickets on the day of their expiration, and to 'scrutinise all these tickets closely and report irregularities'. SAS 1221 R4/0402, Circular issued by Assistant General Manager, Johannesburg, 2 February 1928.

40. SAS 1222 R4/4/5, Memo. by Chief Inspector, Johannesburg, WNLA Natives, 15 June 1910; General Manager, SAR to Secretary, WNLA 22/23 June 1910, 14/15 May 1914, 11 June 1914, 2 November 1915, 14 April 1916; Secretary, WNLA to General Manager, SAR, 29 June 1910, 20 May 1914, 15 June 1914, 5 November 1915.

41. SAS 1222 R4/4/5, Ticket Inspector Watson, Pretoria to Chief Inspector, Johannesburg, 9 March 1917.

42. Though the report cited in Note 41 suggests that "Bob" and "Nikkis" themselves may have been innocent of fraudulent intentions.

43. SAS 1221 R4/0402, Director of Native Labour to General Manager, SAR, 7 November 1919.

44. In the early years of this century, a time of severe labour "shortage", the mining industry stretched its tentacles much further. Supported and assisted by Lord Milner's Transvaal Crown Colony government, the mines in 1904 began importing thousands of Chinese indentured labourers. Following the Imperial government's grant of responsible government to the Transvaal and the election of Louis Botha's Het Volk ministry in 1907, the remaining Chinese were repatriated.

45. The introductory paragraphs of this section are partially based on a number of secondary sources. Special reference should be made to Van Onselen, Chibaro, especially chapters 3, 4 and 8, and to an as yet unpublished manuscript by Alan Jeeves on the evolution of monopsonistic mine labour recruitment in South Africa.

46. African residents of Natal and Zululand were not permitted to travel at the reduced fares immediately after Union, however. This temporary exclusion of Zulus and "Natal natives" from the "special native fare" facilities apparently was the result of

political pressure exerted by Natal interests. White residents of Natal rather disliked the concessionary fares because they were believed to entice local labour to the gold mines. I am not sure when this restriction was lifted, but it was no longer in existence in 1917. See SAS 1219 R4/4, Divisional Superintendent, Durban to General Manager, 4 October 1917.

47. The departure of the "special native fare" scale from the third class passenger scale is illustrated by the following comparison of "special native fares" and third class fares as of 1 March 1931:

Miles	Third Class Fare	"Special Native Fares"	Difference
250	£1.03s.3d.	16s.8d.	6s.7d.
350	£1.12s.9d.	£1.03s.4d.	9s.5d.
450	£1.19s.3d.	£1.10s.0d.	9s.3d.
600	£2.12s.3d.	£2.00s.0d.	12s.3d.
800	£3.09s.6d.	£2.05s.7d.	£1.03s.11d.
1000	£4.07s.0d.	£2.11s.2d.	£1.15s.10d.

Source: SAS 1219 R4/4, General Manager, SAR to Secretary for Native Affairs, 23 November 1931.

48. SAS 1219 R4/4, L R Nightingale to General Manager, SAR, 28 March 1925.

49. Not always, however. In 1912, for example, pressure from the Department of the Interior extracted fare and baggage concessions for white agricultural labourers travelling by rail. SAS 1182 R2/13, General Manager, SAR to Acting Secretary for the Interior, 25 May 1912.

50. SAS 1219 R4/4, Acting General Manager, SAR to Secretary for Native Affairs, 25 February 1928.

51. 'Vehicle Builders and the Railway Department', editorial, South African Commerce and Manufacturers Record, April 1912, 190, 192.

52. Nightingale's request was turned down. See SAS 1219 R4/4, General Manager, SAR to L R Nightingale, 3 April 1925.

53. SAS 1219 R4/4, Memo. by Rates Office, Special Fares for Native Travellers and Umfaans, 15 July 1921.

54. SAS 1219 R4/4, General Manager, Vryheid (Natal) Railway Coal & Iron Co. Ltd. to General Manager, SAR, 10 February 1919, 28 February 1919, 27 August 1919 and report by C A Hadley enclosed in latter piece of correspondence.

55. SAS F15402/8, Memo. by General Manager, Tariff Revisions: 1924, 15 March 1924.

56. SAS 1219 R4/4, Secretary, Transvaal Chamber of Mines and WNLA to General Manager, SAR, 3 March 1931.

57. SAS 1182 R2/13, Sir J H Langerman to Henry Burton, 11 June 1917.

58. SAS 1182 R2/13, copy of letter from I Gordon to Minister of Agriculture, 2 February 1918.

59. These farmers had founded a co-operative association, the 'Transvaalse Landbouwers Arbeids Maatschappy Bpt.', to acquire and distribute such labour. A government regulation forbidding the recruitment of Africans under eighteen years of age initially restricted the operations of the association, but in November 1917 the state relaxed this regulation and magistrates were empowered to authorise the recruitment of African youths by licensed labour recruitors.

60. SAS 1182 R2/13, Secretary, Transvaalse Landbouwers Arbeids Maatschappy Bpt. to General Manager, SAR, 8 November 1915; Memo. by Native Labour Superintendent's Office, Transvaal Agricultural Labour Co., Ltd, 22 November 1917 and enclosed letter from Acting Director of Native Labour to all magistrates, Native Commissioners and Sub-Native Commissioners; Memo by General Manager, Fares for Natives under 18 Recruited for Agricultural Employment 26 November 1917; A M Mostert Ltd to General Manager, SAR, 29 November 1917; Acting Director of Native Labour to General Manager, SAR, 30 November 1917; Railway Board Minute 6813, 30 November 1917; General Manager, SAR to A M Mostert Ltd, 19 December 1917.

61. CAD, Departement van Handel en Nywerheid (HEN) 525 60, Office of Census and Statistics Special Report Series, Report No. 58, <u>Motor Vehicle Statistics for the Year 1928</u>, table on p. 5.

62. SAS 1159 R1/22, Minutes, Meeting of Senior Transportation Officers, 7 July 1927, p. 6. In this case the road and rail fares were about the same but the buses provided a superior service: 'The trouble was that natives were now accustomed to being taken direct from their kraals into Durban and back. The fares were approximately the same as those by rail, but the natives were allowed to take packages of all descriptions without any extra charge, and, generally, the services were more convenient than by rail'.

63. SAS 1219 R4/4, Station Master, Dundee to Native Traffic Inspector, Johannesburg, 30 July 1932. The rail fares for Africans travelling between Dundee and Johannesburg were 17s.4d. for men and 24s.6d. for women at this time. The difference is explained by the fact that women were excluded from the "special native fare" privilge. Taxis carried both men and women to the Rand for fares ranging between fifteen and seventeen shillings. 'Our RAIL fares are too high and allow a margin for Taxi profits', the Station master commented.

64. Detailed correspondence may be found in SAS 1222 R4/4/8.

Politics, Ideology, and the Invention of the 'Nguni'

John Wright

The word 'Nguni' is today commonly used by academics as a collective term for the black peoples who historically have inhabited the eastern regions of southern Africa from Swaziland through Zululand, Natal, the Transkei and the Ciskei to the eastern Cape. These peoples are conventionally distinguished by language and culture from the Thonga peoples of the coastlands further to the north, and the Sotho peoples of the interior plateau to the west and north-west. Use of the Nguni in this extended sense is now so well entrenched in the literature on southern African ethnography, linguistics, and history as probably to make the term irremovable, but, from a historical perspective, it is important to note that it is only within the last half-century that this usage has become current. Previously, the peoples now designated as Nguni had been variously labelled as Zulu, or Xhosa, or Kaffirs, or Zulu-Kaffirs, while Nguni itself had been a non-literary term used by the black peoples of south-east Africa in a number of more restricted senses. Nowhere among these peoples was Nguni used in a generic sense.

The purpose of this paper is to trace the historical process by which the modern literary usage of Nguni became established. It is divided into three parts. In the first, the various historically known meanings of Nguni are identified. In the second, an explanation is suggested as to why specificaly one of these meanings was appropriated by academics from the 1930s onward. In the third, an explanation is put forward as to how and why this particular meaning had developed in the first place.

The earliest known documented usage of Nguni dates from 1589, when survivors of the Sao Thomé, which had sunk off the coast of what is now northern Zululand, found that the region where they made their landfall was known as the country of 'Virangune' or 'Viragune'.[1] This word was regarded by Bryant as a rendering of 'baNguni'.[2] Junod considered that it was not a Bantu word,[3] but present-day opinion would support Bryant's gloss.[4] The survivors of the <u>Sao Thomé</u> apparently gave 'Virangune/Viragune' as the name of what the accounts of their experiences call a kingdom, although, as Hedges points out, another party of shipwreck survivors who traversed the region further inland in 1593 found no such polity in existence. Hedges argues that the word is likely to have applied to 'early residents of lower areas of Zululand' rather than to a specific political unit.[5] Either way, the point to note is that in 1589 the use of Nguni as a designation seems to have been confined to part of the Zululand coast and its immediate hinterland. To the north and south, according to the recorded accounts of the <u>Soa Thomé</u> party, were other 'kingdoms' with quite different names.[6]

The next recorded use of Nguni that the present writer has been able to find is in the papers of Henry Francis Fynn, who, as is well known, operated as a hunter and trader at Port Natal from 1824 to 1834. In a fragmentary note written in or after 1832, he records that the west was known as the wind of the 'Abangoonie'.[7] By whom it was so called he does not specify, but presumably it was by the peoples of the region, extending from Port Natal to the Mpondo country, where

Fynn concentrated his operations and where he established a number of homesteads for his African adherents. In this case the reference to the 'Abangoonie' would be to the Xhosa peoples who lived to the south-west. Certainly this was one of the meanings which the word Nguni had acquired, in Natal colony at least, by the middle of the 19th century, for in the first edition of his Zulu-English Dictionary, published in 1861, Colenso gives Nguni specifically as 'Another name for the Amaxosa'.[8] This definition was retained through to the third edition, published in 1878.[9] Kropf's Kaffir-English Dictionary, first published in 1899, also gives the location form ebunguni as 'in the West; westward',[10] and in the first decade of the 19th century several of James Stuart's informants used Nguni to designate the Xhosa.[11] It was used exclusively in this sense by Soga in his classic work, The South-eastern Bantu, published in 1930. 'The term Ebu-Nguni,' he wrote, 'is used by Natives of Natal to indicate the country of the Abe-Nguni or Xhosas, which lies west of Natal ...'.[12]

The meagreness of the evidence in the sources cited above makes it difficult to specify with any confidence the geographical regions in which, during the period surveyed, Nguni was used to denote the Xhosa peoples. Tentatively, though, it can be suggested that this usage was current predominantly in the region from Natal colony southward, as distinct from the Zulu kingdom and areas neighbouring it to the west and north. As argued above, Fynn's note on the meaning of 'Abangoonie' probably reflects observations he made during his travels in southern Natal and the Mpondo country. Colenso's Dictionary was based on linguistic research conducted primarily in Natal colony, where, apart from a five-week trip to the Zulu kingdom in 1859, he resided continuously during the period when he was preparing this work.[13] Kropf spent forty nine years as a missionary among Xhosa-speakers before the publication of his Dictionary.[14] Of those of Stuart's informants whose statements have been published in the first three volumes of the James Stuart Archive, and who used Nguni as a term for the Xhosa, it is significant that all seven had spent all or most of their lives in Natal or the territories to the south.[15] In Soga's usage, as exemplified in the passage cited above, 'Natal' frequently denotes the region south of the Thukela, as distinct from Zululand to the north.

In the Zulu kingdom, by contrast, a quite different meaning of Nguni seems to have existed for most of the 19th century. According to the evidence given to Stuart by Magidigidi kaNobebe in 1905, a number of the lineages incorporated into the Zulu kingdom by Shaka had been accustomed to designate themselves as abaNguni until the king reserved the term, in its personalized form, Mnguni, as one of his own address- names.[16] It is highly likely that the designation Nguni would thenceforth have been applied exclusively to the Zulu ruling lineage, possibly together with those others, like the Qwabe, that could incontestably claim a close genealogical relationship to it. On the basis of admittedly skimpy evidence, the term does not seem to have been used within the kingdom as a designation for its inhabitants generally. Colenso makes no mention of it: if it had been so used, so acute a student of language would presumably have included this meaning in his Dictionary definition of the word. In similar negative vein, Colenso's protégé, the philologist Wilhelm Bleek, who in 1856 spent three or four months in the Zulu kingdom studying the language, makes no mention of the term Nguni in his published account of his travels.[17] Bryant, who lived and worked both south and north of the Thukela in the years before the publication of his Dictionary in 1905, commented in that work that Nguni was a name adopted only occasionally by the 'Zulu-Kafirs', that is, the inhabitants of Zululand and Natal.[18]

In the Zulu kingdom, then, Nguni had a meaning quite different from the sense in which it was widely used in the regions to the south. At the same time, yet another meaning seems to have existed for much of the 19th century in the territories to the west and north of the kingdom. Presumably by extension from Nguni as an appellation of the ruling Zulu lineage, the Sotho peoples to the west and the Thonga to the north seem to have used the word to designate the inhabitants of the Zulu kingdom generally, together with peoples who culturally and linguistically were closely related to them. Thompson records that in the 1830s Dr Andrew Smith, who led an official expedition from the Cape into the highveld regions in 1834-5, used the word 'Abingoni' to refer generally to the peoples who lived east of the Drakensberg escarpment.[19] Without further details as to the context of this usage, it is difficult to accept Thompson's assertion that Smith employed Nguni 'in precisely the same sense as it was used later by Bryant and modern scholars'. More likely is that Smith noted the same kind of usage as Arbousset and Daumas recorded in the same area a few years later. According to these authors, the Sotho of the highveld usually used 'Bakoni', the Sotho form of 'Abanguni', to refer to the 'Zulus', a term which the authors used to designate the peoples both of the Zulu kingdom and of the newly formed offshoot Ndebele kingdom. Occasionlly, it seems, the Sotho extended the meaning of the term to include 'all the Caffers which they knew'.[20] A similar usage seems to have been prevalent in the Thonga country, where, Bryant recorded in 1905, Nguni designated 'a Zulu-Kafir'.[21]

In sum, during the 19th century there appear to have been three regionally distinct meanings of Nguni. South of the Thukela, the term designated primarily the Xhosa peoples. North of the Thukela, in the Zulu kingdom, it designated the dominant Zulu clan and closely related clans, to the exclusion of the great majority of the clans that had been incorporated into the kingdom. Among the Sotho and Thonga, the word designated the people of the Zulu kingdom as a whole.

By the early years of the 19th century, at the latest, these regional distinctions of meaning appear to have been breaking down. Though, as indicated above, a number of the informants interviewed by Stuart in Natal at this time still used Nguni to mean specifically the Xhosa, in the usage of others the term was now being applied to certain clans living north of the Thukela in what had until 1879 been the Zulu kingdom. Yet others of his informants used it in both senses. The clans most commonly designated as Nguni were the Zulu and the related Qwabe;[22] others were the Biyela, Chunu, Langa, Lagwaza, Mthethwa, Ndwandwe, Nzimela, and Zungu.[23] Certain others - the Hlubi and the Thuli - were mentioned specifically as not being Nguni.[24] But opinion was by no means unanimous on which clans could legitimately be regarded as Nguni, and which not: the Zulu, Methethwa, and Ndwandwe, given as Nguni by some informants, were described specifically as not Nguni by others.[25]

In effect, in Natal and Zululand, the meaning of Nguni was by now being extended to include peoples to whom it had not previously been applied. This extension of meaning was reflected in a number of linguistic and historical works that appeared at this time. In the fourth edition of Colenso's Dictionary, revised by his daughter Harriette and published in 1905, the original definition of Nguni was broadened to read 'Another name for the amaXosa, Qwabe, Zulu, and other kindred tribes'.[26] Where, in the historical introduction to his Dictionary of 1905, Bryant had used the then common terms 'Kaffirs' and 'Zulus' to designate the African peoples of Natal and Zululand generally, in a series of historical articles that appeared in 1910-13 in the newspaper Izindaba Zabantu he was beginning to use instead the word Nguni, usually in compound forms like 'Zulu-Nguni' and 'Tonga-Nguni'.[27] The first work unreservedly to use Nguni as a generic term was Magema Fuze's Abantu Abamnyama, which appeared in 1922, although it had apparently been completed at least twenty years earlier. In this work Fuze used Nguni to denote the African peoples who had populated Zululand-Natal and also the regions to the south.[28]

In the first two decades of the 19th century, then, the modern meaning of Nguni was beginning to gain currency among certain writers in Natal. At this stage it was by no means a generally used term, however. To take three well-known works of the period, it did not appear in Gibson's The Story of the Zulus (first published in 1903), in Stuart's History of the Zulu Rebellion (1913), or in Faye's Zulu References (1923).[29] It was not until the publication in 1929 of Bryant's now classic Olden Times in Zululand and Natal, sub-titled 'earlier political history of the eatern-Nguni clans', that Nguni as a generic term began to become firmly established in scholarly usage. More than half a century later, this is still the standard work on its subject, and more than any other single work it has served to popularize use of the term Nguni to denote the peoples of the area from Swaziland to the eastern Cape. Bryant adopted the term, he explained, 'because abaNguni was the name by which, in times gone by, these peoples generically distinguished themselves from the other two types around them', i.e. the Sotho and the Thonga.[30] No proof of this assertion was offered, and in the light of the arguments put forward above it represents a substantial oversimplification, even a distortion, of the historical picture. This was also the opinion of one, at least, of Bryant's contemporaries, the Government Ethnologist, N J van Warmelo. Writing in 1935, he commented,

> ... though not commonly heard, the tribal name abeNguni occurs, also as isithakazelo (Mnguni), far and wide wherever tribes of 'Nguni' stock are encountered, but exactly what people were originally designated thereby is to my mind still a matter of uncertainty, notwithstanding the conviction of a few authors that they have fathomed the problem.[31]

The usage of Nguni as a generic term, he continued, 'by no means coincides with the original content of the native tribal name abe-Nguni'.[32]

Evidence that older, more restricted meanings of Nguni were still current in African usage when Olden Times was published exists in at least two contemporary works. In his Zulu Dictionary of 1923 R C A Samuelson indicates that the term was still one applied specifically to the Zulu clan,[33] and the statement of Soga cited above (p. 3) suggests that Nguni was being used by people in Natal as late as 1930 as a designation for the Xhosa. But among contemporary academics neither these nor Van Warmelo's points seem to have counted for much against Bryant's assertion, based, as it appeared to be, on the massive and evident scholarship that had gone into the preparation of Olden Times. After the publication of this work, the usage of Nguni as a generic term in place of various combinations of 'Kaffir', 'Zulu', and 'Xhosa' quickly gained academic respectability. It was used by Doke as a linguistic term in a major review of the literature on the southern Bantu languages published in 1933, and as an ethnic term by Schapera in a survey of the ethnographic literature on southern Africa published in 1934.[34] In the latter year Schapera introduced the word to a wider readership in using it in the first comprehensive academic survey to be published on 'the native problem' in South Africa.[35] Two years later it appeared for the first time in an ethnographic monograph, Krige's well-known The Social System of the Zulu.[36]

By the mid-1930s Nguni was also beginning to receive semi-official sanction as an ethnic label. In spite of his reservations about its validity as a generic term, Van Warmelo was prepared to incorporate it into his well-known Preliminary Survey of the Bantu Tribes of South Africa, published in 1935, as a designation for one of the five 'divisions' which he recognized among the country's Bantu-speaking peoples. Though 'used in an entirely arbitrary sense', he explained, the term had already 'received the sanction of several years' usage in scientific literature'.[37] As he went on,

> The main reason for its adoption lies in the absence of any other name that would be equally suitable. However valid the arguments, therefore, that might be adduced against its use as a collective term, these will probably have to yield to this necessity.

Although he continued to express serious doubts about the usefulness of the versions of Nguni history (presumably Bryant's and Soga's) then current, Van Warmelo was himself prepared to use Nguni as a generic term without reservation in his contribution to The Bantu-speaking Tribes of South Africa, an influential composite ethnography edited by Schapera and published 1937.[38]

With the appearance of this latter work, the modern literary meaning of Nguni may be fairly said to have become established in academic and official ethnographic and linguistic usage. The questions arise why it was this particular meaning of Nguni, to the exclusion of its other meanings, that so became accepted, and why it was absorbed into academic usage so rapidly and with relatively little criticism. At one level of explanation it could be argued that Nguni became established as a generic term simply because most academic anthropologists in South Africa were willing to see an apparently scientific designation replace the by then anachronistic and offensive 'Zulu-Kaffir'. From this point of view the introduction of Nguni into academic discourse posed no problems: it was simply a new and historically acceptable name for one of the two broad groupings of African peoples in South Africa that had for a century been recognized as geographically and linguistically differentiated, that is, the 'Zulu-Kaffir' or 'Zulu-

Xhosa', and the 'Basuto-Bechuana'.[39] It could similarly be argued that the parallel absorption of Nguni into official usage was the result of the establishment in 1910 of a unified Department of Native Affairs in place of the four pre-existing colonial departments, with the use of a system of generic nomenclature reflecting the needs of a centralized, as against regionally based, administration.

The approach embodied in arguments of this kind is essentially an ahistorical one, with limited powers of explanation. On the one hand it takes no account of the particular circumstances within which anthropology as a profession was established in South Africa in the 1920s and 1930s. On the other, it fails to recognize that in South Africa (and presumably elsewhere) changes in established ethnic terminology have often reflected shifts in basic socio-political relationships. (One need only think of the political contexts within which usage has changed from Kaffir to Native to Bantu to Black.) The answers to the questions posed above need to be looked for not simply in terms of the volition of a handful of anthropologists but in a consideration of the historical conditions within which the works mentioned in the preceding paragraphs were produced. It is to this issue that the second part of this paper is addressed.

Students of the post-World War I era of South African history are generally agreed that it was a period when a number of deep-seated changes were taking place in the structure of South African society. While there is considerable debate about the precise nature of these changes, there seems to be a broad consensus on two points germane to the argument being developed in this paper.[40]

Firstly, that from World War I onward, the political, economic, and ideological domination that imperial mining capital had exercised in the sub-continent since the early years of the century was increasingly being challenged by the emergence of a South African national bourgeoisie (there is as yet no clear agreement about its composition), in alliance with important sections of the white working class. In her seminal work on the history of capitalist ideologies in South Africa in the late 19th and 20th centuries, Belinda Bozzoli argues that at the ideological level the emergence of this national bourgeoisie was associated with the propagation of what was in effect a new notion of 'development'.[41] Where, in the 1890s and 1900s the 'organic intellectuals' of mining capital had been leaders in ideological innovation, by the 1920s their capacity to generate new approaches to the new problems that by then were facing capital in South Africa had dried up. Where, previously, mining capital had been actively concerned to restructure South African society in its own interests, now, with its objective largely achieved, 'ideologies were not being created through the media of mining capital as much as regurgitated; while social structures were not being "engineered" as much as lubricated'.[42] From this time on, in Bozzoli's view, it was increasingly those intellectuals who spoke for the rising national bourgeoisie, with manufacturing interests in the van, who concerned themselves with producing new ideological guidelines for the capitalist class as a whole.

This shift in the locus of ideological leadership led to a new emphasis on 'development' via industrialization. For the first time in South Africa, the idea began to be extensively and effectively propagated that local industrial growth was a desirable objective. Where imperial mining interests had generally opposed the development of protected heavy industry in South Africa, on the grounds that the mines could import capital goods more cheaply than they would be able to buy them locally, local manufacturers, in alliance with important sections of commerce and agriculture, were increasingly pressing for the expansion of South African industry behind a barrier of a tariff protection. From the time of World War I onward, Bozzoli argues, manufacturing interests and their allies, from a position of growing strength , were expanding their 'ideological network' to propagate what she felicitously calls 'scientific South Africanism'.[43] The nub of their case was that planned industrialization would be for the common good, and would be the solution to South Africa's growing list of social 'problems' - the native problem, the race problem, the poor white problem, the problem of rising worker unrest. In effect, 'a developmental, scientific, and planning-oriented ideology' was being articulated.[44]

The second point is that in the post-World War I period, the domination of capital as a whole was increasingly being threatened by the expansion of an urbanized and, on occasion, militant black working class, potentially in alliance with radicalized elements of the emergent black petty bourgeoisie. In effect, the whole system of control of African labour established in the states and colonies of South Africa in the late 19th and early 20th centuries was threatening to break down under the impact of a massive influx of Africans from the rural reserves to the urban areas, the growth of African worker organization, and the increasingly insistent - if still sporadic - demands on the part of representatives of the African petty bourgeoisie for more political rights.

After the coming to power of the Pact government in 1924, one of the state's lines of response to these developments was to begin revamping the whole system of African administration through a deliberate policy of 'retribalization', as Marian Lacey has put it. In terms of this policy, the administrative system, which at that time still to a large extent reflected the different policies of the four pre-Union states, was to be centralized, strengthened, and made uniform. The assimilation of Africans into an industrializing society was as far as possible to be halted, 'surplus' African in the towns (though not on white-owned farms) were to be pushed back into the reserves, and a system of control in the reserves through 'traditional' African authorities was to be resuscitated, with emphasis on ethnic and cultural separatism.[45]

The contention of this paper is that the penetration of the ideologies outlined above - those associated with development planning and with retribalization - into the sphere of public debate was a necessary precondition for the sudden growth of support, both private and official, for applied research into African cultures and languages that took place in South Africa during the 1920s. Ethnographic and linguistic research in South Africa was nothing new, but for the most part it had been in the hands of untrained non-professionals. From early in the century voices in South Africa had called for the state to fund a more scientific kind of enquiry into the 'native problem',[46] but it was not until after World War I that governments began to respond to these pressures. It is no accident that in this period funds were made available for the establishment of the first departments of what would now be called African studies at South African universities, at Cape Town in 1920, and at Witwatersrand in 1923, with a department of volkekunde following at Stellenbosh in the late 1920s.[47] Nor is it an accident that the journal Bantu Studies (later African Studies) was founded in 1921 in Johannesburg, as a 'clearing agency' (in the words of the first editor, J D Rheinallt Jones) for scientific research into the enthnography and languages of Africans in southern Africa;[48] nor that the South African Institute of Race Relations was established, with private funding, in 1929, in part, at least, as a research body.[49]

The liberal academics who staffed these institutions (with the exception of Stellenbosch) made it quite clear that their researches were to a significant extent motivated by a profound unease about the future of 'white civilization' in South Africa, and a firm belief in the ultimate practical value of scientific ethnographic and linguistic research in aiding the improvement of 'race relations'. Thus in the first issue of Bantu Studies, the newly appointed professor of social anthropology and head of the School of African Life and Languages at the University of Cape Town, A R Radcliffe-Brown, could write,

> In Africa ... social anthropology is a subject not of merely scientific or academic interest, but of immense practical importance. The one great problem on which the future welfare of South Africa depends is that of finding some social and political system in which the natives and the whites may live together without conflict; and the successful solution of that problem would certainly seem to require a thorough knowledge of the native civilisation between which and our own we need to establish some sort of harmonious relation.[50]

In an article significantly entitled 'The need of a scientific basis for South African native policy', Rheinallt Jones expressed very similar sentiments:

> A definite responsiblity rests upon scientific workers in the fields of anthropological and psychological research to collect the data from which general principles may be deduced to guide the country in the adoption of a sound policy in race relationships.[51]

These intellectuals were quite explicit that one of the main aims of ethnographic and linguistic research was to influence, at least indirectly, those whites who were involved on a day-to-day basis in shaping the lives of Africans. The study of African beliefs and customs, Radcliffe Brown wrote in 1923,

> can afford great help to the missionary or public servant who is engaged in dealing with the practical problems of the adjustment of the native civilization to the new conditions that have resulted from our occupation of the country.[52]

The mining industry, too, 'would benefit by the increased expert knowledge of native questions' that would follow from research of this sort, Rheinallt Jones told the Chamber of Mines in 1922.[53]

At much the same time that liberal academics were beginning to involve themselves in scientific ethnographic research, mainly through the state-funded universities, the state itself was beginning to participate more directly in research of this sort. The coming to power of the Hertzog government in 1924 gave impetus to this process. In 1925 the Department of Native Affairs set up its own ethnological section, with the aim of promoting scientific research into African ethnography and linguistics in order to obtain information which, it was felt, 'was likely to prove of the greatest assistance in the smooth and harmonious administration of tribal affairs and in the prevention of friction'.[54] The following year the government began to make funds available for academic research into African life and languages, and set up an Advisory Committee on African Studies, whose members were drawn mainly from the universities, to supervise this work.[55] Though as a result of economic depression these funds fell away in 1930, the government's willingness to finance ethnographic research was an indication that it acknowledged its potential usefulness to the state.

By the late 1920s, then, a body of professional anthropologists to a greater or lesser extent committed to 'practically' oriented research had been provided with an institutional base in South Africa. It seems to have been taken entirely for granted by them and by their sponsors, official and unofficial, that the primary unit of their investigations would be the 'tribe', that is, a group of people which was seen as occupying a specific territory under the political authority of a chief, as being economically more or less self-sufficient, and as being more or less united by ties of kinship, culture, and language. The history of the concept of the 'tribe' in western thought is badly in need of study, but certainly the main tenets of the notion of the bounded tribe as outlined above had been central to British anthropological thought since at least the later 19th century,[56] and its unquestioning deployment by British-trained South African anthropologists in the 1920s and 1930s comes as no surprise. It is easily understandable, too, that for Afrikaner *volkekundiges*, with their emphasis on the historical centrality of the *volk* in human affairs, the ethnic group should represent the primary social unit.[57]

But the uncritical acceptance of the concept of the tribe by South African anthropologists cannot be explained simply in terms of their intellectual predispositions. The point needs to be stressed that for anthropologists and *volkekundiges* alike there was in the 1920s and 1930s a positive disincentive for producing critical examinations of the concept, in that anthropology/*volkekunde* as a socially subsidized profession had come into existence, partly at least, to provide socially useful information on cultures that had long been perceived in administration circles as tribally based. In this context, the continued existence of the notion of the tribe was central to the further expansion or, at the very least, the continued existence of the profession:

To expand on this point, a useful parallel can be drawn between the social contexts within which South African and British anthropologists were operating at this time. Before World War I, anthropological organization in Britain had not been particularly successful in obtaining public or private funding, primarily, Stauder argues, because the historically and speculatively oriented anthropology of the time seemed of little possible use to colonial administrators, missionaries, and traders.[58] After World War I, however, the nature both of British colonial administration and British anthropology changed in directions that brought about a convergence of their respective interests. On the one hand, the period saw the emergence of structural-functionalist anthropology, which rejected the obsession with origins and speculative history which characterized the established evolutionary and diffusionist anthropology, and proposed in its place an approach that sought rather to establish the workings of social 'systems' in a synchronic context. On the other, British colonial governments in Africa were seeking to integrate what they saw as traditional political institutions into their systems of administration, in order to reduce expenditure and as far as possible to avoid direct coercion of the indigenous peoples. The establishment of 'indirect rule' as it was called, required some knowledge on the part of the authorities as to how traditional institutions functioned, knowledge which anthropologists in the field were well placed to provide. Anthropology was now able to recommend itself as of some practical use in colonial administration, with the result that by the late 1920s and early 1930s its practitioners in the British empire were receiving substantial public and private funding, and it was expanding as a profession.[59]

With the existence of the profession depending, in part at least, on the maintenance of the relationship which it had established with a colonial system which emphasized the tribe as the natural unit of administration,[60] it is hardly surprising that, however critical they might sometimes be of the way in which colonial authority was exercised,[61] British anthropologists did not seek to undermine the assumptions on which it was based. This is not to argue that they consciously avoided doing so; rather, that the ideological context within which they operated served to orient their critical faculties in a way which made for the existence of an intellectual blindspot as far as questioning the notion of the tribe was concerned. And as far as South African anthropologists were concerned, the particular ideological context within which their profession had come into being would have served to make this feature of their thinking even more marked.

This section of the paper has attempted to delineate some of the more significant features of the intellectual climate in which Bryant's Olden Times was written and published. The contention here is that it appeared just at a time when there was coming into existence an academic and administrative readership that was likely to be receptive to its main arguments and assumptions. From the professional anthropologist's point of view there could be no doubt that it was a thoroughly scholarly and scientific piece of work. From the administrator's point of view, it could be seen as potentially useful in the formulation and implementation of the 'new' native policy in Natal-Zululand. It is significant that publication of Olden Times was funded (to what extent is not made clear) by the Hertzog government,[62] and certainly one contemporary reviewer, J Y Gibson, himself an ex-magistrate from Natal, was in no doubt about its 'practical' usefulness. Bryant's book, he commented, 'cannot but be of great service to those charged with native administration ... It is worthy of careful study by those who would acquire an understanding of the present-day "Native Question"'.[63]

From the point of view both of academics and administrators, a further recommendation was that Olden Times was cast firmly in terms of tribal histories. It was based, therefore, on a principle that was at once fully comprehensible and acceptable to both categories of readers. And for both it had the further merit of proposing an apparently authentic term, Nguni, for one of the major groupings, until then without a scientific designation, in the system of 'South African Bantu classification' (to use Hammond-Tooke's term) the development of which was then regarded as a research priority.[64] Though individuals like Van Warmelo might express reservations about the validity of Nguni as a generic term, such objections were in the end subordinated to the socio-political need for the creation of a comprehensive tribal taxonomy.

The continued existence, in fact the reinforcing, of a system of administration which emphasized African 'tribal' divisions was presumably one of the major structural reasons why the word Nguni survived so long as a collective term without being called into question. It was not until the later 1960s that some scholars began critically to re-examine its validity. In an investigation of what they recognized as the Nguni 'problem', Marks and Atmore commented,

> ... the latter day inclusive use of the term Nguni may do much to distort the past. Recently historians have used the term rather freely of the peoples in the Natal-Zululand area, in an attempt to avoid the anachronistic "Zulu" for the pre-Shakan period. In fact, it may be masking as great or even greater anachronism. ... it should probably be used to designate only a few of the large numbers of peoples to whom it is now applied.[65]

In similar vein, Marks argued that

> This all-inclusive term with its connotation of timeless homogeneity may well be the first obstacle in the way of our understanding the origins of the layers of people that make up the present day Nguni.[66]

Though Marks and Atmore were well aware that in the 19th and early 20th centuries the meaning of Nguni had varied over time and space, they were not primarily concerned to develop a historical explanation of this phenomenon. In so far as they touched on the emergence of Nguni as a collective term, they attributed it to 'white intervention or invention', particularly on the part of Bryant.[67] While agents like Bryant were of course directly instrumental in creating the modern meaning of Nguni, this line of argument does not go far enough. It does not make the point that what these agents were doing in effect was appropriating and transforming, for their own particular purposes and within a specific historical context, a concept previously used in a number of different ways for a number of different purposes within certain of the African societies of south-east Africa. In the third and final section of this paper an explanation will be suggested as to how and why this concept had come to be amenable to academic appropriation in the first place.

As noted in the first section of this paper, Nguni seems to have been used in the late 16th century to designate certain peoples living on the coast north of the Mfolozi river. There is no evidence available as to how the term was used in the two succeeding centuries. Then, in the Zulu kingdom that emerged in the early 19th century the form Mnguni came to be reserved by Shaka as a designation for the Zulu monarchy. David Hedges has put forward some suggestive comments as to why this happened; as they constitute a useful starting point for a historical explanation of the emergence of the modern usage of Nguni, they will be looked at here in some detail.

At a time that by implication was well before the 19th century, the term Nguni, Hedges suggests, had come to connote 'great antiquity and extensive political authority'.[68] The reasons for this are now lost to history, but it seems clear that at least by Shaka's time Nguni/Mnguni had become 'a sobriquet of leadership and an expression of profound salutation ... in praise of authority'.[69] The word may have had social significance in that 'it described attributes of political authority per se';[70] in any case its adoption by Shaka and his successors may well 'have derived from the need of succeeding royal families to associate themselves with the ancient inhabitants'.[71] As Hedges puts it, 'nineteenth century usage does reflect the contemporary ideological requirements: reinforcing social dominance by appeal to historical primacy'.[72]

On the basis of statements made by certain of Stuart's informants, Hedges argues that the 'ancient inhabitants' were probably what he calls lowlanders as distinct from the up-country peoples of the region north of the Thukela.[73] The particular statements that he cites do not actually substantiate his case: as will emerge below, they may well reflect, rather, a desire on the part of the lowlanders living in the early 20th century to be regarded as Nguni. But there is evidence in the Stuart collection that lends support to his main point: that Nguni carried with it associations of ancient residence in the land. 'The abaNguni do not refer to ever having descended from the north' they say they originated here, i.e. in Zululand', Baleni kaSilwana told Stuart.[74] 'The name Nguni appears to have been applicable to some anciently resident people', commented Magidigidi kaNobebe.[75] Distinct from the supposedly indigenous Nguni people were the Ntungwa, who were generally regarded in tradition as immigrant peoples from 'the north' or from 'up-country'.[76] As Hedges argues, these traditions of migration should not be taken too literally,[77] but the point that emerges from them is that the Ntungwa seem to have been regarded as of lesser status by those who, by the early 20th century at least, were calling themselves Nguni. By these latter the word Ntungwa/Mntungwa was sometimes used as an insult.[78]

The argument here is that the appropriation of Mnguni as an appellation of the Zulu kings, and Nguni as a designation of the ruling Zulu lineage, was consciously initiated by Shaka and the Zulu royal house as a means of legitimizing the lineage's newly achieved political dominance. As the upstart head of a potentially highly unstable conquest state, Shaka would have been deeply concerned not only to maintain control over the means of physical coercion at his disposal, as has so often been stressed in the literature, but also to develop and propagate an official ideology that portrayed the Zulu royal house to its subjects as 'natural' rulers of the kingdom by right of seniority.[79] This line of argument cannot be developed in detail here; what follows is a series of points aimed at demonstrating that the reworking of the meaning of Nguni was not an isolated phenomenon.

The appropriation of Nguni/Mnguni, with its connotations of historical primacy, was only one example of official manipulation of the usage of address-forms to strengthen the Zulu claim to political legitimacy. A similar case was Shaka's reservation of the designation Mntwana, meaning 'prince', for himself alone. As the word umntwana also means child, when using it in the latter sense people throughout the kingdom had to substitute for it the hlonipha (formal avoidance) word ingese.[80] In addition, Shaka took over a range of salutations previously used by other lineages - 'Ndabezitha!' from, variously, the Chunu, Khumalo, or Mbatha; 'Bayede!' from Cele, Mthethwa, or Ndwandwe; 'Gumede!' from the Qwabe.[81] At the same time he was concerned to suppress use of the insulting address-name Lufenulwenja or Lobololwenja, literally dog's penis, which had previously been applied to the Zulu clan in the days of its insignificance.[82]

The importance of symbolic naming in the development of a Zulu ideology of state is further illustrated by Shaka's manipulation of ethnic terminology to typecast as social inferiors certain of the peoples subject to his rule. Particularly, it seems, this applied to peoples on the geographical peripheries of the kingdom who for one reason or another had not been fully incorporated into the body politic.[83] In the emergent official ideology, certain features of the cultures and dialects of these 'marginal' peoples were stressed as symbols which marked them off as at once different from, and inferior to, the peoples of the kingdom's 'core', and derogatory new names, or derogatory new meanings of old names, were applied to them. Thus the partially 'Sothoized' peoples on the north-western borders of the kingdom, like the Hlubi, were called iziYendane, 'the tassles of hair', after their particular manner of doing their hair, or izinGadangqunu, 'those who run about naked', after the nature of their dress.[84] The Tsonga peoples to the north were known as the amaNhlwenga, or destitute persons,[85] while those peoples in the south-eastern border regions of the kingdom who spoke tekeza dialects became known contemptuously as Lala, 'those who sleep (ukulala) with their fingers up their anuses'. The name may have existed before Shaka's time, but, according to several sources, it was during his reign that it became widely used.[86] South of the Thukela, the remnant clans of region became known by the insulting name of iNyakeni, which probably derives from inyaka, a 'commoner' in the derogatory sense, or a 'thoroughly indolent person'.[87] The peoples of southern Natal, who were noted for their practice of facial scarification, became known derogatively as the amaZosha, the face-slitters.[88]

Though very little is known about the history of ideology in the Zulu kingdom, it seems safe to assume that Shaka's successors would have been concerned to propagate as thoroughly as circumstances would allow the official ideologies developed during his reign. It is well documented that the Zulu ruling lineage worked to enforce linguistic and cultural conformity in the core region of the kingdom, with non-Zulu patterns of speech and behaviour being officially discouraged in favour of Zulu ones.[89] It would follow that a high degree of ideological conformity would have been enforced as well, with, among other things, non-Zulu lineages being prevented from contesting the ruling lineage's claim to historical primacy. During the lifetime of the kingdom, then, prohibitions on the appropriation of Nguni by non-Zulu would have been maintained.

It would not have been until the overthrow of the Zulu monarchy in 1879, and the collapse of established structures of authority in the civil wars of the 1880s, that such official prohibitions would have fallen away. One consequence was the re-assertion of pre-Shakan usages of certain terms. An explicit statement to this effect is Ndukwana's comment that the approbrious term Lubololwenja, which had been suppressed by Shaka, reappeared as a designation for the Zulu after the death of Cetshwayo.[90] Clearly its usage had never completely died out among the peoples subordinated to Zulu authority.

Nor had knowledge died out that the Zulu claim to Nguni descent was spurious. This is made clear in statements recorded by Stuart from several of his informants in 1904-5: 'Zulu and Qwabe are spoken of by outsiders as amaNtungwa'; 'The Zulu are not abaNtungwa, for they did not originally use this term in respect of themselves'; 'The amaNtungwa (the Zulus, Qwabes, and Cunus) have a keen desire to speak of themselves as abaNguni ...'; '... the Qwabes and Zulus, who are really amaNtungwa, speak of themselves nowadays as abeNguni'.[91]

If usages of this kind were reappearing in Zululand (as it now was) in the late 19th and early 20th centuries, it is likely that longstanding claims to Nguni descent on the part of certain non-Zulu lineages would also have begun re-surfacing. At the same time, entirely new claims may well have been invented by lineages seeking to prove their antiquity of residence in the region. But it would not have been simply the disappearance of an inhibiting political authority which allowed for this process; it would also have been actively stimulated by the undermining of lineage-based systems of social relationships that was beginning in Zululand and Natal in these years. Under the impact of devastating civil wars in Zululand in the 1880s, socio-ecological disasters in both Zululand and Natal in the 1890s, and a particularly aggressive settler colonialism in Natal from the 1890s and in Zululand from the early 1900s, 'traditional' African societies in the region were beginning to disintegrate. Loss of land and livestock, a rapid increase in the emigration of able-bodied men, changes in family structure, and pressures from the colonial administration all served to undermine the established patterns of authority and ideology that held these societies together.[92] For lineage leaders struggling at once to maintain their standing in their own communities, and groping to find a degree of security for these communities in the new colonial order, the claiming of Nguni descent would possibly have represented one means of attempting to shore up their crumbling authority.

Authorities on oral tradition in Africa seem agreed that in a lineage-based community the view of the past 'officially' sanctioned by its leaders is continually, if often unconsciously, reworked in order to harmonize with changes in the leaders' perceptions of where the community's political interests lie. At times of social crisis the process of manipulating the past in order to legitimize the decisions of the leadership will often become more deliberate. Typically, traditions of origin and chiefly genealogies will be among the first elements of the remembered past to be recast in politically suitable form.[93] Very little has yet been written specifically on the effects which the imposition of colonial rule, particularly of direct settler rule, had on the reformulation of African communities' views of their own past, but a recent study by Henige of the effects of what he calls 'culture contact' on African oral traditions provides some useful pointers. Henige argues that the establishment of 'indirect rule' in British colonial Africa brought about an increased concern on the part of colonial administrators with issues regarding 'paramountcy, seniority, succession, boundaries, and the like'.[94] Presumably this concern would have been even more marked among their African subjects. In Natal and Zululand, in the conditions of the 1890s and 1900s, it is highly likely that similar issues were regarded as of crucial importance by leaders of disintegrating lineages. Ability to demonstrate genealogical seniority and historical primacy would certainly have carried weight with the colonial administration in its appointing of chiefs and headmen, and may also have done so in its allocating of shrinking African land resources. This could well have been a time when lineage histories were more or less consciously being revamped in order to underpin real or fictitious claims to historical primacy, and when claims to Nguni descent would have been proliferating.

It would follow, then, that the numerous - and often conflicting - claims to Nguni descent that were recorded by Stuart in the early years of the 20th century were largely of recent origin. Evidence in support of the contention that the late 19th century saw the beginnings of a conscious recasting of traditional histories among the peoples of Natal -Zululand comes from Bryant's investigations into the genealogy of the Zulu royal house. Writing in Olden Times in 1929, he noted that the genealogies recorded by Colenso, Grout, and Callaway in the third quarter of the 19th century had a maximum of four names in the line of chiefs before Shaka, and that these versions were consonant with information he had himself obtained after he had begun his researches in 1883. Subsequently to this date, however (i.e. in the late 19th and early 20th centuries), numbers of 'modern accretions' had been made to the list of Zulu ancestral rulers.[95]

Though the name Mnguni was not one of the 'accretions' that had crept into the variants of the Zulu royal genealogy recorded by Bryant in Olden Times,[96] information given by one of Stuart's informants indicates that attempts were being made by the early 20th century in some circles, presumably Zulu royalist ones, to incorporate it into the list of remembered Zulu chiefs.[97] Certainly the old Zulu royal usage of Nguni had not died out at this time. R C A Samuelson, who had close links with the Zulu royal house, fixed this usage in print in his King Cetywayo Zulu Dictionary, published in 1923. In this work he gave as one of his definitions of umNguni, an ancient; 'a person belonging to an ancient stock', and wrote of the plural form, Abanguni, 'the Zulus have this appellation in consequence of their tribe being the oldest native tribe from which the others have sprung'.[98] In his autobiography, Long, Long Ago, published in 1929, Samuelson recorded what can be seen as another elaboration of the royal myth of origin in his note that 'the first two known kings of the Zulus, uMdhlani and uMalandela, are known by the Zulus and called by them the "Abanguni"'.[99]

Though Bryant, as indicated above, was sensitive to the genealogical manipulations that were being conducted at the very time when he was engaged in his linguistic and historical research, he seems to have had no overall conception of their historical causes. If he did, it did not extend to an appreciation that the meanings of terms like Nguni were also historically rooted, and therefore liable to change. What did become clear to him as as his work progressed was that Nguni could no longer be regarded simply as a 'name by which the Tongas call a Zulu-Kafir', as he had written in his Dictionary of 1905.[100] Rather, it was a designation of apparently great antiquity, to which numbers of different lineages in Zululand laid claim, and also one which numbers of Africans in Natal applied to the Xhosa peoples to the south. For a scholar working in an evolutionist and diffusionist tradition that focussed on the origins and migrations of non-European peoples and cultures, the temptation to use it as a generic term for peoples of apparently common descent seems eventually to have proved irresistible.

Bryant, then, did not so much invent the modern usage of Nguni as put his own particular gloss on a usage which he had encountered among Africans in Natal and Zululand from the early 20th century onward, and convey this reworked meaning to a readership of academics and administrators which, for historically explicable reasons, was particularly receptive to it. What neither he nor his contemporaries realized was that, far from being of ancient vintage, the senses in which Nguni was used by Africans in Natal and Zululand in the early 20th century were a product of recent history. And far from being a 'neutral' ethnic designation, the word in fact carried a heavy ideological loading.

As appropriated by South African scholars and administrators for their own specific purposes in the 1920s and 1930s, and as used in academic circles for the past fifty years, Nguni remains a politically loaded term. Objectively its main ideological function appears to be to impose a primordial ethnic unity of the African peoples of the eastern seaboard of South Africa, and thus allow them collectively to be portrayed by their European-descended rulers as descendants of recent immigrants, with no more historically established rights to the region's resources than the offspring of immigrants from Europe. It helps conceal the conclusion which recent research into the archaeology and oral traditions of the region clearly points to - that the historically known African societies of the region emerged locally from long-established ancestral communities of diverse origins and of heterogeneous cultures and languages. As a generic label, then, it has no historical validity. While it remains useful as a linguistic label - Nguni languages, Nguni-speaking peoples - as a designation for historically existing peoples it needs to be discarded altogether.

NOTES

1. Accounts of the wreck of the Sao Thomé are to be found in G M Theal, (ed.), Records of South-eastern Africa (henceforth RSEA), vol. 2 (London, 1898; reproduced Cape Town, 1964), 188-224; and in C R Boxer, (ed.), The Tragic History of the Sea 1589-1622 (Cambridge, 1959), 54-104. Both are translations from the Portuguese account, first published in 1736, written by the historian Diogo do Couto in 1611. Couto's account was compiled from information obtained from survivors of the Sao Thomé. A closely similar account, possibly derived from Couto's manuscript, was published in 1674 in the third volume of Manuel de Faria e Sousa's Asia Portuguesa. An English translation of Sousa's Spanish appears in G M Theal, ed., RSEA, vol. 1, 33-5. The word 'Virangune' was used by Sousa (RSEA, vol. 1, 34), and 'Virangune' by Couto (RSEA, vol. 2, 199; Boxer, Tragic History, 70-1).

2. A T Bryant, Olden Times in Zululand and Natal (London, 1929), 289; A T Bryant, The Zulu People (Pietermaritzburg, 1949), 12-13.

3. H A Junod, 'The condition of the natives of south-east Africa in the sixteenth century, according to early Portuguese documents', SA Journal of Science, 10 (1913), 148.

4. D W Hedges, 'Trade and politics in southern Mozambique and Zululand in the eighteenth and early nineteenth centuries', unpublished Ph.D thesis, University of London, 1978, 105.

5. Ibid.

6. Do Couto in Boxer, Tragic History, pp. 70-1, and in RSEA, vol. 2, 199.

7. H F Fynn Papers, Notes, file 29 (Natal Archives). The note is undated, but the paper on which it is written is watermarked March 1832.

8. J W Colenso, Zulu-English Dictionary (Pietermaritzburg, 1861), 334.

9. J W Colenso, Zulu-English Dictionary, 3rd ed., (Pietermaritzburg, n.d., 1878?), 338.

10. A. Kropf, A Kaffir-English Dictionary (Lovedale, 1899), 255.

11. C de B Webb & J B Wright, (eds.), The James Stuart Archive (henceforth JSA), vol. 1 (Pietermaritzburg, 1976), 98; vol. 2 (Pietermaritzburg, 1979) 115, 116, 117; vol. 3 (Pietermaritzburg, 1982), 45, 76, 134, 225.

12. J H Soga, The South-eastern Bantu (Johannesburg, 1930), 82.

13. An account of Colenso's visit to the Zulu kingdom appears in his 'First steps of the Zulu mission' (London, 1860; reproduced in

J W Colenso, *Bringing Forth Light*, ed., R. Edgecombe, Pietermaritzburg, 1982), 43-144.

14. *Dictionary of SA Biography*, vol. 1 (Cape Town, 1968), 443-4.

15. See note 11 above.

16. *JSA*, vol. 2, p. 97.

17. W H I Bleek, *The Natal Diaries of Dr W H I Bleek 1855-1856*, ed. O H Spohr (Cape Town, 1965).

18. A T Bryant, *A Zulu-English Dictionary* (Pietermaritzburg, 1905), 430.

19. L Thompson, *Survival in Two Worlds: Moshoeshoe of Lesotho 1786-1870* (Oxford, 1975), 333.

20. T Arbousset & F Daumas, *Narrative of an Exploratory Tour to the North-east of the Cape of Good Hope* (Cape Town, 1846; reproduced Cape Town, 1968), 133-4, 271.

21. Bryant, *Dictionary*, 430.

22. On the Zulu as Nguni see *JSA*, vol. 1, 29, 335; vol. 2, 28, 60, 254; vol. 3, 42. On the Qwabe see *JSA*, vol. 1, 118; vol. 2, 28, 60, 117, 254; vol. 3, 42, 45, 225, 262, 263.

23. The Biyela are given as Nguni in *JSA*, vol. 3, 42; the Chunu in vol. 2, 60, vol. 3, 42, 263; the Langa in vol. 3, 42; the Magwaza in vol. 3, 42; the Mthethwa in vol. 2, 28; the Ntombela in vol. 3, 42; the Nzimela in vol. 2, 280; the Zungu in vol. 2, 104.

24. The Hlubi in *JSA*, vol. 2, 15; the Thuli in vol. 2, 282.

25. The Zulu in *JSA*, vol. 2, 117, vol. 3, 262, 263; the Mthethwa in vol. 3, 76; the Ndwandwe in vol. 1, 345.

26. J W Colenso, *Zulu-English Dictionary*, 4th ed. (Pietermaritzubrg, 1905), 395.

27. These articles appeared in *Izindaba Zabantu* from the preliminary issue of 17 October 1910 to the issue of 15 March 1913. They were subsequently republished under the collective title *A History of the Zulu and Neighbouring Tribes* (Cape Town, 1964).

28. M M Fuze, *Abantu Abamnyama Lapa Bavela Ngakona* (Pietermaritzburg, 1922). An English translation by H C Lugg, edited by A T Cope, was published in Pietermaritzburg in 1979 under the title *The Black People and Whence They Came*.

29. J Y Gibson, *The Story of the Zulus* (Pietermaritzburg, 1903); J Stuart, *A History of the Zulu Rebellion 1906* (London, 1913); C Faye, *Zulu References* (Pietermaritzburg, 1923).

30. Bryant, Olden Times, 4.

31. N J van Warmelo, A Preliminary Survey of the Bantu Tribes of South Africa (Pretoria, 1935), 59.

32. Ibid.

33. R C A Samuelson, King Cetywayo Zulu Dictionary (Durban, 1923) 316, 864.

34. C M Doke, 'A preliminary investigation into the state of the native languages of South Africa', Bantu Studies, 7 (1933), 1-98; I Schapera, 'The present state and future development of ethnographical research in South Africa', Bantu Studies, 8 (1934), 219-342.

35. I Schapera, 'The old Bantu culture', in I. Schapera, ed., Western Civilization and the Natives of South Africa (London, 1934), 3-36.

36. E J Krige, The Social System of the Zulus (London, 1936), 3-6.

37. Van Warmelo, Survey, 59.

38. N J van Warmelo, 'Grouping and ethnic history', in I Schapera, ed., The Bantu-speaking Tribes of South Africa (Cape Town, 1937), 45-6, 48-50.

39. See for example A Smith, Andrew Smith's Journal of His Expedition into the Interior of South Africa 1834-36, ed. W F Lye (Cape Town, 1975), 20n.

40. The discussion that follows draws especially on M Legassick, 'South Africa: forced labor, industrialization, and racial differentiation', in R Harris, ed., The Political Economy of Africa (New York, 1975), 244-56; R Davies et al, 'Class struggle and the periodization of the state in South Africa', Review of African Political Economy, 7 (1976), 4-13; R Davies, Capital, State and White Labour in South Africa 1900-60 (Brighton, 1979), chapters 4 and 5; B Bozzoli, The Political Nature of a Ruling Class: Capital and Ideology in South Africa 1890-1933 (London, 1981), chapters 3-5; M Lacey, Working for Boroko (Johannesburg, 1981), passim.

41. Bozzoli, Political Nature, esp. chapters 3 and 4.

42. Ibid., 9-10.

43. Ibid., 158 ff.

44. Ibid., 164.

45. Lacey, Working for Boroko, 67 ff, 84 ff.

46. See for instance H Junod, 'The best means of preserving the traditions and customs of the various South African native races', Report of the SA Association for the Advancement of Science, 1907, 141-59; H L Jameson, 'An ethnographic bureau for South Africa', ibid., 160-7; W A Norton, 'The need and value of academic study of native philology and ethnology', SA Journal of Science, 14 (1917-18), 194-200.

47. E A Walker, The South African College and the University of Cape Town, 1829-1929 (Cape Town, 1929), 106-7; N J van der Merwe, 'African Studies', in A Lennox-Short & D Welsh, (ed.), UCT at 150: Reflections (Cape Town, 1979), 62; B K Murray, Wits: the Early Years (Johannesburg, 1982), 125, 137; J S Sharp, 'The roots and development of volkekunde in South Africa', Journal Southern African Studies, 8 (1980-1), 29.

48. Editorial in Bantu Studies, 1, 1 (October 1921), 2.

49. P Rich, 'The South African Institute of Race Relations and the debate on "race relations", 1929-1958', African Studies, 40 (1981), 14-16.

50. A Radcliffe-Brown, 'Some problems of Bantu sociology', Bantu Studies, 1 (1921-22), 38.

51. J D Rheinallt Jones, 'The need of a scientific basis for South African native policy', SA Journal of Science, 23 (1926), 91.

52. A R Radcliffe-Brown, 'The methods of ethnology and social anthropology', SA Journal of Science, 20 (1923), 142-3.

53. Cited in Murray, Wits: the Early Years, p. 137.

54. H Rogers, Native Administration in the Union of South Africa (Johannesburg, 1933), 250-1. Significantly, this work was published as a special number of Bantu Studies.

55. Schapera, 'Ethnographical research', Bantu Studies, 8 (1934), 227-8.

56. R Thornton, 'Evolution, salvation and history in the rise of the ethnographic monograph in southern Africa 1860-1920', Social Dynamics, 6 (1980), 14-23.

57. Sharp, 'Volkekunde', Journal Southern African Studies, 8 (1980-1), 16-36.

58. J Stauder, 'The "relevance" of anthropology to colonialism and imperialism', Race & Class, 16 (1974-5), 30.2. See also S Feuchtwang, 'The colonial formation of British social anthropology', in T Asad, (ed.), Anthropology and the Colonial Encounter (London, 1973), 73-84.

59. Stauder, 'The "relevance" of anthropology', 32-8; Feuchtwang, 'Colonial formation', 84-6.

60. See Feuchtwang, 'Colonial formation', 89-90.

61. W James, 'The anthropologist as reluctant imperialist', in Asad, (ed.), Anthropology, 41-69.

62. Bryant, Olden Times, xii.

63. J Y Gibson, review of A T Bryant's Olden Times in Bantu Studies, 4 (1930), 140.

64. W D Hammond-Tooke, 'The present state of Cape Nguni ethnographic studies', in Ethnological and Linguistic Studies in Honour of N J van Warmelo (Dept. of Bantu Administration and Development, Pretoria, 1969), 81. See also Schapera, 'Ethnographical research', Bantu Studies, 8 (1934), 248.

65. S Marks & A Atmore, 'The problem of the Nguni: an examination of the ethnic and linguistic situation in South Africa before the Mfecane', in D Dalby, (ed.), Language and History in Africa (New York, 1970), 120,

66. S Marks, 'The traditions of the Natal "Nguni": a second look at the work of A T Bryant', in L Thompson, (ed.), African Societies in Southern Africa (London, 1969), 126.

67. Marks & Atmore, 'The problem of the Nguni', 125.

68. Hedges, 'Trade and politics', 255.

69. Ibid., 256-7.

70. Ibid., 257.

71. Ibid.

72. Ibid.

73. Ibid. 256.

74. JSA, vol. 1, 29.

75. JSA, vol. 2, 87.

76. JSA, vol. 1, 29, 126; vol. 2, 45, 46, 119, 203, 280-1; vol. 3, 105, 134, 150, 211, 213, 259, 263.

77. Hedges, 'Trade and politics', 28.

78. JSA, vol. 2, 72, 119, 168, 254, 289; vol. 3, 264.

79. The development and function of state ideology in northern Nguni-speaking politics in the pre-Shakan and Shakan periods is currently being investigated by Carolyn Hamilton of the University of the Witwatersrand.

80. JSA, vol. 3, 86.

81. For Ndabezitha see JSA, vol. 1, 104, 174-5, 199, 292, 298; vol. 2, 254; vol. 3, 146. Cf. Bryant, Dictionary, 410; Bryant, Olden Times, 221-2. For Bayede see JSA, vol. 1, 104; vol. 2, 53, 76, 79. For Gumede see JSA, vol. 3, 243.

82. JSA, vol. 1, 104, 174, 208; vol. 2, 12, 254; vol. 3, 146. Cf. Bryant, Olden Times, 13, 221-2, 369-70; Fuze, Black People, 43.

83. My thanks to Carolyn Hamilton for discussion on this point. See also her unpublished seminar paper, 'The amaLala in Natal, 1750-1826' (University of the Witwatersrand, 1982).

84. JSA, vol. 2, 20, 21, 96, 277; Bryant Olden Times, 147, 181, 281.

85. JSA, vol. 1, 24, 63, 342; vol. 2, 254; Samuelson, Dictionary, 188; Bryant, Olden Times, 280.

86. JSA, vol. 1, 118; vol. 2, 54, 55, 130, 254; vol. 3, 150, 158; Bryant, Dictionary, 26.

87. JSA, vol. 1, 118; vol. 2, 55; vol. 3, 227; Colenso, Dictionary, 4th ed., 431; Bryant, Dictionary, 462, 469.

88. JSA, vol. 1, 118; vol. 2, 12, 113, 119; Bryant, Olden Times, 501.

89. JSA, vol. 2, 70, 97; Bleek, Natal Diaries, 76; J L Döhne, A Zulu-Kafir Dictionary (Cape Town, 1857), xv; Van Warmelo, Survey, 70.

90. JSA, vol. 1, 202.

91. Respectively in JSA, vol. 1, 104; vol. 3, 263; vol. 2, 97; vol. 2, 281.

92. See S Marks, Reluctant Rebellion (Oxford, 1970), chapters 1-6, 12; C Bundy, The Rise and Fall of the South African Peasantry (London, 1979), 183-92; J Guy, 'The destruction and reconstruction of Zulu society', in S Marks and R Rathbone, (eds.), Industrialisation and Social Change in South Africa (London, 1982), chapter 6.

93. See for example J Vansina, Oral Tradition (Harmondsworth, 1973), chapters 4 and 5; J C Miller, 'Listening for the African past', in J C Miller, (ed.), The African Past Speaks (Folkestone, 1980), chapter 1; D P Henige, The Chronology of Oral Tradition (Oxford, 1974), chapter 1.

94. D Henige, 'Truths yet unborn? Oral tradition as a casualty of culture contact', *Journal of African History*, 23 (1982), 405.

95. Bryant, *Olden Times*, 34.

96. On 32-3.

97. *JSA*, vol. 3, 225.

98. Samuelson, *Dictionary*, 316.

99. R C A Samuelson, *Long, Long Ago* (Durban, 1929), 390.

100. On page 430.

African Customary Law — Its Social and Ideological Function in South Africa

Raymond Suttner

'Even though there has not been an attempt to abolish Bantu customs directly, the attempt was actually made to replace them surreptitiously with our own law. I have stated before that there was really a deliberate attempt - especially through liberalistic influences - to lead the Native away from what was fine in his Native rights and customs ... I want to allow him to develop his own law according to changed circumstances, but starting from a system of law which is his.' - Dr. Verwoerd, 1955.[1]

'It is perhaps superfluous to say that retention of customary African legal systems for Africans is fully consonant with South African Government policy: paradoxically, perhaps, a desire to move away from these tribal systems is typical of South African liberal thought.' - P.M.A. Hunt, 1963.[2]

'... Customary law is now my devoted study, not because I willed it so, nor because I am one with those who bleat: "Let the natives develop along their own lines", but because up in the Maluti Mountains, and in several pockets of low-land-dwellers, Custom is very much still <u>the</u> law and no amount of contempt for it by others can alter this fact.' A.M.R. Ramolefe, 1969.[3]

The study of the terms and mode of application of African customary law in South Africa has generally been neglected both by lawyers and African Studies scholars. In the case of lawyers, there is little interest in a law potentially relevant to seventy per cent of the population - where that seventy per cent is for the most part unable to pay lawyers' fees.[4]

In the case of students of African studies, the segregated legal and judicial system may seem of marginal consequence, in the light of the more serious disabilities that people experience through more patently repressive laws, such as those regulating influx control, resettlement, banishment etc., let alone laws concerning directly political activities. It would nevertheless be wrong, I shall try to show, to dismiss this area as unimportant or innocuous.

This paper seeks to demonstrate how the special court and legal system set up to deal with civil cases between Africans contributes ideologically, economically, and socially[5] to the national oppression of the African people.

While in any class or class-based social formation, coercion may be used or held in reserve, it is obviously preferable to the ruling classes to govern without the use of force. It is better to have the oppressed classes accept their subjection, to have them understand that 'it is so', that it can be no other way, that there is no alternative to the existing relations of production and domination. This, Althusser argues, is achieved (or attempted) through ideology.[6]

It may be objected that in a colonial-type society (where one encounters not only class exploitation but also national oppression, consequent on the denial of self-determination to the majority of the population) there is much more recourse to repression of the oppressed than ideological domination. This is true. In South Africa the government of whites is broadly by 'consent', whereas blacks experience the state in the form of control, regulation and a variety of other forms of coercion. Yet, even for blacks, ideology is not dispensed with.[7] There are constant attempts, through a variety of means, to 'win over' blacks to the institutions of apartheid. Every period of extreme repression coexists with or is succeeded by renewed attempts to 'win over' the population.

Althusser has argued that ideology operates through interpellating (constituting, hailing) concrete individuals as subjects. Through ideology, individuals recognize themselves as subjects. They recognize their constitution as specific types of subjects as 'obvious' - 'The category of the subject is the constitutive category of all ideology, whatever its historical date - since ideology has no history.'[8]

In any social formation one is interpellated in a number of different ways by a number of different subjects - as citizens, mothers, daughters, Christians etc. The peculiarity of the South African social formation lies in the mode of interpellation of subjects by the state. Unlike conventional bourgeois states where interpellation by the state as subject carries important ideological consequences, connoting equality and citizenship for all, the South African state interpellates individuals not merely as South African subjects. They are also interpellated - by the state - as specific types of 'racial subjects' with varying rights - as 'Whites', 'Indians', 'Coloureds', and 'Blacks'. In the case of Africans, furthermore, they are not only interpellated as 'Blacks' but also as specific 'tribal' subjects - as Xhosa, Tswana etc. (In the case of the Xhosa, this process of subdivision goes even further with the separate constitution of Ciskeian and Transkeian Xhosa.)

At one moment the African is treated as an ordinary bourgeois subject. When he or she enters into a contract, the labourer, X, is legally equal to Anglo-American. Professors H.R. Hahlo and Ellison Kahn write that 'equality' is an 'offspring of reasonableness. Since law consists of reasonable rules and not arbitrary ad hoc judgements, persons in the same legal condition can expect to be dealt with alike.'[9]

In other words, X, being a contracting party 'in the same legal condition' as Anglo, cannot expect any account to be taken of actual differences in negotiating power. 'The power given to one party by its different class position, the pressure it exercises on the other - the real economic position of both - all this is no concern of the law ... That the concrete economic situation compels the worker to forego even the slightest semblance of equal rights - this again is something the law cannot help.'[10] This attitude is well illustrated in the judgement of Kuper, J. in De Beers v Minister of Mines[11] (cited by Hahlo and Kahn):[12]

> 'Counsel said that justice to all parties required that Sir Ernest should be called. On two occasions he told the court

> that the fact that Sir Ernest Oppenheimer is a very wealthy man should not influence the court against calling him as a witness. First of all, there is no evidence that Sir Ernest is a wealthy man: even if he is I think that the suggestion that this might influence the court should not have been made ... It hardly requires to be said that the financial standing or status of any particular person is completely and entirely irrelevant when it comes to the question of the rights of any citizen in this country.[13]

Obviously such statements contain a progressive element, for example, the right of an impoverished black person to damages is, in theory, as great and meant to be awarded on an equal scale to that of Sir Ernest. But this approach to class differences - 'There is no evidence that Sir Ernest is a wealthy man ...' - also means that the notion of surface equality must coexist with an unacknowledged substantial inequality and capacity to coerce.[14]

For purposes of much of criminal law, also, Africans are treated as South African subjects. A charge of theft, murder, treason, etc., does not require a specifically racial or tribal subjectivity. Yet here too the non-racial category conceals actual discrimination. In the first place, social conditions in the townships may predispose impoverished blacks to commit offences, especially against property.

But the mode of policing and punishing such offenders may also be discriminatory. Harry Morris KC has remarked: 'A White man is rarely hanged. The privilege is reserved for the Native. Lashes for the White man have almost been entirely forgotten, and caning is only half-remembered ...'[15]

In aspects of the Roman-Dutch civil law and general South African criminal law, therefore, a formally non-racial/non-class law actually discriminates or may discriminate against blacks and workers or it conceals unequal relations behind a juridical form of equality.

At another moment, however, the criminal law specifically constitutes Africans as 'Blacks' - as a condition for criminality. One cannot be an accused under certain laws, unless one is a 'Black'. In the case of pass offences, only a 'Black' has to carry a pass and is liable to penalization for failure to have it in his/her possession.

Though such statutory criminal law constitutes Africans as 'Blacks' and therefore potentially liable for offences that do not apply to 'non-Black', it generally does not specifically differentiate between particular 'tribal' categories. Along with Radio Bantu, Bantu education, bantustan administration etc., it is one of the functions of the special system of civil law for Africans to constitute Africans as specific tribal subjects.

Only cases between Africans may be tried by the special courts set up under the Black Administration Act[16] — the 'independent' bantu-law courts.[17] All parties must be 'Blacks'. Although the courts have a discretion to apply 'Black law', it will be argued, below, that they tend to favour it over the Roman-Dutch law.

This 'Black law' is not a general law (although there is a great deal of similarity between the various customary tribal laws).[18] The Black law applied is the law of particular 'tribes' There are special rules for resolving disputes where parties belong to different 'tribes'.[19]

Not only is there a preference for 'Black law' but there is a tendency to apply a rigid, frozen form of original customary law.

The undue preference for 'Black law', in unchanged form, seeks to halt or set back the process whereby many/most Africans have reduced or ended their identification with tribal values and allegiance to 'tribal authorities'. It further seeks or serves to undermine the process whereby Africans have tended to reduce inter-tribal tensions and identify with one another as Africans. The policy of retribalization through bantustans and associated institutions has sought to disorganize this growing national movement and to disrupt the development of national consciousness.

This attempt to halt the process of emancipation from 'traditional' life and to re-establish the coherence of the 'tribal order', with Africans having an allegiance to 'their' bantustans, does not go uncontested. This process is challenged in the first place by the reality of African life itself, by the fact that Africans do not generally live as tribespeople any more. But it is also challenged at the political level by the growing strength of forces working for democracy, which interpellate Africans as South Africans.[20]

At the level of the economy, the encouragement of 'traditional' customary law has consequences for the capacity of families in the reserves to contribute towards the subsidization of the wage levels of migrant workers.[21] The encouragement of customary law means the refurbishing of the patriarchal, joint family system of the tribe. To the extent that 'Black law' impedes female emancipation (e.g. it prevents their emergence as 'free legal subjects', generally treating women as perpetual minors), it consolidates the family-centred, male-dominated 'tribal' redistributive system. This subjection and confinement of women as inferior members of a family group helps to perpetuate the subsidization of the capitalist mode of production by production processes in the reserves.

Characteristically, the African civil court and legal system is not merely segregated but is also inferior in status and in the quality of the justice dispensed (that is, the degree to which its judgements satisfy the needs or/and expectations of litigants in their specific social situation today). Far from alleviating disabilities, it will be argued that decisions of these special courts often add to the problems of men and women (but mainly women) who use them.

In personal relations one expects the law to regulate such questions as marriage, divorce and guardianship in a manner that provides certainty as well as sufficient flexibility to encompass new living patterns.

The dualistic legal structure does not meet these needs. There is much uncertainty in the law as to who is married or unmarried. The terms of recognition of customary law, as a subsidiary legal system, have also produced negative side effects, such as the non-recognition of customary marriage as a lawful union for many purposes.[22]

I have referred to the 'special system of civil law' applied in cases between Africans. In such litigation courts may apply 'Black law' (previously called Native law/Bantu law). 'Black law' is not synonymous with original customary law. It represents those aspects of African customary law that have been recognized and applied, subject to various modifications, by South African courts and legislatures.

The existence of a separate court and legal system to regulate civil relations between Africans is a specifically colonial phenomenon.[23] Colonizers invariably declare their own law to be the 'law of the land'. The law of native peoples has to be specially 'recognized'. In the case of South Africa, the existence of legal and judicial dualism is merely an aspect of a wider bifurcation of state functions with separate state structures existing for white and black in education, politics and most other facets of their existence.[24]

The diagram below contrasts the court system[25] for non-Africans, that in the 'independent' Bantustans, and the special system established for Africans in the rest of South Africa.

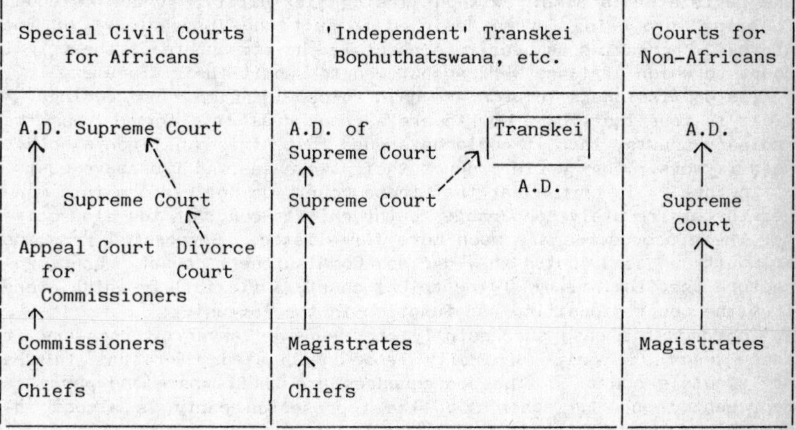

There is not space here to give a full description of such questions as the jurisdiction of the various courts. I want to stress a few factors only.

While Commissioners are at the same 'level' in the judicial hierarchy as Magistrates, they have a much wider jurisdiction as to amount than do magistrates.[26] What this means is that whereas for cases between non-Africans, litigation involving large sums of money would have to be tried by the Supreme Court judges, for Africans such cases would be decided by the equivalent of magistrates, that is officers with much lower status and qualifications.[27]

For non-Africans there is practically automatic appeal to the Supreme Court and then the Appellate Division in civil cases. For Africans there is an appeal to the special Appeal Court for Commissioners (appointed from the ranks of Commissioners) and only very limited possibilities of appeal to the Appellate Division.[28]

There is a widespread feeling amongst academics (echoed to some extent by practitioners and social workers) that the Commissioners' Courts are in crisis.[29] Speaker after speaker in evidence before the Hoexter Commission into South Africa's court system mounted criticism against the operation of these courts. Many speakers recognized that Africans regard 'their' judicial 'dispensation' as inferior and unsatisfactory. They feared that this would lead to (or increase?) disrespect for the law.[30]

Part of this expression of anguish is a result of the inability of these courts to meet the goals set for them. When the special courts were established, they were presented as providing unique advantages to Africans. Thus the president of a division of the Appeal Court remarked in 1929 that he saw in the new courts a 'system of judicature ... embodying a simple and convenient form of procedure, stripped as far as possible of legal niceties and technicalities, designed to meet the needs of the situation, one of the central ideas of which is to bring the machinery within easy reach of and accessible to, the highest as well as the lowest members of the Native community ... with comparatively little expense'.[31] On a later occasion he elaborated on the legislature's aims: without losing flexibility, it was intended to bring into being forums designed to suit the 'psychology' of the African, recreating as nearly as possible the atmosphere of the tribal court to which Africans were accustomed to submit their disputes.[32]

The Commissioners' courts are said to provide simple proceedings.[33] If it is true that these courts are a great deal less formal than the ordinary courts, then it could be argued that African litigants do not need laywers. They could conduct their own cases and thus save costs.

In fact it is quite clear that these courts do not perform in a manner that is remotely comparable to the chief's court in the old society. Their procedures are much more formalistic. Segregated from the community whose disputes they decide, Commissioners' courts cannot recapture the flexibility of the tribal court, a flexibility which arose from the court's position and function in the community.[34]

To conduct a case successfully one needs a lawyer. Procedure in these courts is only marginally less complicated than that in the Magistrate's court.[35] The consequences are that, where one party is represented and the other not, the represented party is almost invariably successful.[36]

Whether litigants need a lawyer or not may be an 'open question' for the academics, but it is not for the ordinary people who realize that they need to be able to pay for their 'justice'. One hundred years ago Ntabeni Magabela, Headman of Peelton Mission Station, King William's Town, told the Cape Native Laws and Customs Commission:

> 'Yes. There are many points in which they [i.e. principles of customary procedure] differ from those of the colony:-
>
> First, in the Colony a person goes with money to the lawyers in order that his case may be entered upon. He who has no money is in perplexity about how his case will be heard.'[37]

Cases are regularly dismissed or repeatedly delayed because of formal deficiencies. Sometimes these defects are the result of the clerk of the court drawing up summonses incorrectly.[38] On other occasions, litigants stand bewildered while Commissioners, before dismissing pleas, applications or arguments, ask what are confusing and formalistic questions.[39]

Related to the alleged simplicity of procedure in these courts is the claim that costs are substantially lower than in ordinary courts.[40]

Where litigants appear without a lawyer (and with consequent disabilities), it may be true that their costs will be relatively low. Yet even this may have to be qualified, for repeated delays and problems with jurisdiction (especially in the special divorce court) may mean many days away from work and possible loss of earnings.[41]

Where a lawyer is employed, it is doubtful whether such services would be any less expensive than for cases involving non-Africans. The tariff of costs (i.e. court fees etc.) is lower in the special courts than in the ordinary courts. This does not, however, stop attorneys from charging their usual fees on a 'party to party' basis for their own services.[42]

These courts may, then, be cheaper than those for non-Africans if the litigant appears without a lawyer (and, that is, with reduced chances of success). Where a lawyer is employed, costs are not substantially lower than for other races.

It is also claimed that these courts are staffed by experts.[43] In the debate preceding the passing of the Black Administration Act in 1927, the Minister said that he envisaged in these courts 'a man specially versed in native law.'[44]

In fact, the presiding officers hold very low qualifications (lower civil service law examination)[45] and display the conservative, sometimes racist attitudes which seem characteristic of the Department of Cooperation and Development.

Despite these low qualifications, Commissioners adjudicate many matters that, in the case of non-Africans, can only be decided by Supreme Court judges whose minimum academic qualification is an LLB.

Commissioners do not have to be proficient in a Bantu language - yet it is claimed by some officials that this total reliance on interpreters had led to 'miscarriage of justice'.[46]

Although it is not a 'claim' made for these courts, I want to consider a final characteristic of the special court system, that is, the type of contribution made by practitioners and academics to the quality of their justice.[47] Professor Ellison Kahn has remarked that:

> 'The process of producing a judgement in a law suit is a co-operative enterprise. Counsel is there to cite the relevant authorities and from the cut and thrust of argument points may emerge that were hitherto latent. In the words of Justice Louis D. Brandeis, one of the greatest judges of the United States Supremem Court, a "judge rarely performs his functions adequately unless the case before him is adequately presented"'.[48]

Quite obviously this principle cannot be realised where the vast majority of litigants cannot afford to employ legal representatives. Even where litigants do have the funds, attorneys in South Africa prefer not to handle these cases. Not only do 'Black law' cases pay far less well than cases in such areas as company law and tax, but 'Black law' cases are often very complex and make demands on the attorney's time that are considered out of proportion to the financial rewards.[49]

Even where they are willing, can one say that attorneys and advocates are competent to make a contribution to the law suit if it is seen (as Kahn says) as a 'cooperative enterprise?'

In the ordinary courts, attorneys and advocates often argue 'hammer and tongs', not only over the facts, but also over the meaning of the law and the way it is to develop. In Commissioners' courts, however, the tendency is to only argue over the facts and to leave law to the Commissioner, to let him decide what the law is, whether or not to apply 'Black law' etc. In practice, therefore, the Commissioner is left free to apply his own static version of customary law.[50]

The shallowness of the intervention of legal representatives is largely a result of their training. On the assumption that lawyers are there to serve the more wealthy twenty per cent of the population, very few law syllabuses demand a compulsory course in the law governing the civil relations of the most impoverished seventy per cent of the population.[51]

Where lawyers have studied 'Black law', it has generally been through positivistic textbooks which ignore the changed social conditions in which customary law operates today. This means that even where lawyers know something about customary law, their orientation is so narrow that their contribution is likely to reinforce that of the Commissioners.[52]

Is judicial integration the solution?[53] Some of the scholars giving evidence to the Hoexter Commission have called for the scrapping of the separate system of courts for Africans.[54] In the Transkei, Ciskei, Bophuthatswana and Venda a formally integrated structure has been established.[55]

It is not inconceivable that the Hoexter Commission will call for an end to judicial segregation, and it is also not impossible that the government will agree to the integration of the special courts as a special 'division' of the Magistrates' Courts.[56] The Riekert Commission has already suggested that 'the administration of justice function at present exercised by the Department of Plural Relations and Development can be transferred to the Department of Justice. Such a step can only be conducive to uniformity in the country's administration of justice. Apart from the transfer of commissioners to the Department of Justice, some adjustments can be made to the curricula for law examinations in order to ensure that magistrates are properly prepared to deal with the questions in which Native law arises ...'[57]

Under such a system, especially if the wide jurisdiction granted to Commissioners at present[58] is retained, the division handling African civil cases would remain effectively isolated. It would, of course, be able to continue the ideological function (as it does in the 'independent' bantustans) of interpellating/constituting subjects tribally.

It is true, nevertheless, that if the special Appeal Courts were abolished and appeals went to the Supreme Court, there would be greater opportunities for influences from outside the Department of Co-operation and Development on the development of African civil law - that is, in the very small number of cases where litigants know that they are able and can afford to appeal to the Supreme Court.

What effect will judicial integration have, assuming that it will entail, at least, greater access to the Supreme Court? Judges have higher academic qualifications than members of the (special 'Black') Appeal Court, but whether they know much about customary law (considering that few have ever studied it or handled cases concerning it) is questionable. Whether they would pursue a more progressive policy towards customary law is also doubtful. Such creativity runs counter to basic tenets of their training, which is very antagonistic to 'judigical lawmaking'.[59]

The fundamental problems that Africans face in civil cases will remain unresolved, irrespective of whether the hierarchy of appeal is segregated or integrated. Africans generally cannot afford the legal representation that they, like whites, need, in order to litigate effectively. Even those who can afford a lawyer, we have seen, cannot always obtain one who knows much about customary law. Certainly there are few practitioners who would be able and willing to contest the Commissioner's or judge's interpretation of the law and to urge modifications in accordance with changed social conditions.

An integrated court structure would solve little in itself. To respond adequately to the personal law needs of Africans one requires a mainly African bench[60] - trained to respond more dynamically, together with adequate provision of legal representation of all who require it. This cannot be realized in the present state structure.

Having provided a brief critique of the courts which decide African civil law cases it is necessary to give a fuller picture of the way in which they have operated in practice and the adequacy of their decisions, given the nature of the social conditions today.

The Black Administration Act of 1927 gave Commissioners' Courts a discretion to apply customary law. Section 11(1) reads:

> 'Notwithstanding the provisions of any other law, it shall be in the discretion of the Commissioners' Courts in all suits or proceedings between Blacks involving questions of customs followed by Blacks, to decide such questions according to the Black law applying to such customs except in so far as it shall have been repealed or modified: Provided that such Black law shall not be opposed to the principles of public policy or natural justice. Provided further that it shall not be lawful for any court to declare that the custom of lobola or bogadi or other similar custom is repugnant to such principles.'

This section provides for a discretion which operates only in cases between African and African (in the 'independent' bantustans, however, the discretion operates in cases involving all races).[61] Where an African sues a white/'Coloured'/Indian or vice versa, the section has no application and Roman-Dutch Law must apply.

Courts do not have to apply Black law in cases between Africans. There is a choice ('discretion'). Nevertheless, for a number of years in the 1930's and 1940's the Appeal Court interpreted this section to mean a mandate for a policy of 'legal segregation' - that is, that Black law had to be applied as far as possible.[62] In 1948 the Appellate Division of the Supreme Court, following a question put by the Minister, reversed these decisions.[63] (Where he doubts the correctness of any Appeal Court for Commissioner's decision, the Minister may submit it to the Appellate Division to decide what the correct decision should be.)[64] They held that sec 11(1)[65] provided no basis for the view that 'native law should be treated as _prima facie_ applicable in cases between natives ...'[66]

That is the law (laid down by the highest court) - but there are nevertheless indications in later decisions that the special courts are still giving an undue preference to Black law.[67] This preference is partly a result of their tendency to depict Africans as an undifferentiated mass, all of whom act and contract, and lead their lives generally according to 'tribal' patterns. Thus in one case, when deciding to apply Black law rather than Roman-Dutch to a case of defamation arising from an imputation of witchcraft, the court held:

> 'But amongst Bantu an imputation of witchcraft is a most serious matter and may result in the most dire consequences to the person so accused so that any claim based on such an imputation is essentially a matter to be dealt with under Bantu law and custom and in my view the Commissioner was wrong in not having done so.[68]

It may well be true that most Africans do believe in witchcraft and that allegations of witchcraft would cause serious social inconvenience in many African communities.[69] What the court was required to do in terms of its mandate, however, was to establish the circumstances of the specific litigants, whether an allegation of witchcraft would be significant in their particular case.[70] That it does not do so serves, obviously, to reinforce the constitution of Africans as tribal subjects - people living in a community to which the court attributes specifically tribal values.

The discretion arises in cases 'involving questions of customs followed by Blacks'.[71] How one interprets the term 'customs' is crucial in determing whether customary law is to be frozen in supposedly 'pure', 'traditional' forms or whether it is allowed to retain its dynamic qualities.[72] Thus Julius Lewin remarked in 1947:

> 'The customs recognised as Native law are ancient ones. But in actual fact many of these customs or certain features of them are changing as the social and economic conditions of Native life change. Nowhere in the world has social change been as swift and as far-reaching as it has in Africa in the last two or three decades. Where customs of marriage or family life have undergone significant change, which form of the custom shall the courts recognise as Native law? Shall they countenance only the practice of the oldest generation? Or shall they seek to find current or contemporary custom in the practice of younger people? ...'[73]

The courts and academics have generally tended to treat the term 'custom' as synonymous with immemorial usage.[74] Thus, in one case, the court speaks of the rule of succession (male primogeniture) as 'entrenched, sacrosanct'. The court regarded it as a dangerous doctrine to allow a modern local custom to oust 'a law which had its genesis in the ancient policy of the founders of the race and has been universally recognised and generally applied down through the ages to the present time'.[75]

This is not to say that there have not in fact been judicial innovations. The courts and legislature have superimposed on tribal society common law categories such as majority status and individual rights to property. In Sijila v Masumba,[76] for example, President McLoughlin introduced the common law term 'majority' and declared a woman incapable of owning any category of property, all being vested in the only 'major', the 'kraalhead' or her husband, as the case may be. Though the decision diminished the rights of women, this was regarded as a natural result of European judicial administration of the indigenous law:

> 'It is when recourse is had to European courts with a procedure foreign to the Native system that complications and confusion results. The European individualistic system regards one man as outright owner, and it is in deference to the principles of that system that the present-day idea of personal ownership in a kraalhead has taken root.'[77]

The combined impact of the introduction of individualistic categories from the common law and the courts' conservative approach to the formation of custom has been to strengthen the patriarchal domination over women. This has meant that the rights of women are often reduced in comparison to those which they enjoyed in the pre-colonial tribal society.[78]

The more general problem, however, is that courts are not dealing with people who are living in the same manner as the 'founders of the race'. Many men and women are finding that the male/female relationships of the old society are not always viable or suitable in the conditions which they experience today. When both men and women are independent wage-earners, women tend to demand a more egalitarian marriage relationship; or if unmarried, an independent female wage-earner, deriving little in the way of protection or few benefits from her male guardian, will resent his power over her personal life or her property.[79]

A woman's guardian may be her father, her husband, brother or even someone much more remote who never makes an appearance except when it is time to collect lobolo or an inheritance.[80] He has to consent to her customary marriage[81] (in Natal and, since 1972, also in the Transvaal, he must consent to her civil (Roman-Dutch law) marriage even if she is over twenty-one).[82] He is no longer allowed to force her to marry[83] but he can make it impossible for her to marry the man of her choice, through making unreasonable lobolo demands.[84]

This 'guardian', no matter how remote his actual connection with the woman may be, is entitled to damages for seduction from the father of her child[85] and he (the guardian) is entitled to lobolo when she marries. If she is an unmarried mother he is entitled to lobolo for her children, even if he contributes nothing to their support.[86]

The law regarding divorce from a customary union also reflects this patriarchal dominance over women. The guardian may come to an agreement with the husband to dissolve his daughter's/ward's marriage - even without her consent.[87] A man may simply repudiate his wife - provided he is prepared to forego the lobolo he has paid.[88] The woman has no such right. Normally she has to try and persuade her guardian to return the cattle/money (or whatever the lobolo comprised).[89] She can, in theory, obtain a divorce if she has been driven out by her husband, with the intention of ending the relationship.[90]

The courts, however, are reluctant to conclude that a husband's behaviour constitutes 'repudiation' and this leads them to condone violence against the wife. In one case, an application for dissolution of a customary union was rejected - despite the fact that the husband had assaulted his wife on a number of occasions, threatened to stab her, told her to go away and said that he would kill her if she returned. The court declared that the husband had not intended to drive her away 'in the legal sense'.[91] In another case, the court again reinforced the standards of the most reactionary section of the African community, by depicting them as 'customary':

> 'It is not uncommon for a Native husband to chastise his wife. Unless this is done brutally and with a reckless disregard of the consequences, Natives do not regard chastisement as a rejection of the wife.'[92]

To summarize: 'customs' has been interpreted by the courts to mean the custom of the most reactionary sections of the community and to reject the formation of new, more progressive (and less narrowly tribal) customs, born of changed living patterns. This reinforces the patriarchal strucutre of the traditional family and, in a modest way, adds coherence to the attempts to re-establish 'tribal' order.

Section 11(1) also imposes limitations on the application of 'Black law'. Black law may only be applied where the customs out of which the law arises are not repugnant to natural justice or public policy.[93] Although natural justice normally has a fairly precise meaning, the courts have taken this provision to mean that they should intervene where particular customs outrage their sense of morality. In the early days of white administration of customary law, courts sometimes went so far as to outlaw customary marriage altogether because of its intrinsic connection to the lobolo and polygyny institutions.[94] These were said to reduce women to the level of slavery while their menfold enjoyed lives of 'indolent sensuality'.[95] At one time it was impossible for Africans in the Boer republics to contract lawful customary or 'common' law marriages.[96] It was to avoid such excesses in the new climate of tolerance of African customs (born of virtually completed land seizure, etc.) that the legislature specifically prevented the courts from declaring lobolo repugnant.[97]

Since then, the repugnancy clause, where it has been invoked, has often served a relatively progressive function. Through invoking this provision, courts have outlawed a variety of coercive relationships, such as forced marriages.[98] One of the problems has been that they have been unwilling to use this 'repugnancy clause' to play a more ambitious reformative role.[99] In consequence, the 'Black law' that is applied retains many practices that are very oppressive in relation to women.[100]

Lawyers concerned with the development of customary law in the Transkei have attacked the repugnancy clause, using anti-colonial rhetoric.[101] They argue, correctly, that the clause has often been used in the past to enforce Eurocentric values.[102] They say (also correctly), that the fact that the customary law and not the common law is subject to the repugnancy clause, reflects the customary law's inferior status.[103] Digby Koyana, a former member of the Transkei 'cabinet' writes:

> 'As the sleeping giant of Africa awakens these restraints are gradually being removed. Thus, in Tanzania and Ghana the repugnancy clause has been dropped. It was considered unfitting to the dignity of the indigenous laws of the people of these countries to suggest that repugnancy existed ...'[104]

In principle, there is no reason to object to the view that Africans (like whites) do not need their customs to be measured against a repugnancy clause, that their values should be respected and that repugnancy clauses tend to negate such respect and to substitute European values for their own.

But this is not an abstract question about Africans or African values 'in general' but about what the proposal of Koyana and others, to remove the repugnancy clause, would signify in South Africa today.

Koyana, we have seen, points to post-independence developments in Ghana and Tanzania in support of his contention that this clause should be scrapped. If the position in the Transkei or in South Africa generally were analogous to that in Ghana or in Tanzania there would be no reason to object, for I think that these states were correct (as independent states) to get rid of the repugnancy clause.

But the position in South Africa is (obviously) different. Getting rid of this clause would (at most) serve to foster an illusory feeling of emancipation. In reality its effect, in present circumstances, might be undesirable and retrogressive.

Even if (as indicated) the courts have been reluctant to use this clause for reformist purposes, what effect will it have, to remove it now? In an area like the Transkei, where the power of chiefs is entrenched, one possibility is that without a repugnancy clause there is room for the introduction or reintroduction of a variety of customs allowing for coerced relationships and a further degradation of the status of women.[105] Courts and the repugnancy clause have an erratic record but they have nevertheless provided a measure of protection.

We have seen that there appears to be a continued tendency on the part of the courts to deny the diversity (and the direction) of contemporary African social patterns and especially to ignore the substantially changed lives of many people. This sometimes leads them to give an unwarranted preference to (their version of) customary law, instead of Roman-Dutch law. There is also an unwillingness to recognize that customary law has a diminished relevance (or no relevance at all) in many peoples' lives.

In responding to such tendencies, it is important that one does not overreact and assume that customary law is a Nationalist Party creation, and that it has no relevance at all. There is a tendency amongst liberal academics, under the guise of supporting 'equality before the law' to adopt a chauvinistic position towards customary law. Thus, in line with the view of P M A Hunt, quoted at the beginning of this paper, it was suggested at a law conference in 1962 that 'the Roman-Dutch law should be made of general application for all racial groups in South Africa'.[106]

Nor is it acceptable when Professor Carmen Nathan writes:

> 'The attitude of the South African government is a reflection of its policy which denies not only the permanence of

> the Black people in urban areas but also the fact that many Black people have lost all tribal identity. This attitude shows a lack of understanding of the indigenous law and the fact that it can function only in a traditional setting. The time for allowing the indigenous system to develop and adapt through the medium of judicial decision has long since passed . . .'[107]

While not denying the relevance of customary law, this view presents a rigid geographical division of the spheres of operation of Roman-Dutch and customary law. People in the urban areas are presumed to choose Roman-Dutch law (or if they don't choose it they should, since, according to Nathan, the customary law cannot 'function' in urban areas). The operation of customary law, according to this view, should be restricted to rural areas.[108]

Such an approach underrates or ignores the complexity of living patterns in both rural and urban areas. Just as rural people are not unaffected by the changes that are most marked in the towns, equally there are many urban dwellers who retain a degree of adherence to 'traditional' ideas and behaviour patterns. Ellen Hellman wrote:

> 'There is no one pattern of urban African family life. There are many changing patterns of behaviour within the family, many different adaptations between the traditional and modern. Income, occupation and education, length of urban residence - quite apart from personal attributes - affect these patterns.'[109]

What this means is that it is not satisfactory to present people with the type of either/or choice that Professor Nathan provides: either one lives with the consequences of a customary union - unmodified (because 'the time for allowing the indigenous system to develop and adapt through the medium of judicial decision has long since passed ...') or one chooses the Roman-Dutch law marriage.

Now there are a great many Africans who prefer customary marriages to common law ones[110] and they are unlikely to be dissuaded by talk about the inability of customary marriages to 'function' in urban areas. And they are right, because the basic problem does not lie in the incapacity of the customary union for reform. (As it happens, independent African states have successfully modified and developed that law.)[111]

The problem lies rather in a different kind of incapacity - that the recipients of Commissioners' Court justice are unable to influence the course of 'their own' law. The Roman-Dutch law marriage operates in an environment quite different from that in which it originated. But it was developed by courts and recently by parliament in order to cope better with present conditions. Africans, a people who are unrepresented in parliament, and hardly represented on the bench, cannot rely on a similar sensitivity to their needs. This is not so much a result of the government's 'lack of understanding of the indigenous law' - but rather a result of the wider relations of national and class domination, as a result of which Africans cannot legally influence most of the fundamental circumstances of their lives.[112]

I have tried to show that the civil justice system established for Africans by whites in South Africa has generally failed to meet the actual needs of the overwhelming majority of the population. But it was not established to meet their needs. During the nineteenth century, when tribal chiefdoms were still vital structures, there was a much less tolerant attitude towards African custom than one finds in Government circles today.[113] It was only after the seizure of African land and the subjugation of almost all the chiefdoms that a unified and generally 'benign' policy towards customary law started to evolve. Having created the conditions for the gradual dissolution of tribal politics, the South African state sought to breathe new life into discredited chiefdoms through pseudo-tribal structures, such as the Bantu Authorities system.

The Bantu law/court system articulates with this wider policy of retribalization and helps to maintain the 'tribal' family. Its continued viability is important if the patriarchal family production is to continue its subsidization of the capitalist mode of production.

Ideologically, the special courts seek to constitute individuals as specific tribal subjects and this serves or seeks to splinter attempts at developing a national movement and/or national consciousness. It is sought to blur the contradiction between Africans and the white 'colonial bloc', through promoting specific tribal identities.[114]

Like much else in the (special) colonial state structure, the court system is in crisis. It has for some time been patently ill-suited to the needs of the communities whose lives it is intended to regulate. Its direction of development is in contradiction to the emerging social patterns of the African community. The current state of the law of marriage, divorce and the status of women seeks to perpetuate social categories (e.g. perpetual minority of women) that are glaringly incompatible with the lives that many women actually lead. This legal inadequacy tends to result in many people taking the view that their *de facto* disabilities are less onerous than those likely to result from recourse to the law courts. Taken together with the other barriers in the way of successful litigation, it is not surprising that many people who are separated do not try to get divorced, nor that many who cannot get their guardian's consent to marry (often through his making excessive lobolo demands) form loose unions. All of this contributes to the already very high levels of illegitimacy and attendant social problems.[115]

One of the most crucial barriers to adequate civil justice for Africans, that of adequate legal representation, cannot be solved while the legal profession operates on a basis that puts their services out of the reach of all save a minute number of Africans. This problem might be solved in the future by the socialization of the legal profession, i.e. provision of legal representation as a necessary social service to all who need it. That any substantial moves in that direction cannot be envisaged under the existing state structure, is made abundantly clear by a statement of the Minister of Justice in 1978:

> 'Legal aid does not exist to be given to every person who wants it. The idea behind the legal aid is that when a person cannot afford the costs of legal proceedings and he has a good case - and I want to stress that - a case which he ought to bring before the court, the richer sector of

> society helps the poorer sector of society to allow the administration of justice to take place. I do not want a legal aid which is available to all and sundry. We are surely not a socialist society.'[116]

The future of customary law and of the civil justice system within which it oeprates are tied to the future of the African people generally. Though it is possible that limited improvements may be made in present conditions, adequate resolution of the problems of African civil law await the satisfaction of the wider aspirations of the African people in realizing their self-determination in a democratic system of government.[117]

NOTES

1. Union of South Africa, Senate Debates, 3rd Senate (Fifth Senate) March 17, 1955, col. 751.

2. 'South Africa: The Faculty of Law, University of the Witwatersrand, Johannesburg', Journal of African Law, 7 (1963), 125.

3. 'Sesotho Marriage, Guardianship and the Customary Heir' in Max Gluckman (ed.) Ideas and Procedures in African Customary Law (Oxford, 1969), 197.

4. See R S Suttner 'African Civil Law - Special Legal Aid Problems' in Legal Aid in South Africa (Proceedings of a Conference held in the Faculty of Law,University of Natal, Durban, from 2nd - 6th July 1973) (Durban, 1974) 189, where a survey of the opinions of practitioners is presented.

5. These categories are somewhat crude, but neverthless useful.

6. cf. Louis Althusser 'Ideology and Ideological State Apparatuses. Notes towards an investigation' in Louis Althusser, On Ideology (London, 1984), 1-60.

7. See Gerhard Maré, Ideology and Ideological Struggle: Hegemony, liberation and revolution (unpub. 1980) note 3, 5-6, and Raymond Suttner, 'The Ideological Role of the Judiciary in South Africa' Philosophical Papers, 13, (1984) 28.

8. Althusser, op. cit., 45. He continues (ibid): 'I say: The category of the subject is constitutive of all ideology, but at the same time and immediately I add that the category of the subject is only constitutive of all ideology in so far as all ideology has the function (which defines it) of "constituting" concrete individuals as subjects. In the interaction of this double constitution exists the functioning of all ideology, ideology being nothing but its functioning in the material forms of existence of that functioning.'

9. H R Hahlo and E Kahn, The South African Legal System and its Background (Cape Town, 1968), 34.

10. Engels, Origins of the Family, Private Property and the State, quoted in Maureen Cain British Journal of Law and Society, 1 (1974), 142.

11. 1956 (3) SA 45 (W).

12. Hahlo and Kahn, op. cit., 34.

13. Ibid., 50. Emphasis inserted.

14. See Maré, 2-3.

15. Quoted Barend van Niekerk South African Journal of Criminal Law and Criminology, 3 (1979), 154.

16. Sec. 11(1) Act 38 of 1927, as amended, (henceforth referred to as "The Act").

17. See note 61 below.

18. See e.g. G M B Whitfield, South African Native Law, (Cape Town) 2 ed. (1948) at 4.

19. See Sec. 11(2) of the Act and J C Bekker and J J J Coertze, Seymour's Customary Law in Southern Africa 4 ed. (Cape Town, 1982), 65-67.

20. See e.g. The Freedom Charter (1955) and the Declaration of the United Democratic Front (1983).

21. Cf. H Wolpe 'Capitalism and cheap labour power in South Africa: from segregation to apartheid' Economy and Society, 1 (1972), 425, where the process through which the mode of production in the reserves has subsidized the dominant capitalist mode, is described. While Wolpe virtually concludes that this subsidization has ended, my assumption is that it continues, though the contribution may have diminished in some respects. Without pretending to an exhaustive critique, I think that Wolpe focuses on the diminished relative contribution of the reserves, while ignoring its increased absolute contribution. According to official statistics, in the period 1959-1974, there was a relative decline in the importance of agriculture in the reserves, but its absolute value trebled. (From R45,5 m to R123,9 m. In 1973, 89,5% of agricultural production was reckoned to be subsistence production (i.e. of produce that was not marketed but consumed by the producers themselves). According to Benbo (Black Development in South Africa: The Economic Development of the Black Peoples in the Homelands of the Republic of South Africa (Pretoria 1976 at 81): 'During the period 1968/69 -73/74 the gross value of agricultural and forestry production increased at an average rate of 11,7% p.a., whereas the production prices of agricultural products during the same period increased at an annual rate of 8,6%. The increase in production thus averages 3,10%. Equally he pays insufficient attention to the contribution of factors other than agriculture to the reproduction of labour power. Finally, the fact that production in the reserves may not any longer constitute an independent mode of production, does not mean that production processes in the reserves do not continue the subsidization function. See also (anon) 'Colonialism of a Special Kind and the South African State' (1983, African Perspective 23, (1983) 81-82, note 7, 92.

22. See e.g. Sec. 195(2) of the Criminal Procedure Act, No. 51 of 1977. Here the status of the 'customary union' is treated quite bluntly:

'195(2) Anything to the contrary in this Act or any other law notwithstanding any person married in accordance with Bantu law or custom shall, notwithstanding the registration or other recognition under any law of such a union as a valid and binding marriage, for the purposes of the law of evidence in criminal proceedings, be deemed to be an unmarried person.'

23. cf. e.g. Antony N. Allott, Essays in African Law (London, 1960), T O Elias, British Colonial Law (London, 1962).

24. This 'bifurcation' is remarked on by the influential Riekert Commission (Report of the Commission of Inquiry into Legislation Affecting the Utilisation of Manpower (excluding the legislation administered by the Departments of Labour and Mines) RP 32/1979, Republic of South Africa, Pretoria. Chairman: Dr. P J Riekert) which describes the Department of Plural Relations and Development (as it was then called) as a '"public service within a public service" in respect of the administration of matters affecting Black persons' exercising control over them and performing 'services for them that are undertaken by the functional departments for the other population groups ...' (p. 200).

One of the purposes of the present 'reform initiative', of the Botha regime appears to be to create the impression of 'deracialization', to imply that there is a common administration for all South Africans (i.e. excluding citizens of 'independent' bantustans). The concept race is apparently removed from labour legislation, labour movement is increasingly regulated as 'foreign relations' i.e. unwanted Africans are 'deported' to 'their' states. Departments that deal with 'racial affairs' e.g. group areas, black education etc., are now designated by neutral-sounding names e.g. Dept. of Community Development, Cooperation and Development, Education and Training etc. Such a tendency may lead to the integration of the "special courts" into the ordinary legal system.

25. The courts have previously been critically examined by Professor Ellison Kahn in H R Hahlo and Ellison Kahn South Africa: The development of its laws and constitution (Cape Town, 1960), Julius Lewin, Studies in African Native Law (Cape Town, 1947), R S Suttner, 'Problems of African Civil Law Today' 78-79 (1974), De Rebus Procuratioriis 266-268, 311-315 and The System of Civil Justice for Africans in South Africa (unpublished 1983), 17-27.

26. There is no limitation as to the amount that can be involved in a case tried by Commissioners. In the case of magistrates once the issues involve more than a certain amount, it must be tried by Supreme Court.

27. See below.

28. To appeal to the Appellate Division litigants need permission of both the Appellate Division and the Appeal Court for Commission-

ers itself. Very few appelants reach the Appellate Division (whether for lack of funds or lack of permission). See R S Suttner, The System of Civil Justice, 14-15.

29. See evidence of academics and social workers reported in press during 1981, e.g. 'Hoexter - Kommissie van Ondersoek na Howe: Geïntegreerde hofstelsel nodig', Die Transvaler, 29 August 1981, 'Judicial officers' "ignorance" slated, Rand Daily Mail, 29 August 1981.

30. See evidence of Professors R verLoren van Themaat, F A de Villiers and C J Maree to Hoexter Commission. Beeld, 19 May 1981.

31. 1929 Native Appeal Court (Natal and Transvaal) 3-4, *per* Stubbs, (President).

32. 1930 Native Appeal Court (Natal and Transvaal) 9 at 12.

33. Ibid.

34. See discussion of tribal courts in Suttner, System of Civil Justice, 3-7 and 'Discussion' in Legal Aid in South Africa, 206.

35. See Lewin, Studies in African Native Law, 16-20, R S Suttner, South African Legal Journal 85 (1968), 445, note 61 where the rules are illustrated. According to the Rand Daily Mail, 12 June 1981 Mr L J Make, public relations officer for the Zionist Christian Church in Pietersburg told the Hoexter Commission that the 'court procedure was totally alien to most rural blacks ...' These rules have led to the publication of a book, now in its third edition, aimed at their elucidation for practitioners. See J A N Khumalo, The Civil Practices of All Courts for Blacks in Southern Africa 3rd ed., (Cape Town, 1984).

36. See R S Suttner, 'African Civil Law - Special Legal Aid Problems' in Legal Aid in South Africa *op. cit.*, 189-191, 201-202.

37. In reply to a circular from the Cape 1883. G-4 Government Commission on Native Laws and Customs, Appendix C at 211.

38. The clerk sometimes/often helps unrepresented clients.

39. See reference note 36 above.

40. See e.g. statements of Stubbs, (President) above and Howard Rogers, Native Administration in the Union of South Africa 2 ed. (1949) 203.

41. See Suttner System of Civil Justice, 21-22.

42. Lewin *op. cit.*, 19-20, Hahlo and Kahn, South Africa: The Development of its laws and constitution, 332. See also Zubi Seedat 'Lead-in Address' in Legal Aid in South Africa *op. cit.*, 204-205.

43. cf. Suttner, *op. cit.*, 23-24.

44. Union of South Africa *House of Assembly Debates*, vol. 9, col. 2907, 28 April 1927.

45. cf. Suttner, *op. cit.*, 23-24.

46. See 'Many "found guilty" by interpreters' *The Star*, 21 October 1981, 'Courts misled by poor interpreters probe told', *Rand Daily Mail*, 21 October 1981.

47. cf. Suttner, *op. cit.*, 24-26, Suttner, 'African Civil Law - special legal aid problems', *Legal Aid in South Africa* *op. cit.*, 189ff.

48. 'The Judges and the Professors OR Bench and Chair' *South African Law Journal* (1980), 571, quoting Brandeis 'Living Law' in *Illinois L R*, 10 (1961), 470.

49. See Suttner 'African Civil Law' *Legal Aid in South Africa* *op. cit*. 191-196.

50. *Ibid*. and see below.

51. cf. Suttner, *op. cit.*, 196ff.

52. See remarks of Mr Mu Ashekele, 'Discussion', *Legal Aid in South Africa*, *op. cit*. at 206.

53. The view adopted here is much more sceptical of the advantages of judicial integration than expressed in Suttner, 'Towards Judicial and Legal Integration' 445ff.

54. See e.g. "Hoexter-Kommissie van Ondersoek na Howe: Geïntegreerde hofstelsel nodig", *Die Transvaler* 19 August 1981.

55. See above.

56. See J M T Labuschagne and D.J. Swanepoel 'Regspleging van die Stedelike Swartmens in Suid-Afrika' *De Jure* 12 (1979), 27-28, where the establishment of such specialized divisions is in fact advocated.

57. Riekert Commission, 208.

58. See above.

59. For a wider examination of this aspect of 'judicial ideology' see the works of John Dugard, esp. *Human Rights and the South African Legal Order* (New Jersey, 1978).

60. 'Appointment on merit' is not adequate unless merit includes knowledge of and sympathy for the problems of the community most affected by the law. There is, at present, a general lack of con-

confidence amongst blacks in the law and the courts. The establishment (in a democratic South Africa) of a bench composed primarily of people from the black community, will, it is suggested, be part of the process of establishing confidence.

61. See Sec. 53(1) Republic of Transkei Constitution Act, No. 15 of 1976, Sec. 67(1) of Republic of Bophuthatswana Act, No. 18 of 1977, Sec. 51(1) Republic of Venda Constitution Act, No. 18 of 1979, Sec. 61(1) Republic of Ciskei Constitution Act, No. 20 of 1981.

62. See e.g. Matsheng v Dhlamini, 1937 Native Appeal Court (Natal and Transvaal) 89 at 91, Kaula v Mtimkulu 1938 Native Appeal Court (Natal and Transvaal) 68 at 70, and discussion in Julius Lewin op. cit., 22ff.

63. cf. Ex parte Minister of Native Affairs: in re Yako v Beyi 1948 (1) SA 388 (A) (hereafter: Yako v Beyi).

64. Sec. 14 Black Administration Act.

65. Quoted above.

66. per Schreiner, JA at 397 - in note 63.

67. See Twala v Ngoqo and Ngoqo - 1968 Bantu Appeal Court (North-Eastern Division) and Kumalo v Mbata 1969 Bantu Appeal Court (North-Eastern Division) 69 and discussion in Suttner, System of Civil Justice for Africans, 30-34.

68. Twala v Ngoqo and Ngoqo supra at 12-13.

69. See e.g. B.A. Pauw 'The Influence of Christianity' in W D Hammond-Tooke (ed.) The Bantu-Speaking Peoples of Southern Africa London, (1974) 437.

70. In Yako v Beyi, Schreiner, JA said (at 398) that it would not necessarily be an improper exercise of 'class distinctions' if the court were guided in its decision to apply the common law by the fact that 'the parties or either of them were educated, civilized, urbanised or detribalised ...'

71. See Sec. 11(1) quoted above.

72. cf. Brun-Otto Bryde, The Politics and Sociology of African Legal Development Frankfurt, (1976), 108ff.

73. Lewin, op. cit., 107.

74. Regarding academics, see R.S. Suttner 'The Study of "Bantu law" in South Africa', Acta Juridica, (1968), 147, and Suttner, 'African Civil Law', 199-201.

75. Mazibuko v Mazibuko 1930 NAC (N & T) 143 at 146, 145.

76. 1940 NAC (C & O) 42.

77. Ibid., 47.

78. In contrast to the courts and the Natal Code (at least until its 1982 amendment) denying women any rights to hold property, various scholars have shown that their rights were not so restricted in the old society, cf. David Welsh, The Roots of Segregation, (Oxford, 1971), 162ff Monic Hunter, Reaction to Conquest, (Cape Town, 1961), 119, N J van Warmelo and M W D Phophi, Venda Law (Government Printer, Pretoria, 1948), parts 2 and 3, H J Simons, African Women: Their Legal Status in South Africa (London, 1968), 83, 92, 187ff, 194ff, 198ff, 202ff.

79. See Ellen Hellmann, 'The African Family Today' in South African Institute of Race Relations, African Family Life (Johannesburg, 1968), 1, Ellen Hellmann, 'Social Change among Urban Africans' in Heribert Adam (ed.) South Africa: Sociological Perspectives (Oxford, 1971), 158, Ellen Hellman, 'African Townswomen in the Process of Change' South Africa International, 5 (1974), 14 and H J Simons, op. cit., generally.

80. H J Simons, op. cit., generally, R.S. Suttner, 'African Family Law and Research in South Africa Today: Prospects and Problems'. Paper presented to the Afrika-Studiesentrum Seminar, 'New Directions in African Family Law', Leyden, Netherlands, September 30 - October 4, 1974 (henceforth referred to as 'African Family Law'), 13ff, Hellmann 'African Townswomen', 20-21.

81. Bekker and Coertze, Seymour's Customary Law in Southern Africa, 106 and ch. 5 generally.

82. See Sec. 22 ter of Black Administration Act, as amended by Sec. 2 of Act No. 23 of 1972.

83. cf. N J J Olivier, Die Privaatreg van die Suid-Afrikaanse Bantoetaalsprekendes, (Durban 2 ed. 1981), 43ff, Bekker and Coertze, 107.

84. H J Simons, op. cit., generally, Suttner, 'African Family Law', 18ff.

85. If there is also a claim for maintenance it must be brought under the common law by the woman herself. The customary law does not provide damages for maintenance. As a result of their lack of training, some lawyers bring actions under 'Black law', where it would be quite possible to bring a successful action under the common law. See case recorded in Suttner, 'African Civil Law - Special Legal Aid Problems' 194-195.

86. cf. Suttner 'African Family Law', 23-24, Z.K. Seedat, The Natal Code of Bantu Law as it Affects African Women in the Changing Situation Today, (1969) 84. B.A. Honours dissertation, University of Natal, Durban, 1969, 84.

87. Nkabinde v Mlangeni and Another 1942 NAC (N & T).

88. Olivier op. cit., 160ff, H J Simons, op. cit., 130, 131.

89. H J Simons, op. cit., ch. 12.

90. Ibid. and Olivier, op. cit. 173ff.

91. Mokoena v Mofokeng 1945 NAC (C & O) 89.

92. Stolleh v Mtwalo and Another 147 NAC (C & O) 33 at 34. The principle of 'moderate corrective chastisement' is recognized by leading academic authors. See Bekker & Coertze op. cit., 190 and Bekker 'Grounds of divorce in African customary marriages in Natal' (1976) 9 Comparative and International Law Journal of Southern Africa 346 at 350, where he states: 'It is a well-known fact that a Zulu husband will punish his wife for neglecting her marital duties.'

93. See above.

94. See E R Garthorne 'Applications of Native Law' Bantu Studies, 3 (1929), 256-7.

95. See Natal 1852/3 Commission appointed to inquire into the past and present state of the kaffirs in the District of Natal. Proceedings and Report. (Pietermaritzburg, J Archbel).

96. cf. H J Simons, op. cit., ch. 3.

97. See Sec. 11(1) quoted above.

98. cf. Olivier op. cit., 612ff.

99. The wife-beating cases (above) are a good example.

100. cf. generally H.J. Simons, op. cit., Suttner, 'African Family Law'.

101. See Nicola S Peart, 'Application of the Repugnancy Clause', Institute for Public Service and Vocational Training Bulletin, (1980), 52-53, 51 at 52-53, D S Koyana, Customary Law in a Changing Society, Cape Town (1980), 112-113. In a recent personal communication Peart has indicated that she no longer adheres to the view expressed in the article that I criticize.

102. Peart, op. cit., 54-55, 58. Koyana op. cit., 112-113. See similar remarks of Mr Mu Ashekele in 'Discussion', Legal Aid in South Africa, op. cit., 205.

103. loc cit.

104. Koyana, loc cit.

105. This wariness appears justified, among other things, by the recent report that the Transkei Marriage Act had removed the right of a wife to maintenance after a divorce. Mr George Matanzima is quoted as saying: 'We prefer the lobola system which gives a woman all the security she needs. If she leaves her husband she can go home - which is why the husband pays her father for her hand'. (Sunday Tribune, 11 September 1983).

While this does not constitute a reversal of some of the changes introduced by the repugnancy clause, it is an indication of the Transkeian orientation.

106. A S Mathews in 'Verslag van 'n Noordelike Streekskonferensie van die Vereniging van Universiteitsdosente in die Regte in Suid-Afrika (1962) 25 Tydskrif vir Hedendaagse Romeins-Hollandse Reg 195 at 297.

107. 'The Legal status of Black Women in South African Society' in A J G M Sanders (ed.) Southern Africa in Need of Legal Reform Durban (1981), 6. Emphasis inserted.

108 See also Julius Lewin, Outline of Native Law Cape Town (1966) 30.

109. Hellmann, 'The African Family Today', 7, Koyana op. cit., xx.

110. Most Africans who enter into legal marriages in South Africa still marry according to 'Black Law'. See e.g. Reep verLoren van Themaat 'Die verfyning van die reg vir swartes in Suid- Afrika' (1980) 43 THRHR at 241ff. On page 242 he remarks that the customary union 'is die huweliksvorm van ongeveer twee-derdes van die swart bevolking wat behoorlik getroud is'.

111. See Arthur Phillips and Henry F Morris, Marriage Laws in Africa London, (1970), 35ff.

Domination by Consent: Elections under the Representation of Natives Act, 1937-1948

Mirjana Roth

The elections which were held under the Representation of Natives Act in 1937, 1942 and 1948 warrant examination for two reasons. Firstly, because they were the only elections ever held in South Africa on a national level in which blacks took part. And secondly, because the holding of free elections in a country which denied the electorate many of the other basic freedoms such as freedom of movement, of speech and of assembly was an anomaly in itself and ought to be examined for this reason alone.

The first of these elections was held in 1937. The electorate were male black tax payers over the age of eighteen who, by an elaborate voting system, were to elect their representatives to the three institutions where they could make their wishes known to the government. The Cape voters, who had been removed from the common roll, could now elect three white representatives to the House of Assembly. The whole of the black electorate could vote for the four senators, as they could for the members of the newly formed third body, the Natives Representative Council. Twelve of the sixteen black members of that Council could be elected (four were nominated by the government). The Council's purpose was to consider and to comment on all new legislation on black affairs before it was tabled in either the House of Assembly or the Senate.[1]

The main emphasis of this paper will be on the elections to the Natives Representative Council (NRC), because it was this feature of the Representation of Natives Act which Africans themselves emphasised, both in their newspapers and in their political organisations. To understand the importance which the black electorate attached to the election of the NRC, it must be made clear that although the functions of the Council as laid down in the Act made it a totally advisory body, it was nevertheless felt to have the semblance of a third chamber of Parliament. This idea that the NRC might one day assume the guise of a parliament for blacks was first postulated by Smuts (although this was later disputed by him) and assiduously repeated by both black and white politicians.[2] Newspapers published for black readers repeatedly referred to the Council as a "black parliament" throughout its fifteen years of existence. A National Party spokesman even gave as one of the reasons for the necessity for the Council's abolition the fact that such a "parliament" would be a danger to white domination.[3]

An indication of the importance which councillors attached to their membership of the NRC was the addition of the letters "MRC" behind their names in the same way that members of Parliament were "MP's".[4] Both Dr Moroka, who was a councillor and African National Congress (ANC) president, and A P Mda, who was Congress Youth League president in the 1940's, emphasised the status attached to being a member of the NRC. They held the opinion that far more status was attached by blacks to the councillors than to the heads of any of the black organisations of that time, including the ANC.[5]

The electoral process itself was a very elaborate one, due mainly to the attempts by the authorities to circumvent the fact that the vast majority of the electorate was illiterate. No attempt has been made here to analyse the whole of this in detail. This would entail a paper on its own; certain aspects of it only, when considered important, are however explained.

Voting was by a show of hands and the actual result of the vote was recorded in writing, placed in a sealed envelope and handed to the relevant authorities, so that the vote was in effect a secret one. No whites were allowed to be present during the proceedings of the voting units.[6] The results of the first election were published in detail in the Government Gazette. Unfortunately this procedure was not followed in the same detail in the 1942 and 1948 elections, and no accurate figures are accordingly available for these two elections, making statistical comparisons of any kind very difficult. Although many of the results were published in the newspapers, the figures given differed considerably from each other, compounding the difficulties in this connection.

The elections had two separate stages: the first was what was called nomination day, when the electoral units nominated their candidates to the Council. These candidates were often local notables who, receiving no support from anyone else, would then withdraw. The advantage of nomination day for the more successful candidates lay in the fact that they could gauge their support well before the day of voting and also recognise who their most important opponents were. This was of importance because the size of the electoral areas made it difficult and expensive for candidates to canvass the whole of them unless compelled by reason of the paucity of their support. J D Rheinallt Jones was not considered as having canvassed unusually extensively in having travelled 8 000 kms. through the Transvaal and Orange Free State in March 1937 when standing as a senatorial candidate.[7]

Besides largely travelling through the electoral areas themselves, all the candidates appointed black political agents to canvass those rural areas which they themselves could not cover. At times the NRC candidates would align themselves with others (there were two rural seats for each of the four Provinces), or with the Senatorial candidate for that area or his agent, and act as a team. This enabled them to interview and address a greater audience than would otherwise have been possible in the available time.[8]

The candidates who worked as a team were not both necessarily elected. In 1937, Dube, who was the most influential African in Natal at this time, stood with W W Ndhlovu as rural candidates and both succeeded. In 1942, however, Dube abandoned Ndhlovu and gave his support to Albert Lutuli. Dube retained his seat but Lutuli was defeated, as was Ndhlovu. The seat was won by George Champion. It was felt by the candidates that the support of a national figure like Dube was a distinct advantage in the elections but from results like this it seems obvious that this alone did not ensure any candidate's election.[9]

The attitude of the authorities towards the freedom of speech of the electoral candidates was ambivalent. There is no doubt that the type of speech made by the candidates during the election campaign was of the sort not normally tolerated by the government. A typical example was a speech made by Thema in Benoni in 1937, in which he stated *inter alia* that the Africans would be perfectly justified in overthrowing their white persecutors and when making reference to the police said that they would be shooting children next. The nominated members of the Council like Mishiyeni Dinuzulu spoke in a similar fashion.

In August 1939 the Department of Native Affairs was considering promulgating a proclamation designed, as they put it, "to counteract the activities of those who might exercise subversive influcences over the African". The parliamentary representatives protested that this proclamation would have meant that a member of the NRC would have had to get permission from the Department before being allowed to address his own constituents, a measure which would have destroyed the very basis of their representative function. With the change of government in September 1939, the measure was dropped. The government, however, had an alternative method of keeping a close watch on the speeches and activities of both elected councillors and candidates in the 1942 and 1948 elections. Before any meetings were held by them, they were expected to give notice of their intentions to the Native Commissioners in the rural areas and the location superintendants in the urban areas.

In this way the freedom of speech both during and after the election campaigns was maintained but the contenders in these elections were closely watched. Those considered to be the most extreme were given "agitator" numbers. During the fifteen years of the Council's existence at least five of the councillors had such numbers.[10]

Thomas Mapikela can be taken as an example of the type of candidate who successfully contested a seat in the 1937 election. His election manifesto was not based on any clear ideological or political outlook. The most that can be said for it was that it had a mildly liberal tone with an emphasis on matters of social welfare.[11] Mapikela was a founder of the ANC and a leading politician in Bloemfontein; he had taken part in some of the fruitless attempts by blacks to interest the British government in their plight and had led the agitation against instituting passes for black women. At the time of his election he was prominent in the Advisory Boards Congress and above all he had been one of the leaders in the recent protest against the Hertzog legislation.[12]

Nearly all of the successful candidates at this election had been the leaders of the 1936 campaign against the abolition of the Cape franchise. Were they elected because of their prominence during the campaign? A puzzling feature of the black opposition to the 1936 legislation was the absence of any mass protests. Why were there no riots or strikes? A political organisation had after all been specifically formed for this purpose, namely, the All African Convention (AAC). If the African masses had protested they would not have been leaderless but they did not protest. It may be concluded from this that only that small section of the black population that could have benefitted from the pre-1936 situation was prepared to protest against the change. Those who had no direct stake in the status quo, by far the greater part of the electorate, remained quiescent. If there was no mass support for this attitude then it must be concluded that it was their past record in general rather than their recent opposition to the 1936 legislation which was instrumental in these persons being elected. Godlo, in fact, did not believe that a recommendation by the AAC would be of much value in the 1937 election and there is also some evidence that these candidates were unpopular in the Cape. It ought not to be overlooked that the AAC had been singularly unsuccessful in its effort in 1936 and thus to have taken part in its campaign could hardly have been an advantage.[13]

The ANC also endeavoured to get its candidates elected, although often the nominations were the same as those for the AAC. This was probably due to the fact that neither of these organisations had clearly defined policies and that the prominent black politicians who were relatively well-known were limited to a small number of men. John Dube, R V Selope Thema and R H Godlo were all members of both the AAC and the ANC. Godlo was, in addition, the head of the Advisory Boards Congress, which endeavoured to get its nominees elected to all the urban seats allocated to the Council. The disorganised state of both the ANC and the AAC makes the influence which these organisations had on these elections even more difficult to ascertain. All that can be said with some certainty is that the Africans who were elected to the Council in 1937 were, on the whole, proven leaders of long standing. They were more probably elected on their own "track records" than because they were the chosen candidates of any political party. In any event those elected were regarded "as the accepted mouthpiece of Africans in their respective chambers" by both the AAC and the ANC.[14]

The Communist Party had also put up candidates in the 1937 elections. They were Hyman Basner for the Senate and Edwin Mofutsanyana for the NRC. Unlike the other candidates, and parties, the Communist Party had a definite policy which it never attempted to disguise. It had little success in the elections. Basner attempted to get elected apparently without appealing to the chiefs in the rural units. His resultant massive defeat, polling only 66,234 votes against Rheinallt Jones's 404,447, cannot thus necessarily be attributed to any lack of support for the Communist Party.[15]

Edwin Mofutsanyana, the other Communist candidate, was a fairly prominent black leader who at the time of these elections was also general secretary of the Communist Party. He was the only head of a political party ever to stand as a NRC candidate. Mofutsanyana was not a dynamic leader and it was perhaps unfortunate that he was chosen to represent the Communist Party not only in these elections but also in the elections of 1942 and 1948.[16]

Mofutsanyana himself attributes at least part of his lack of success at the polls to harassment at the hands of anti-Communist location superintendents during his campaigns. At Reitz, for example, he was prevented from using a hall to address an election meeting and at Messina the police even prevented him from entering the black location. However, from his own account it seems that he generally found a way round these difficulties and succeeded in addressing a number of meetings.[17] There were thus other factors which prevented Communist Party candidates from succeeding at the polls in 1937 although the extent to which their defeat can be attributed to them is uncertain.

Besides Basner and Mofutsanyana there were three candidates in the 1937 elections whose views at that time can be described as being more radical than those of the other candidates. They were George Champion, Josiah Gumede and W G Ballinger, the husband of the successful Cape Eastern candidate, Margaret Ballinger. Both Gumede and Champion played down these views in their manifestos. Champion stated that he was now "trying to act within the law and be respectable".[18] Gumede mentioned neither socialism nor his visit to Russia in his manifesto, although he exaggerated the scope and importance of his other visits to Europe.[19] Thus neither Champion nor Gumede, if one cares to judge from their election manifestoes, considered that an emphasis on radicalism would get them any votes. Both were defeated. Dube had 311,638 votes cast in his favour, W W Nhlovu got 161,647, Champion 154,609, and Gumede trailed after Champion. William Ballinger found that his nomination for senator was so little supported that he withdrew his candidature.[20]

Those successful in the 1937 elections of the parliamentary candidates were whites who professed liberal attitudes such as Rheinallt Jones, the director of the South Africa Institute of Race Relations, and Margaret Ballinger. Among the blacks were many of the foundation members of the ANC like W W Ndhlovu, John Dube, Thomas Mapikela and R V Selope Thema. Both the founder of the Advisory Boards Congress, A M Jabavu and the then president, R H Godlo were chosen to represent the urban areas. The Transkei had chosen three of its most prominent members, who in 1937 were the sitting members of the General Council's Executive Committee. These were Charles Sakwe, Jeremiah Moshesh and Elijah Qamata. Sakwe was also the chairman of the Transkei Native Voters' Conference and influential on the Cape Native Voters Association. Jeremiah Moshesh had been a member of the Transkeian General Council since 1918. The last councillor elected from the Transkei, Elijah Qamata, was the most popular of the three, having gained more votes in the Transkei than any other candidate.

The two remaining members of the 1937 NRC for rural areas were Richard Baloyi, a landlord and bus owner active in ANC circles and Bertram Buxton Xiniwe, chairman of a large electoral committee in the King William's Town area and shortly to be Cape ANC president. A J Sililo, the councillor for the urban Natal seat, was not elected until 1940, due to the anomalous position of the urban voting unit in that province.[21]

The electoral units responsible for the election of the three members of the Council who represented the urban areas were the advisory boards. The suspicion with which the Native Affairs Department tended to regard urban Africans found expression in the unwillingness of its officers to approve the formation of these boards. However, not only was the Department tardy in this respect but the municipal authorities allowed only a very small number of blacks to register as urban dwellers.[22] Some magisterial districts had only one taxpayer registered in a whole area.[23] Durban had twenty-seven voters from some 70,000 Africans, Johannesburg had 719 and Benoni 1,653.[24] The situation was absurd but in the case of the Transvaal and Cape elections not crucial because so long as the total number of voters for the urban seat was 2,000 Africans a candidate could still be chosen. It soon became apparent, however, that the whole of Natal did not contain 2,000 Africans who were registered in urban areas and thus no member of the NRC for urban areas could be chosen until the Act had been amended.

D L Smit, the Secretary for Native Affairs, maintained that it was a simple matter to transfer a man's tax registration (which determined his voting area) from a rural to an urban area. But in actual practice this must have been difficult because in 1937, of a total of 1,408,362 voters, only 14,865 in the whole of the Union outside the Transkei were registered as urban taxpayers.[25]

The black population which the authorities were so unwilling to acknowledge as urban voters had to be placed in another category for voting purposes and this resulted in large numbers of urban Africans being placed in the voting units known as electoral committees. These electoral committees consisted of large numbers of urban Africans, especially those centred in Johannesburg and the Witwatersrand area generally, as well as those blacks living outside the reserves in small towns and on farms throughout the country. It is noteworthy that even in 1937, before the large-scale industrialisation of the post-war years had taken place, that these "detribalised" blacks comprised nearly half of the total voting population outside the Transkei, namely 597,105 voters.[26]

The electoral committees were thus filled on the one hand by the politically well-informed Africans of the urban areas (the Orlando Electoral Committee, for example, at one stage had Dr. Xuma as its chairman) and on the other hand by people who had never before participated in politics or elections, the blacks in the white farming areas. In those areas inhabited by the more politically aware blacks, the electoral committees became effectively mere extensions of the urban vote. Because such a great number of urban Africans were placed in these committees, it meant that urban Africans had the greatest influence on the election. In this election it was not the number of units who voted for any candidate which mattered, but the actual number of voters.[27]

The rural electoral committees were dominated by the only educated segment of the rural black population, the teachers. It was they who explained to the often illiterate voters the implications of the elections and guided them in their voting. The provincial educational authorities viewed this with some alarm; they threatened to dismiss all such teachers on the grounds of their participation in politics, and their attitude was fully endorsed by the Department of Native Affairs. This came too late to affect the 1937 election but the teachers were expressly forbidden from participating in any future elections, except as voters.[28]

In 1940 the Representation of Natives Act was amended and the chairmen of the electoral committees could now be appointed by the local Native Commissioner; he could also explain to the voters the way these committees were meant to function. This was an attempt by the government to rid the electoral committees of the influence of the teachers who it presumably felt were partly to blame for the election of 1937 resulting in a black Council comprising all the better-known black politicians who had put themselves up for election. This amending legislation, however, still provided that no white person could be present at the actual voting. Since the vote was still secret, it is doubtful whether the government succeeded in this attempt at "guiding" the voters. The government on the one hand was intent upon ensuring that the politically aware section of the rural community was unable to dominate the electoral proceedings (that domination it wanted to preserve for itself) but on the other hand by preserving the secrecy of the voting procedure the government seemed to want to ensure that an element of consensus was preserved.[29]

A cardinal event which took place during the tenure of the first Council was the outbreak of war in 1939. It led to the most important of the debates in which the councillors participated: the merits of black participation in the Defence Force. The NRC was divided between those who asked for an amendment to the Defence Force Act to include black soldiers on terms of equality with whites, and those councillors who disagreed, contending either for unconditional participation or for complete non-participation. It became clear to those who disagreed that the electorate was totally behind the motion of equality. The motion was proposed by R H Godlo and its main opponents were T Mapikela, A M Jabavu and Elijah Qamata. Godlo himself thought that public opinion would lead the opponents of his motion to lose the next election.[30]

The outbreak of war had also led to a change of government in South Africa. Jan Smuts, who took over as Prime Minister from J B M Hertzog, centred his policy towards blacks on attempts to improve their social and economic conditions. He stated, however, that these improvements would be dependent on the country's financial situation. As his government was a war-time administration, there was not a great deal of money available and little was done during the war to provide social services for blacks. Politically Smuts was in favour of some liberalisation of the administration being carried on but at what he termed "a modest pace and determined by (white) public opinion".[31]

In January 1942 Smuts made a speech before the South African Institute of Race Relations. As Piet van der Byl, the Minister of Native Affairs, later wrote, Smuts was in the habit of giving an audience what it wanted to hear and on this occasion said in his speech that in his opinion segregation as a policy had failed to keep Africans out of the cities and that perhaps another method ought to be tried to achieve this. However, the phrase "segregation has failed" was taken out of context and false hopes were raised that the segregation policy had breathed its last.[32]

By 1942 the drive to the cities was already under way, mainly as a result of the economic plight of blacks in the rural areas.[33] Economic conditions in the urban areas, however, could by no means be regarded as satisfactory. In the latter months of 1942, thirty-four strikes involving black workers took place. In nearly every one of these strikes the workers were pressing for higher wages and an improvement in their working conditions. The dissatisfaction which the African worker was expressing was probably not only the product of war-time economics but also the result of the reformist ideas expressed at this time by the pronouncements of Allied statesmen and in documents like the Atlantic Charter.[34] Thema's statement in the NRC that the men fighting up North did not expect to come back to the same conditions which had prevailed before they had left the country, was yet another expression of a common feeling that conditions must improve in the future.[35]

It was probably against this background that it had become clear to William Ballinger that the limit of voluntary concessions had been reached and that in future Africans would have to fight and make sacrifices for what they wanted.[36] This seems also to have been clear to the electorate because the men returned in the 1942 elections were by and large of a more radical turn of mind than those of 1937. This applied, however, mainly to the blacks returned to the NRC rather than to the Senators and black elected members of the House of Assembly.

The second elections were scheduled to take place on 4 November 1942. As has been mentioned, very little official information was published on this election, the main sources being newspapers and some private correspondence. There is some doubt as to whether all the councillors even stood for re-election: according to William Ballinger, Mapikela did not seek re-election but (rather surprisingly, considering his former attitudes) urged his supporters to vote for the Communist Party candidate, Edwin Mofutsanyana.[37]

The Communist Party in 1942 had originally put forward three candidates for the elections. They were E Mofutsanyana, A M Mabela and one Lekgetho, who toured the rural areas together in an attempt to gain the rural vote.[38] In an article in the Guardian mention is made of a pamphlet issued by a black organisation, the "African Election Committee", which urged blacks not to elect communists because the Communist Party was multi-racial and could thus never speak for black interests alone.[39] Although this article was addressed to the voters of Advisory Boards, this aspect of the election campaigns of the Communist Party candidates was an important one. It is evident from the campaigns of these candidates that racial divisions were ignored and that white communists campaigned on behalf of their black comrades. It is also evident that among some sections of black opinion, African communists were regarded as nothing more than puppets of Moscow.[40] The multi-racialism of the Communist Party and its known association with the USSR, as well as an impression that the Party was dominated by whites, probably contributed to its lack of success at the polls. As in 1937, electioneering by the communists was again accompanied by intimidation from the authorities. This time it was Moses Kotane who was arrested after making a speech on behalf of the Communist Party candidate.[41]

Although the communists were as unsuccessful in 1942 in the NRC elections as they had been in 1937, their white senatorial candidate for that election, Hyman Basner, now won a decisive victory over the incumbent, J D Rheinallt Jones. Basner won by the large majority of 332,798 votes to 237,199. Only three of the Reef advisory boards, not one local council and only eleven out of fifty-eight chiefs had voted for Rheinallt Jones. There were various contributory factors which may help in understanding his defeat. Rheinallt Jones had initially been uncertain whether he should seek re-election and entered the campain at a relatively late stage. He had visited only seven districts and had spoken at only seven meetings during his entire campaign. Another possible reason for his poor showing in the rural areas was that during his five years as senator he had apparently told his black constituents that he was in favour of abolishing the black reserves. This was probably misunderstood by them to mean that he was in favour of their land being taken away from them and could not have increased his popularity.[42]

Basner had left the Communist Party over the war issue, but was nonetheless considered to have taken a radical stance in his campaign. Lord Harlech, the British High Commissioner, believed that the election of Basner was a sign of impatience with the liberal outlook among a large section of black opinion and that the authorities viewed it as a gesture of revolt and dissatisfaction. Xuma was certainly impatient with the liberal outlook as personified by Rheinallt Jones. He had wanted his defeat in the elections but did not seem to attach any particular significance to the election of Basner in his stead.[43]

It is difficult to see Basner in quite such a radical light when taking into account his subsequent statements in the Senate. He stated, for example, that he was in favour only of a qualified franchise for blacks. His conduct in the Senate when he refused at times to follow parliamentary discipline seems not so much the result of his radical turn of mind as plain bad manners.[44] Basner was thus not as much the radical as he was pictured at the time of his election. That Rheinallt Jones lost the election was more due to slack campaigning than to the ideology of Hyman Basner, especially when one takes into account that all the other returned parliamentary candidates were of a liberal outlook. On the other hand it should be said that the area in which Basner was elected did include the Witwatersrand, which had a vast number of those very voters who were at the forefront of the industrial unrest of 1942; this may have been an important element in Basner's success. Without firm statistical evidence such conclusions can, however, only be tentative. Basner's view can, however, still be regarded a more militant one than that of the average liberal black elected parliamentarian. He was certainly regarded in this way by the authorities who in 1943 went so far as to put him on trial for interfering with the police during the Alexandra bus boycott.

The AAC had also put up certain candidates at this election, all of whom apparently were defeated. Dr. Moroka, who won a seat in 1942 and was the AAC's treasurer, was not, it would seem, put forward by the AAC as one of their official candidates. Joe Matthews was of the opinion that the defeat of their candidates turned the Convention against the NRC and that this was the reason that that organisation, in 1943, adopted a resolution to boycott the Council. A P Mda disagreed with this view and said that the resolution was passed as a matter of principle rather than pique at the the AAC's lack of success at the polls. He did, however, admit that the status of the members of the Council was resented by certain sections of black opinion and may have been the reason for the NRC being singled out in this way.[45]

The attitude of the ANC to the 1942 elections was quite different from both the AAC and the Communist Party. Before the holding of the 1941 annual conference at Bloemfontein, it appeared that Congress would put up its candidates as the other organisations were doing. James Calata, the secretary-general of Congress, had in fact already asked the various branches to submit nominations for the forthcoming elections.[46] At the conference itself, however, a decision was taken not to sponsor any candidates, although individual Congress members could vote for whom they liked.[47]

This ruling was made at the suggestion of Xuma, at that time its president-general, who did not want the ANC publicly to support candidates for the Council, in case they were defeated. A defeat of this nature would reflect badly on the support which ANC decisions received from the black voters. Privately, however, the ANC was eager to have certain candidates elected. Xuma himself was a member of a Johannesburg electoral committee and thus took an active part in the election. Xuma felt that the election of both Moroka and Z K Matthews, in particular, would be of benefit to Congress. He thought that the election of these two candidates would enable Congress to guide the activities and attitudes of the Council. After the election he received a congratulatory letter from James Calata expressing his satisfaction that Congress had succeeded in placing its candidates on the Council without appearing to do so.[48]

Xuma was later criticised by Paul Mosaka for this decision, Mosaka accusing him of giving no lead to the people for the 1942 elections. Initially, however, Mosaka had responded to Xuma's personal appeal for the newly elected Council to take a more active interest in the ANC. The success of Mosaka and Basner in the 1942 elections, which they had fought as a team, convinced them that they would be equally successful after the elections and it was this that led them to form the African Democratic Party.[49]

Other ANC members who were elected in 1942 were the two most radical members of the first Council, and its leaders, R V Selope Thema and R H Godlo. Three of the councillors who had not supported Godlo's motion asking for equality in the Defence Force were defeated and replaced by more radical men, these being Thomas Mapikela, A M Jabavu and Elijah Qamata. Richard Baloyi was replaced by the more outspoken James Moroka. In Natal George Champion was elected, defeating W W Ndhlovu. As has been pointed out, Ndhlovu was now no longer supported by John Dube in his fight for election. It is not certain why this was so but Ndhlovu did display some racialist attitudes in certain Council debates. In addition to this, Champion himself was now standing for a rural seat and not an urban one as had previously been the case. The rural seats, as has been noted, had a large number of urban workers amongst whom Champion had been carrying out extensive trade union work since the lifting of his banning order.[50]

Many of the men elected in 1942 were to rise to positions of eminence in the ANC. Champion and Z K Matthews were to become provincial presidents of Natal and the Cape respectively and Moroka became president-general in 1949; others like Xiniwe, Godlo and Thema held office or were part of the national executive during the time they were members of the NRC.[51] Thus the second NRC consisted of a majority of ANC members. It has been noted that Xuma's view was that the ANC could now influence the views of the Council. This was indeed the case but Congress did not influence the Council in the way that a political party usually did, by guiding its members on policies they should pursue once they had been elected. This was because Congress was at all times reluctant to define its position in case this should imperil its always shaky facade of unity. To continue to regard itself as the mouthpiece of all African opinion meant that it had to forego any definite political outlook. Inkundla Ya Bantu was of the view that the only reason the councillors did indeed look to the ANC for advice was because it was the only completely African body of any standing.[52]

The years between the holding of the second election in 1942 and the third in 1948 were the most crucial of the Council's history. As has been noted, the new members of the NRC and those former members who had been returned were of a more militant turn of mind than those of 1937. They showed this not only in their speeches in the Council but also in their activities outside. It was in this period that it became apparent that although they were permitted to hold election meetings, political activities were not regarded with the same equanimity by the government once the elections had been held. Both Paul Mosaka and Thema were arrested in this way: Mosaka when he took an active part in the Alexandra bus boycott of 1943 and Thema in Cape

Town during the Anti-Pass Campaign.[53] In addition, freedom of speech at political meetings outside the election period was frowned upon. In 1944 Mosaka had referred to the government as a "Nazi government" at a meeting of his African Democratic Party in Kroonstad. He was immediately warned by the authorities that such "subversive" conduct would not be tolerated.[54] Freedom of assembly was also at this time not permitted after the passing of Proclamation 131 of 1945 which prohibited black gatherings of more than ten people.[55]

The only activity that the black councillors were permitted to undertake as part of their duties was to act as liaison in some cases of dispute. Mosaka assumed this role in the case of the Orlando squatters when he negotiated on their behalf.[56] On no account, however, were the councillors permitted to act in this capacity in more explosive situations. In 1950 the councillors offered to reduce tension during riots in the Bethanie location by entering that location (for which they had to seek permission) and talking to the inhabitants, but the Native Affairs Department refused to allow them to do so.[57] There was a marked contrast between the freedom of speech and the freedom of movement granted the councillors during electioneering and during their term of office.

On Dube's death in 1946 a by-election was held in Natal and his seat was won by Albert Lutuli, the man whom Dube had suported in 1942 as a Natal rural candidate. Lutuli's chief opponent in this by-election was Henry Selby Msimang. Msimang was supported by George Champion, who was attempting to assume the Natal leadership left vacant by Dube's death. Lutuli, however, won by a massive majority of 132,808, gaining 231,926 votes to Msimang's 99,118.[58]

The most far-reaching influence on the 1948 elections was the launching of the Anti-Pass Campaign by the Communist Party in November 1943. Xuma gave this campaign his support in 1944 and then became its conference chairman and president. In spite of a great deal of effort by Xuma, the campaign proved a failure. A number of councillors were also involved in the campaign, the most prominent among them being Thema, who was arrested for unlawful assembly when he led a procession in Cape Town. The final conference on the Anti-Pass Campaign was held in June 1946 at which it must have been obvious to all that the campaign had been a dismal failure.[59]

The only possible source of influence left the leaders of the Anti-Pass Campaign was the NRC, a meeting of which was scheduled for August 1946. Between June and August of that year a meeting of the national executive of Congress was held in Bloemfontein. It seems that Thema, a member of the ANC executive who had recently been jailed for his efforts on behalf of the campaign, was understandably most adamant that the matter should be taken further through the offices of the NRC. As a leader of the campaign in Cape Town he must have been humiliated by the refusal of Hofmeyr, the Acting Prime Minister, and Piet van der Byl, the Minister of Native Affairs, to receive him or to even see the Anti-Pass petition. By pursuing the matter through the Council he probably thought that the government would be compelled to take some notice of his efforts and not dismiss them in such a cavalier manner. It is not known exactly what was discussed at this meeting but the general opinion seems to have been that Thema was eager to take the matter further by somehow involving the NRC. It was probably here that it was decided to stage a formal protest at the next NRC session.[60]

Cyclostyled letters were then sent by Xuma informing the councillors of the ANC decision to adjourn the next meeting of the Council as a form of protest.[61] According to Dr. Bokwe, it took a great deal of persuasion before unanimity on this directive by the councillors was reached.[62]

Secrecy concerning this decision was, of course, essential, but if the Native Affairs Department had been more alert they would have realised that something unusual was afoot from the mere fact that whereas in previous years over one hundred separate motions were often received, for the opening of this ninth session of the Council only twenty-two had been tabled. Of these, three were Thema's. One asked for an "eleventh hour" appeal to the Minister of Native Affairs to hold a round table conference on the pass laws, the other two asked for the abolition of segregation and the removal of the colour bar. The Native Affairs Department realised that the session would be shorter than usual but attached no significance to this.[63]

At the caucus meeting held prior to the opening of the session, Matthews asked Dr. Moroka if he would present the motion for adjournment, thus catapulting Moroka into instant acclaim as the mover of what was later termed the "freedom resolution". It is surprising that Thema himself did not present the motion but from Moroka's remarks it seems as if the councillors were unsure as to what the government's reaction would be; perhaps Thema felt that as he had so recently been imprisoned for his activities, presenting such a motion would unnecessarily draw the attention of the authorities to him yet again.[64]

On the 15 August the NRC met for the opening of its ninth session. The adjournment motion was passed almost immediately. It was supposed by those who did not know the true state of affairs (including all the parliamentary representatives of the blacks), that the adjournment was a spontaneous action prompted by the gold miners' strike which had coincidently occurred at the same time.[65]

This decision of the NRC to suspend its operations indefinitely until the government decided to abolish its policy of discrimination was reflected in the way in which the adjournment resolution was couched and in this form received widespread support. In October 1946 Xuma called a special conference in Bloemfontein to discuss the NRC's action. Over four hundred people were said to have attended the meeting. The number present is attested by a number of sources and is of interest in that the annual conferences of Congress did not attract a quarter of this number. It seems that the action of the NRC had a large measure of support and did give Xuma and the other black leaders some of that prestige which they may have lost through the failure of the Anti-Pass Campaign.[66]

At this meeting it was decided to allow the councillors to attend further meetings of the Council convened for the purpose of receiving the government's reply to the adjournment resolution. At the same time voters were called upon to embark upon a boycott of all elections under the Representation of Natives Act of 1936.[67] The decision to boycott the elections was achieved with some difficulty, nobody wanting an unconditional boycott except Lembede and the Congress Youth League and even they were not unanimous in their opinion on the matter.[68]

The talk of boycotting the elections was nothing new. Besides the decision on the matter taken in 1943 by the AAC, the matter had also been discussed as early as 1936, when the legislation had originally been passed. What made the boycott so attractive to the Congress Youth league at this particular time was the impact created by the boycott by the Indian community of the Asiatic Land and Representation Act. The ultimate objective of the African boycott movement was full citizenship rights. As Matthews pointed out, for the committed boycotters the question of whether they would ultimately succeed or fail was irrelevant, it was an act of faith. On a more practical note it was hoped that if the boycott campaign grew it would eventually develop into a vast civil disobedience movement.[69]

What had been overlooked by the boycotters, Paul Mosaka wrote, was that the struggle of the Indian people was not at all "passive". It was an active act of resistance by which they voluntarily undertook to show the government the hardships they were prepared to undergo in order to demonstrate the intensity of their hatred for this piece of legislation and the strength of their determination to resist it. Xuma and Thema had had to abandon the Anti-Pass Campaign because it had failed to elicit from Africans the very qualities which made the Indian movement a success - organisation, a strength of will and the determination to undergo hardship for the sake of one's principles. There was no reason to believe that the boycott movement would be any more successful than the Anti-Pass Campaign had been, something which Xuma and most of the national executive (especially those who were also members of the Council), were quick to realise.[70]

In 1947 Gordon Hemming, a black elected member for the Transkei of the House of Assembly, died and the boycott resolution was put to its first test. Douglas Buchanan, a liberal of similar outlook to Margaret Ballinger, stood unopposed for the seat. During his electoral campaign, Buchanan had been constantly heckled by his audience and after his election he decided to test the strength of the boycott movement and sent a voting paper to the 2,375 voters in his constituency. Only 144 of these papers were returned stating that they were in favour of the boycott.[71] At the head of the boycott movement in the Transkei was Govan Mbeki, secretary of the Transkeian Organised Bodies, who had obviously found it an easy task to organise the Transkeian voters into a comparatively effective boycotting instrument but it was evident that even in the case of such a small number of voters sufficient unanimity could not be obtained to ensure that no-one at all voted for Buchanan, a step which alone would have made the boycott successful.[72]

The representatives of the Africans in Parliament were not in favour of the boycott. Basner went so far as to state at a meeting of the Transvaal ANC that he thought the boycott resolution "so silly" he did not think that grown men would waste a whole day discussing it. He added that if the boycott resolution was passed, then he would not stand for re-election in 1948. Basner did not stand for re-election. It was at this meeting that William Ballinger was attacked by Ramohanoe, the president of the Transvaal ANC, for wishing to contest the Transkei seat vacated by the death of Hemming.[73] Ballinger withdrew his candidacy. Donald Molteno, the Cape Western representative of the Africans in the House of Assembly, had accompanied Buchanan on his tour during the latter's election campaign in the Transkei and had thus had first hand experience of the boycott. As a result both of this tour and of the heckling which Molteno himself experienced at election meetings, he began to voice some doubts on the suitability of whites representing blacks in Parliament and at one stage even contemplated resigning. He did not give this as a reason for his decision not to seek re-election in 1948, but it must have played some part.[74]

Molteno's decision not to seek re-election disturbed the liberal representatives who felt that this vacancy might, given the climate of black opinion in his constituency, lead to the seat falling to a Communist Party candidate. This was the reason that Douglas Buchanan, who had won the Transkei seat in 1947, decided to contest the Cape Western seat in 1948 instead.[75]

The boycott resolution of the ANC had placed some of the 'blacks parliamentary representatives' in a quandary but did not have the same effect on the black members of the NRC. None of the incumbents of that body ever contemplated resigning before the election or not seeking re-election in 1948. This was the result not only of the lack of influence of the ANC at this time on its members but also of the importance which the councillors attached to the NRC as the only direct link between the government and the Africans.[76]

At the ANC conference in December 1947 the delegates voted sixty-seven to seven in favour of adopting the resolution of the national executive to intensify the boycott campaign.[77] But by January 1948 the ANC had thought better of its boycott decision and had now decided to participate in the elections on a "boycott ticket", the basic reason being that the ANC had found itself quite unable to carry out the boycott, even on a small scale as with the advisory board elections. By "boycott ticket" was meant that the members of the NRC should, as far as possible, be returned in the 1948 elections so that they could continue to discuss reform measures which the Smuts government was proposing to introduce.[78]

An added complication in the 1948 elections was that the white voters were also participating in an election in that year, an election which some influential blacks thought might well result in a change of government, and that this election was taking place before the elections under the Representation of Natives Act. It was felt that an aggressive boycott campaign would embarrass and weaken the present more liberal government and lead to its downfall thus helping the National Party into power.[79]

The AAC did not particpate in the 1948 elections. The Trotskyite elements under Tabata and his followers who had taken over that organisation were advocating a total boycott and did not veer from their original 1943 decision. Furthermore, it was probably due to their influence that the total poll in the Cape Western constituency was only 53%. Tabata's followers would obviously have refrained from voting in spite of the efforts of the communist candidate, Sam Kahn, to get his constituents to the poll.[80]

The attitude of the Communist Party to the 1948 election was initially ambivalent. On the one hand it was clear that the most radical section of African opinion favoured the boycott but at the same time they did not want to pass up the opportunity of getting their own people elected to the NRC and to Parliament.[81] The Communist Party had certainly tried to implement the boycott resolution as far as it could do so but when this was seen to be impossible[82], they then put up their own candidates for the 1948 elections. This was in conflict with the ANC resolution, to which both Moses Kotane and J B Marks, as members of the national executive, had agreed, which had advocated the return of the 1942 elected councillors. In its arguments for this decision, the Guardian pointed out firstly, that the vote was a right which ought not to be voluntarily suspended and secondly, that the black voters must realise that at this juncture a boycott policy could only play into the hands of the National Party (the white election had at this time been won by them). They could abolish the franchise by pointing out that the blacks themselves were advocating a boycott and therefore did not want it.[83]

The Communist Party had put up three black candidates for the 1948 NRC elections, Edwin Mofutsanyana, Alpheus Maliba and A S Damane. Both Mofutsanyana and Damane were members of the Party's central committee.[84] Mofutsanyana had been an unsuccessful NRC candidate as far back as 1937. He had also been heavily defeated in the 1947 Orlando Advisory elections when the Sofasonke Party defeated the Communist Party candidates by 4,947 votes to 1,688. It seems that the Communist Party hoped that it was not its candidates as much as its policy which would ensure electoral victory.[85]

The elections of 1948 were apparently as well supported (in spite of the boycott), as the other elections had been. The Transvaal-OFS seats, for example, had twenty candidates for the one urban seat and fifty-two for the two rural seats. Besides the incumbent members of the NRC, men like L K Nhlabati, a Bloemfontein Congress organiser, and J S Mpanza were nominated in this constituency. As in previous elections, the Communist Party again experienced difficulty during this one: Michael Harmel was assaulted by the location superintendent when he attempted to address a meeting in support of Edwin Mofutsanyana.[86]

The policy of the ANC, together with the reputation and publicity that the members of the NRC had got from their adjournment resolution of 1946, ensured the re-election of almost all of them in 1948. The only exception was Natal where Champion, by this time in firm control of the Natal ANC presidency, succeeded in ousting L P Msomi from the urban seat and getting Henry Selby Msimang elected in his stead.[87] The 1948 election results indicated the confidence of the electorate in the retiring members of the Council and their support for the policy pursued by them.[88]

The main interest in these elections lay in the fact that firstly, a Communist Party member, Sam Kahn, was standing for Molteno's seat and secondly, that all the other seats of the parliamentary representatives (including Molteno's seat) were being contested by National Party candidates. This situation had come about because the National Party majorities in the House of Assembly and the Senate were so small (the Senate majority was only one), that it would have been useful to them to win additional seats, besides giving them a mandate, if they had won, for their policy of apartheid.

The National Party Secretary in Johannesburg, some would think perhaps a little optimistically, approached Xuma to gain his support for that Party's candidates, in the 1948 election.[89] The National Party candidate in the Transvaal-OFS was one J H J (Kosie) van Rensburg, an Afrikaans farmer from the Orange Free State, who opposed William Ballinger. Xuma reacted to this request by writing a personal letter to all the electoral units asking them to vote for Ballinger and in addition reminding them that the ballot was secret.[90] Presumably this was because the black electorate did not feel at ease voting against a candidate openly sponsored by the white party in power. In spite of Xuma's efforts, fully twenty-five electoral units did vote for Van Rensburg, including Alexandra Township.[91]

The National Party published a pamphlet explaining its aims to the black electorate. It stated that the aim of apartheid was the granting of responsible government to Africans. The reason it gave for the National Party putting candidates forward in this election was that the actions of the present parliamentary representatives had placed African representation in Parliament in danger of being abolished but that this could be retained if the electorate voted for National Party candidates.

In Natal J J van Rooyen stood against Edgar Brookes. Van Rooyen had approached Champion and the Natal ANC in an attempt to gain their support for his candidature. His political agent was a founder member of Congress, W W Ndhlovu, who had been a member of the NRC from 1937-1942. It seems that the National Party even applied pressure on the Zulu chief, Cyprian, by making it clear to him that his paramountcy was dependent on him voting for Van Rooyen rather than for Brookes.[92] Members of Congress in Natal like Henry Selby Msimang made every effort to see that Van Rooyen was not elected. In a roneoed election newsheet signed by E G Jansen as leader of the National Party in Natal, it was stated that Van Rooyen was the candidate who supported the government and that the government wanted the electorate to show that it approved of its plans for them and wanted them to be carried out.[93] They wanted the African voters' consent to apartheid.

In the Transkei W H Stuart was opposed by J D L Kruger who stood for the National Party. Stuart was a member of the well-known and liberal Cape family, the Schreiners, and on this account gained the support of George Champion, councillor and head of the Natal ANC and of Paramount Chief Victor Poto of the Transkei. The only three cornered election was in the Cape Western Constituency where D M Buchanan, a liberal, stood against Sam Kahn of the Communist Party and A P van der Merwe of the National Party. All the five apartheid candidates in the election lost their £50 deposits because they failed to poll one fifth of the winning candidate's total. Prof. P J Schoeman of Stellenbosch, for example, received 222 votes in the Cape Eastern constituency against Margaret Ballinger's 2,920. The Communist Party candidate won the Cape Western seat by a comfortable majority - 3,780 for Kahn, 754 for Buchanan and 194 for van der Merwe.[94]

Kahn was the first communist member of the House of Assembly, chosen by the blacks to represent them. This was a development of importance in that there was no doubt that in the one constituency where the electorate had been given a choice between a liberal, a member of the National Party and a member of the Communist Party, they chose the Communist Party member. However, as has been shown in the case of the Transkei, in the absence of a Communist Party candidate a man with liberal sympathies was more likely to be chosen by black voters than one who was not a liberal.

It is of some significance that whereas a white Communist Party member was acceptable as a Native Representative, no communist ever became a member of the Representative Council. The reason for this may have been that the parliamentary representatives were chosen because of their ideology and what this represented to the voters, while the councillors were chosen for themselves. If it had been possible for J B Marks, the leader of the African Mineworkers' Union in the 1946 strike, to stand as a candidate in 1948 instead of Edwin Mofutsanyana, he would certainly have polled more votes than the latter and might even have been elected. J B Marks could not stand for the Council as he was a Coloured and thus did not fulfill the criteria of what constituted a permissible candidate for the NRC.

The government attempted to use both the parliamentary representatives and the NRC to aid it in its domination of the black population. The parliamentary representatives themselves admitted that the only useful work they did in Parliament was when they attempted to either postpone proclamations or to add some slight amendment to existing or new legislation. Edgar Brookes himself gives two examples of such amelioration: the lifting on the restrictions on the gathering of wood in government forests and the introduction of pedigree bulls to black farms. For the government their main utility was in providing an indication of which measures would be tolerated by the African population and which would have to be revised in order to avert any possible confrontation. This was probably also the purpose of giving all new legislation to the NRC first, before it went to either the Senate or the House of Assembly. If the councillors vehemently protested against the measure, then the government could predict the way it would be receivd by the black population.

As has been noted the black elected parliamentary representatives were all staunchly liberal in 1937. By 1942, the election of Hyman Basner, although by no means a radical, can certainly be seen as a swing to the left in the Witwatersrand area. The Native Representatives, lack of ideological unanimity was evident in the conflicting views expressed by them during the 1947 boycott campaign. William Ballinger who stood for Basner's seat in the 1948 elections held similar political opinions to Basner. He said that he would not have opposed Basner had Basner stood for re-election. Ballinger's political agent was Bennett Ncwana of the Springbok Legion and he also received the support of the Communist party. Thus both his election to the Senate and Sam Kahn's to the House of Assembly may be seen as a final repudiation of liberalism by the black electorate. It is true that parliamentary representatives like Margaret Ballinger and Edgar Brookes, who held liberal views, were never defeated but on the other hand they were never opposed by candidates of more militant views. In any case Margaret Ballinger's popularity must to some extent be attributed to her continual stress on such proletarian issues as wages in industry, which she emphasised both in her parliamentary speeches and in articles in the press. The potential these elections contained for serving as a mechanism for consent to domination reached its culmination in the 1948 election which saw the National party put forward candidates who espoused the policy of apartheid. They held out the promise of saving the black franchise but only on the humiliating terms of electing a National Party candidate.[95]

The members of the NRC were, in 1937, the representatives of the politically unsuccessful method of pleading with the authorities to ameliorate the conditions under which the black electorate lived, rather than asking for any specific political rights.

From 1939 demands for equality began to be heard and the 1942 election results clearly indicated that the black electorate was now choosing militant representatives who openly asked for political equality. Their demands culminated in the showdown of 1946 when equality was no longer asked for but demanded. The stand of the Council was fully endorsed in 1948 when nearly all of them were returned by the black electorate.

To the National Party government, which came into power in 1948, the views of the Councillors proved to be of inestimable value because through their attitudes they were able to gauge with great accuracy[96] the temper of the black people over whom they were to govern. The elections had shown that blacks had categorically rejected the policy of apartheid, and were demanding equality. It was a clear presage of the turbulant black-white confrontations of the years to come.

NOTES

1. M Roth, "Formation of the Natives Representative Council", unpublished M.A. thesis, University of South Africa, 1979, 54-55.

2. Ibid., p. 60.

3. Union of South Africa, Senate Debates, 6 September 1948, cols. 300, 304, J M Le Roux; Umlindi We Nyanga, 16 December 1940; Imvo Zabandsundu, 11 July 1942; Umteteli Wa Bantu, 16 December 1939.

4. An examination of the ANC letterheads of the period shows the members of the NRC who were also on the Congress national executive.

5. Interview with J S Moroka, November 1980.

6. M Roth, op cit. p. 100.

7. Umteteli Wa Bantu, 3 April 1937.

8. Ibid., 17 April 1937; F Bridgman, "The Native Franchise in the Union of South Africa", unpublished D.Phil. thesis, Yale University, 1939, 420.

9. Forman Papers, University of Cape Town, Bc 581 A1. 188, G Champion to H Selby Msimang, 17 August 1942.

10. SAIRR Papers, B 100.4.1, E Brookes to D L Smit, 3 October 1939, E Brookes to Rheinallt Jones, 12 October 1939; NTS 2762, 89/276(3), Memorandum, 3 May 1962; Ibid., 2708,89/276(3), Secretary of Native Affairs to Director of Native Labour, 3 July 1932; NTS 1781, 89/276, SAP report of a meeting held at Ixopo by Mshiyeni, Dube and Ndhlovu, 6 August 1938; Ibid. E J Baker, Native Commissioner Benoni to Director of Native Labour, Johannesburg 19 October 1937; Ibid., J N O Spence, ... Deputy Commissioner commanding Witwatersrand ... to Commissioner of the South African Police, Pretoria, 8 December 1937; Ibid., D L Smit to ... Chief Deputy Commissioner of Police, Pretoria; Ibid., B W Martin, Chief Native Commissioner, Witwatersrand to Secretary of Native Affairs, 20 Otober 1937.

11. Umlindi We Nyanga, 15 March 1937; Ibid., 16 August 1937; Imvo Zabandsundu, 16 October 1937.

12. Ibid.

13. M Roth, op. cit. p. 97.

14. Ibid., 94-99.

15. Ibid., 173.

16. Karis and Carter, From Protest to Challenge, (Stanford, 1977), v. 4, 92.

17. Interview by Bob Edgar with Edwin Mofutsanyana, Lesotho, 1981.

18. Ilanga Lase Natal, 20 March 1937.

19. Ibid., 13 March 1937.

20. Umteteli Wa Bantu, 3 April 1937; Ilanga Lase Natal, 3 July 1937.

21. M Roth, op cit. 114-135; NTS 89/276, Welsh to D L Smit, 20 April 1937.

22. Ibid. 25-27.

23. Smuts Papers, v. 127(7), 'Opmerking oor die Wysginge wat deur die Naturelleverteenwoordigende Wetsortwerp beoog is.'

24. Langa Lase Natal, 19 November 1938; Union of South Africa, Government Gazette, 5 February 1937, 250-251.

25. Ibid., pp. 242-255; Union of South Africa, Natives Representative Council Debates, 24 November 1938, 401-403; Umlindi We Nyanga, 15 July 1937.

26. M Roth, op cit., 88.

27. Ibid., 88-89.

28. Ibid.

29. Prime Minister's Papers, URU 1910, Minute, 19 October 1940.

30. Natives Representative Council Debates, 8 December 1939, 577-597; Ibid., Report of the Committee Proceedings War Issue, 5 December 1940, 17; Xuma Papers, University of the Witwatersrand, ABX400119, Godlo to Xuma, 19 January 1940.

31. Hofmeyr Papers, A1 DB, Smuts to Hofmeyr, 29 September 1946.

32. Smuts Papers, 229(310), cutting from the "Evening Standard", 16 March 1943; Ibid., 235(131), Smuts to Hofmeyr, 29 September 1946; Piet van der Byl, From Tophat to Velskoen, (Cape Town, 1973), 216.

33. Senate Debates, 4 March 1942, col. 442, C H Malcomess.

34. D.O 116/8, Despatch no. 19, 15 February 1943, Lord Harlech, High Commissioner to the Union of South Africa, to the Dominion Office.

35. Natives Representative Council Debates, 29 November 1941, 269.

36. SAIRR Papers, University of the Witwatersrand, Lynn Saffrey Correspondence, W Ballinger to Lynn Saffrey, 1 December 1942.

37. Ibid.; Guardian, 8 October 1942.

38. Ibid.

39. Ibid., 29 October 1942.

40. Inkululeko, February 1948; Transkeian General Council Debates, 19 April 1947, 60, Gordon Dana asked Govan Mbeki whether he was expecting a reply from Marshall Stalin in Moscow.

41. Guardian, 5 December 1942.

42. D.O 35/588/444, Lord Harlech, South African High Commissioner to C P Atlee, 18 November 1942; Molteno Papers, Bc 579 A54.49, "An Open Letter to Rheinallt Jones by H M Basner", 10 September 1942. This gives the polling results as 309,274 for Basner and 205,716 for Rheinallt Jones; Senate Debates, 14 February 1950, cols. 421-422, G Heaton Nicholls.

43. DO 35/588/44, Lord Harlech, South African High Commissioner to C P Atlee, 18 November 1942; Xuma Papers, ABX 421231d, 31 December 1942, A B Xuma to A Hoernlè; Ibid., ABX 420912a, 12 September 1942, A B Xuma to A Hoernlè.

44. Senate Debates, 16 May 1945, col. 1849, Basner; Ibid., 8 January 1945, cols. 3033-4.

45. Inkundla Ya Bantu, 30 November 1943; Interview with A P Mda by S Buthelezi, Botswana, February 1982; Ballinger Papers (UCT), M Ballinger to D D T Jabavu, 5 November 1941.

46. Izwi, 14 January 1942, Calata to the Provincial Secretary of the Cape ANC, 5 November 1941.

47. Molteno Papers, BC 579 A54.36, "African Parliamentary Election 1942; Ibid., Bc 578 C2.286, Xuma to Molteno, 20 December 1941.

48. Karis and Carter microfilms, 2:XM66:94, 19 March 1964, G Carter's interview with Z K Matthews; Ibid., 2:XX2:41/21, 1 August 1942; Xuma Papers, ABX 421126b, J Calata to A B Xuma, 26 November 1948; Ibid., ABX 421116b, P. Mosaka to A B Xuma, 16 November 1942.

49. Inkundla Ya Bantu, 30 November 1943; Xuma Papers, ABX 421111a, A B Xuma to R T (Bokwe?), 11 November 1942; Ibid., ABX 42111b, P Mosaka to A B Xuma, 16 November 1942.

50. Natives Representative Council Debates, 27 November 1941, p. 154, W W Ndhlovu; Forman Papers, Bc 581 A1.183, G Champion to E Brookes, 11 June 1942; Ibid., Bc 581 B.16.3, G Champion to Mayor of Durban, 26 June 1941.

51. T Karis and G Carter, op. cit., vol. 4, 19, 81, 156, 32; Xuma Papers, ABX 401001, official ANC letterhead, 10 October 1940.

52. Inkundla Ya Bantu, 21 January 1948.

53. Guardian, 11 January 1945; Inkululeko, 9 June 1945.

54. Department of Native Affairs, NTS 9686, J H Eliot, Chief Control Officer to Secretary of Native Affairs, 28 July 1944.

55. House of Assembly Debates, 16 March 1945, col. 3585, J S Marwick.

56. D Harris, "Princes, Homes and Transport", Belinda Bozzoli (ed.), Town and Countryside in the Transvaal: Penetration and Popular Reponse, (Johannesburg, 1983), 40-41.

57. Natives Representative Council Debates, 4 December 1940, 327-328. R Baloyi.

58. Inkundla Ya Bantu, Second Fortnight, July 1946.

59. P Walshe, The Rise of African Nationalism in South Africa: The African National Congress 1912-1952, (London, 1970) 312-315.

60. Guardian, 15 August 1946.

61. Xuma Papers, ABX 460726, Cyclostyled letters sent to the members of the NRC, 26 July 1946.

62. Guardian, 25 December 1947.

63. NTS 1791, 89/276(2), NRC Agenda, 14 August 1946; Ibid., Secretary of Native Affairs to Secretary for Public Works, 6 August 1946; Ibid., 1790, 89/276(3), NRC Motions for August, 1946 session.

64. Interview with J S Moroka, November 1980.

65. P Walshe, op. cit. 282-283.

66. See, for example, Inkundla Ya Bantu, First Fortnight, October 1946; Bantu World, 26 October 1946.

67. Karis and Carter Microfilms, University of the Witwatersrand, 2:AK 5/11:96/3, "A Chronological Account of the Events Connected with the Deadlock between the Government and the Natives Representative Council ..."

68. SAIRR Papers, AD189, ANC Notebook vi.

69. Inkundla Ya Bantu, 12 May 1948.

70. Inkundla Ya Bantu, 17 July 1947, "The African National Congress and the Boycott of the Native Representation Act", by Paul Mosaka.

71. Molteno Papers, Bc 579 A54.67, "Transkei Voters Boycott".

72. Guardian, 21 August 1949.

73. Guardian, 12 June 1947.

74. Molteno papers, Bc 579 C6.202, Moletno to Xuma, 8 March 1948; Ibid., Bc 579 C6.142, D D T Jabavu to Molteno, 23 September 1947; The Torch, 1 September 1947.

75. Molteno Papers, Bc 579 C6.205, Telegram from Brooks to Molteno, illegible date.

76. Interview with J S Moroka, November 1980; Interview with A P Mda by S Buthelezi, Botswana, February 1982.

77. Guardian, 25 December 1947.

78. Inkundla Ya Bantu, 21 January 1948; Interview with J S Moroka, November 1980.

79. Ilanga Lase Natal, 1 November 1947; Guardian, 10 July 1947.

80. Guardian, 25 November 1948.

81. SAIRR Papers, AD 189, ANC notebooks vi. Moses Kotane and J B Marks, for example, display here completely contradictory attitudes towards the boycott.

82. Inkululeko, September 1947; Ibid., Second Issue, July 1947.

83. Guardian, 30 September 1948; Ibid., 4 November 1948.

84. Ibid., 15 January 1948.

85. Bantu World, 4 January 1947; Report of the Deparment of Native Affairs, 1947-1948, U G 35-49, p. 19.

86. Guardian, 22 January 1948.

87. T Karis and G Carter, op. cit., vol. 4, 105.

88. Karis and Carter Microfilms, 2:AK 5/12/89/5, "The African Attitude to the Smuts Proposals".

89. Inkundla Ya Bantu, 18 December 1948; House of Assembly Debates, 18 May 1949, M Ballinger.

90. Guardian, 21 October 1948; Ibid., 11 November 1948; Bantu World, 21 August 1948; Ballinger Papers, BC 47 C211 Ballinger's election bulletin, 16 September 1948.

91. Ibid., 25 November 1948.

92. Ballinger Papers (University of Cape Town), Izwi Lama Afrika, pamphlet published by the National Party; J H van Rooyen Papers, 6, H Selby Msimang to D J Potgieter, Provincial secretary of the National Party, 18 October 1948; Ibid., 4, W W Ndlovu to J H van Rooyen, 24 September 1948.

93. Ibid., 14, "To the Native People of Natal; "Karis and Carter Microfilms, 2:XC9:41/210, H Selby Msimang to G Champion, 3 November 1948.

94. Champion Papers, 1948, W H Stuart to Champion, 26 July 1948; Ibid., V Poto to G Champion, 5 July 1948; Guardian, 2 December 1948; Inkundla Ya Bantu, 31 August 1948; Guardian, 25 November 1948.

95. Senate Debates, 7 June 1951, col. 5562, H F Verwoerd; E Brookes, "Natives Representatives and the Senate", SAIRR, Political Representation of Africans in the Union of South Africa, (Johannesburg, 1942) p 16; E Brookes, A South African Pilgrimage, (Johannesburg, 1977) p 80; Ballinger Papers, A410 B2.8.3, E Brookes to M Ballinger, 1 October 1948; Guardian 22 April 1948; See, for example, Imlindi We Nyanga, 15 February 1939, for M Ballinger's stress on black wages.

96. Senate Debates, 7 June 1951, col. 5562, H F Verwoerd.

Explanations of the Mau Mau Revolt

John Lonsdale

My intention is to suggest an outline of an historical process, specific to the Kikuyu people of Kenya but which is intelligible within the general rubrics of colonial nationalism and peasant revolt. The process is important, but only as a field for the operation of human intention and the organisation of power.

In the 1940s, and as a direct result of the Second War, Kenya was the scene of rising conflict. There was increased white settlement and political ambition, founded upon expanding markets, increased participation in the business of government, and secure access to crop financing through the Land Bank and production boards. African farmers had also done well out of the war, the Kikuyu especially. The Kikuyu were unique in colonial Africa, in being an agricultural people settled on well-watered, fertile land, whose Reserve was at the centre of a communications system designed to benefit white settlers, and on the doorstep of the capital city, Nairobi. They numbered about one million in 1950, about one fifth of Kenya's black population. One third of them lived outside the Reserve, some of them as bachelor migrant workers in the towns, but most of them as squatter families on the farms of the White Highlands. Over three-quarters of squatters' incomes, comparatively high by the standards of the day, was derived from the sales of their own agricultural and animal produce rather than farm wages. Perhaps half of the 'White' farmlands was under black production. Their occupation stood in the path of white ambitions and threatened white security. The third competitor in post-war reconstruction was the colonial government. It saw increased white production as the main safety-valve for black population increase. But it was also convinced that black agriculture had to be saved from soil erosion, at first by physical remedies such as contour terracing, though by 1950 it was moving towards a policy of allowing Africans (but only in the Reserves) to grow high-value cash crops (coffee, tea, pineapples) under the guidance of an expanded agricultural extension service. A corollary was the stabilisation of African urban labour with a family wage. These would be the economic foundations of a 'multi-racial' polity in the long term, of which the outlines could only dimly be seen. Africans were given their first direct, nominated, representative on the Legislative Council in 1946; they were co-opted on to various government boards. For government, the trick was to bring on Africans while not disturbing Europeans and the capital market. But while Europeans began to grow suspicious, Africans became frustrated and alarmed, both Highland squatters, urban workers, and the notables in the Reserve.

The outbreak of the revolt is a controversial matter. Earlier accounts stressed the British declaration of Emergency in October 1952, a pre-emptive strike against the forces of revolution which in fact galvanised them into action once the moderates had been incarcerated. This viewpoint stresses the inchoate nature of 'Mau Mau' prior to that date - if indeed it can be said to have existed at all. More recent work suggests that the Emergency did not so much bring the movement into being as consolidate it about a nerve centre in Nairobi, which supplied the strong arm in the forests. Prior to that date one has to envisage three 'starting-points', insofar as such can ever be said to exist:

1944 in the White Highlands/Rift Valley: as squatters resisted new labour contracts which reduced their rights to cultivation and grazing while increasing their days of labour service;

1946 in the Kikuyu Reserve, as veteran members of the Kikuyu Central Association (founded 1924) started administering an oath of loyalty (of which there had been two previous versions) designed to secure political control in the new competitions of postwar politics;

1947 in Nairobi, as militant Trade Unionists came to realise the need for more than mere trades unionism in the desperate and violent conditions of the main towns, Nairobi and Mombasa, with real wages dropping sharply in the post-war inflation, and the skills of longer-term migrants being threatened by a large influx of the rural poor.

There are many explanations. I make brief mention of eight. Each makes assumptions about the colonial situation, the nature of Kikuyu society and the quality and ambitions of its leadership.

1. Official/settler/missionary

All later explanations have been a reaction to the contemporary white one, which has in consequence acquired the status of caricature. There were in fact several different white explanations at the time, but they had a core of agreement. They assumed the benevolence of colonialism and the necessary tutelage of settlers, officials and missionaries (although these had had their own violent rows in the past). They admitted that social change was traumatic; but they were increasingly agreed that 'firm measures' had to be taken to combat soil erosion and to recover social control both in the Reserves, where chiefs were (as always) losing authority, and in the towns, where active unionism, 'the guerilla army of the underemployed', was a new and alarming phenomenon. White opinion was divided on the nature of the levers of social control to be employed (whether autocratic or consultative) until the educated African leadership disqualified itself from co-optation by opposition to soil conservation etc. measures which were, to whites, self-evidently beneficial. Autocracy then became a condition for progress and its African opponents became cast as selfish manipulators of mass grievance. They were selfish because as the educated, as traders, clerks and 'politicians', they were naturally opposed to colonial solutions which involved producer co-operatives, communal labour on anti-erosion works and much anxiety over the rapidly growing trend of land purchase by Africans; they also lived, so it was thought, by political levies. Kikuyu society in the mass was thought to be full of hidden depth, easily duped into evil ways but full of enormous potential for industrious wellbeing if only the key could be found - which did not involve, as Kikuyu politicians demanded, the reopening of the issue of white landownership, which was the cornerstone of the government's development policy. Kenyatta, the LSE graduate, with an English wife he had left behind and deserted for a chief's daughter, the man with friends in Moscow, the spellbinding orator, became the arch-schemer in the minds of a political administration which was increasingly uncertain of its way. The administration's uncertainty derived from the puzzle over who should be its African allies. The educated progressives were obviously the men of the future, but they seemed to be too powerful to be led. The older chiefs and Christian gentry, the collaborating class of the inter-war era, were just as keen to engross their holdings at the expense of the mass of the peasantry as any wily trader-politician. Moreover, the old chiefs were reluctant to push their people too hard on contour-terracing labour. The administration recruited increasingly from its own junior ranks, promoting clerks and agricultural instructors to chiefships. In its perplexities the government was withdrawing into itself and casting the blame for failure upon others. 'Mau Mau' was the screen on which it projected its anger and fears - an all-encompassing conspiracy of disobedience to the laws of improvement, which intimidated more moderate politicians, bewitched the masses and began, before the Emergency, to employ selective terror against the most upright chiefs and the staunchest of the Kikuyu Christians. Nevertheless, the novels of Robert Ruark should not be taken as a faithful guide to the official mind. Their stridency is a product of the brutalities of the Emergency years when 'Mau Mau' had narrowed down to the forest fighters. That the British counter-revolution to Mau Mau included the most vigorous programme of agrarian reform in colonial Africa is a much better indication of the complexity of the official view. Mau Mau's barbarity was a necessary attribute of a political movement which had to be destroyed.

2. Liberal nationalist historiography

The standard view was presented by Rosberg and Nottingham (1966). Their book was very much a product of its time. The 'colonial' view has been that Mau Mau represented the resentful agony of a backward society caught up in too rapid modernisation. Rosberg and Nottingham nailed this as 'myth'. It could be said that they invented a counter-myth, of Mau Mau as the militant wing of modernizing nationalism. The radicals were simply those who were fired by nationalists' institution-building but frustrated by colonial immobility. The opposition between moderates and militants was a matter more of tactics than fundamental society strategy. Africans, on this view, were divided more by region and tribe than by class position. The Kikuyu dominated politics because they had been the most mobilised by economic and educational change; they also had the strongest grievance in their 'stolen lands'. Their natural, highly competitive and decentralised egalitarianism had been accentuated by white settlement. Generational conflict had become sharper, social competitiveness had generally turned in upon itself. But political violence did not really gather force until after the British declaration of Emergency, which removed the men of moderation from the scene and induced a mood of defensive despair. Mau Mau was a resistance movement of an ambitious tribe under siege.

3. Radical nationalist historiography

This tradition of explanation also first appeared in 1966, with

Barnett and Njama's book, an edited autobiography of a Mau Mau leader in the forests. It has been followed by Kaggia's autobiography (1955) and two Kikuyu historians, Kinyatti and Ng'anga (both 1977). All these argued not that the educated moderates were removed from leadership but that they actively betrayed a movement which they had helped to set in motion but whose social radicalism they increasingly feared. They wrote in a context not of triumphant nationalism but of a cynical neo-colonialism in which the post-independence elite exploited the sufferings of the poor whose sacrifices had broken the colonial-settler alliance. The underlying assumption of this historiographical tradition was that Kikuyu society was becoming increasingly class-divided, the main index of class formation being educational privilege. This division gave to the British the levers of political and economic co-optation in their efforts to make African nationalism safe for continued settler - and, by extension, capitalist - domination.

4. High politics among the Kikuyu

Two American scholars, Spencer (1977) and Glough (1978), free from nationalist triumphalism and radical anger, began to give some historical depth to the radical analysis of political competition between the Kikuyu leadership, but without its teleological hindsight. Rather, the competition was between 'ins' and 'outs', between chiefs and senior mission teachers who satisfied personal ambition and hoped to promote general social improvement through a critical accommodation with the colonial administration, and those of their colleagues who were like them in every way save in their exclusion from the narrow ranks of the collaborative establishment. 'Politics' was initiated by that establishment. After the Second War, the educated moderates did not so much betray the wider enthusiasms which they had evoked but, rather, retreated from the frustrations of political failure into individually profitable accommodations with colonial reality. The movement which they created became a hollow shell, available to be taken over by their permanent opposition, men who were driven to ever greater extremes more by the need to keep up with their followers than by their own radical vision of the future.

All these interpretations had in common an attempt to see Mau Mau as a whole. They gave priority to political leadership and intention. More recent work has assumed that social processes were at least as causatively significant as political leadership. It has also investigated the three separate regional bases of Kikuyu politics and has been uncertain how they became, or even whether they became linked by organisation and strategy.

5. Social differentiation in the Kikuyu Reserve

This was first investigated by Sorrenson (1967), who has been followed by Ng'anga (1977) and Njonjo (1977). Sorrenson argued that the main conflict was between the big men of Kikuyu lineage groups and their clients. The former repudiated the land rights of the latter, as land values in the Reserve rose not only due to the constrictions imposed by land alienation to whites but also because of the rising opportunities of the produce market, especially in Nairobi and among the labour forces on white plantations. Bundles of rights to land became forcibly simplified, lineage membership became more narrowly defined. Sorrenson reached the cautious and by no means unqualified conclusion that, in the Reserve, Mau Mau gathered together the resentments of the dispossessed against the expropriators, the gentry. The corollary was that any political movement originated by the gentry for constitutional redress was likely to pass out of their control and turn against them. The weakness of his argument was the lack of detailed, oral, social and political data, lineage by lineage. To some extent this deficiency was made good by Njonjo's researches.

There have been two variations on this general theme:

a) Greet Kershaw's material, gathered in the 1950s but as yet unpublished, suggests very strongly that there was not so much a clear process of social differentiation as generalised uncertainty over rights to land where Kikuyu land law, premised on the availability of land as the reward of political allegiance, ceased to have any relevance. The implication of her argument is that the British declaration of Emergency both unified Kikuyu political opinion where there was no unity before, and created conditions of social panic and opportunist murder rather than social revolution. Her data is by far the most detailed that we possess, and her argument is the one on which I mainly build in my own explanation, below.

b) David Throup (also unpublished) argues that the most important process after the Second War was not so much land concentration as agrarian police action, as the gentry-chief enforced the colonial government's corvée-labour solution to soil erosion. The mass of the peasantry, peasant women especially, had to do two days' work per week on the hillside terraces. It was hard and unproductive labour for them. But the rural roads which they also constructed were of direct benefit to the gentry with a surplus to sell.

Throup's emphasis on what I have elsewhere called 'the second colonial occupation' provides three important insights. It links the preoccupations of the colonial state with mass rural unrest in the Reserves. It shows how rural resentment at agrarian rules provided the urban militants with a ready-made constituency when they invaded the moderate politicians' rural base in 1947. And it provides the most concrete linkage between the Kikuyu gentry and the workings of the colonial state.

6. Peasant resistance in the White Highlands

Kikuyu tenant farmers had been under pressure from their white landlords in the late 1920s. In the depression of the 1930s and, still more, during the Second War, they had regained a great deal of freedom to enlarge their own domestic production. At the end of the war the white settlers' district councils moved decisively to impose new, more restrictive labour contracts as the settlers' greater capitalisation freed them from their former dependence upon their black tenants. Squatter communities reacted with oaths of solidarity to resist the new contracts, with arson, cattle-maiming and machine-breaking. To the squatters their white landlords were guilty of breaking what they saw as the moral community between big men and clients. They had supposed that they were the joint heirs to the Highlands. Now white farmers were repudiating their squatter rights in much the same way as the Kikuyu gentry had earlier repudiated their lineage rights in the Reserves. If the squatter resistance movement was Mau Mau, it was for several years highly successful. Right up until 1952 most squatters seem to have retained their customary rights to cultivation and grazing in despite of the new contracts. Their labour was too valuable to be repudiated by their employers; they also moved from farm to farm (or from manor to manor), exploiting the differences between Europeans who were at different stages of the intensification of production, and who had different combinations of agriculture and pastoralism, with different tolerances of squatter livestock. Mau Mau was first given its name in court proceedings in the Highlands.

There are three different interpretations of the squatter movement.

a) Furedi (1974) clearly sees the squatters as 'middle peasants', defending viable family smallholdings with the aid of a working network of natural leaders, the farm foremen, dairy clerks and independent squatter produce traders who had contacts all over the farm districts, focused upon markets and independent churches. His implicit comparison is with Captain Swing, 'the last peasants' revolt' in early nineteenth-century England.

b) Manogo (1980) prefers to see the squatter communities as more egalitarian and secretive, coming together in ignorance of their 'leaders' whom indeed they saw as potential quislings. Furedi saw the leaders as the oath administrators, Kanogo saw them as amongst the first to be murdered. Both used much the same oral material, and their divergence of interpretation is not easily explained.

c) Tamarkin (1976), in his study of the Highland market town of Nakuru, also questioned Furedi's thesis that the squatter resistance movement was controlled by its natural leaders. For in the town, the most successful members of Kikuyu society were ex-squatters who had become urban traders. They were too solid to be radical, and too vulnerable to white retaliation. But their moderate politics was outflanked and then spurned by the unemployed youths whom they had first introduced to political organisation as guards and errand-boys.

There is, then, perhaps a growing consensus that Mau Mau in the White Highlands, is to be understood in the context of political movements which outstrip the intentions of their originators, as popular perceptions of the possible and desirable overtake established perception.

The problem which faces historians who perceive Mau Mau primarily as a squatter resistance movement is how, if at all, it was connected with the more central political direction which was located elsewhere, whether among the moderate nationalist gentry in the Reserves, or among the militant trade unionists in Nairobi, who were their increasingly impatient rivals.

Most of the answer seems to lie in the history of the Olenguruone settlement scheme for 'surplus' farm squatters which the colonial government established on the western forest fringe of the Highlands during the war. All interpretations are on this point agreed. The

Colonial Office had insisted that this safety-valve be opened before any moves were made to restrict squatter rights. But both the Colonial Office and the colonial government were agreed that the settlement should be used as a pilot scheme for the greater official control over African land husbandry which was seen to be more generally necessary. Olenguruone became the site of a bitter clash between its Kikuyu tenants who insisted that the land was theirs by right of compensation for the land they had lost thirty years earlier to white colonisation, and the government which insisted that they were there as tenants of the state and subject to its agrarian rules of good husbandry. These determined oppositions were carried to the point of a mass oath of solidarity among the Kikuyu settlers and their subsequent mass eviction by government in 1948. The refugees dispersed, some to white farms, but most to the towns or as unwelcome clients on the land of distant relatives back in the Reserves.

Fund-raising for litigation and the interest of the vernacular press made Olenguruone a common cause for all the various strands of Kikuyu politics, but only for as long as it was an external grievance. The Kikuyu political notables in the Reserve were descended from those dominant families whose tenantry the squatters had once been. They were willing therefore to give them all support short of that which actually counted, absorbing them back on to the land from which they had been squeezed out a generation earlier.

7. **Urban violence especially in Nairobi, 'the county town of Kikuyuland'.**

The Kikuyu formed over half Nairobi's black population. Many more commuted thither daily, as workers, market gardeners and stallholders. The Kikuyu fed black Nairobi, they owned much of its lodging, controlled its retail-trade, transport, short-term credit, and prostitution; they had a good hold on the skilled and clerical occupations, they ran the trade unions. It was in Nairobi that politics acquired much of its violence; but it was in Nairobi's competitive ethnic political economy that divisions between Africans ensured that militant politics would be confined largely to the Kikuyu. One has to look at two contexts. The first, trade unionism, has been investigated by Stichter (1975) and Spencer (1977). Here, Kikuyu unionists found themselves fighting a rearguard action between their own, home-grown general unionism, and the officially sponsored industrial-craft unionism to which non-Kikuyu leaders tended to be co-opted. Membership drives overflowed from the shopfloor into the African residential locations, enforced by strong-arm visitors at dead of night. The second context, the retail trade in goods and services, has scarcely begun to be investigated and it will be very difficult to elucidate. The starting point might be the fact that moderate politicians and shopkeepers from non-Kikuyu peoples were the first victims of political terror in the early 1950s and in the first months of the Emergency. The defence of established commercial territory and organised crime were closely linked, and African Nairobi was virtually a no-go area for the security forces from October 1952 until April 1953.

Nairobi was the arena in which establishment politics was most decisively overturned by militant action. When the urban militants were invited by the rural gentry, Kenyatta among them, to assist in the general process of political mobilisation they proceeded to overturn its strategic premise, changing it from a weapon of political control to a lever for direct action.

One still has to uncover the linkages, the sense of strategic direction, in these three different strands of politics. To look for unswerving intention and absolute control would be to chase a mirage, to expect Mau Mau to be quite unlike any other political movement in history. It would be to fall into the trap of the colonial interpretation and the radical nationalist one as well. What one can reasonably expect is both more modest and more difficult to analyse: a growing sense of the unity of the political field on which these various conflicts were enacted. So, and this is where my own ideas begin to take off from earlier investigations, I am looking for two keys to a process. These seem to be provided by:

i) a concept of political periodisation; and ii) a concept of cultural boundary-laying, which defines the issues and the competitors. These come to tie the different strands, <u>not</u> into a unified movement, but into a unified field of competition. The competitors can be defined as follows:

- <u>defensive</u> 'middle' and poor peasants in the Reserves and White Highlands;
- <u>aggressive</u> traders and trade unionists in the towns;
- <u>dominant</u> elites in the Reserve, gentry, chiefs, senior mission teachers.

The first resisted the interventions of state and white settlers; the second were attempting, with increasing desperation, to gain more purchase on the workings of the state, if needs be by overturning its rules of collaborative access; the third were attempting to use their already established position to moderate the procedures of the state on the first two, so as to preserve their own dominance.

This search brings me to:

8. The growth of Kikuyu ethnicity

This is implicit in but not positively explored by Buijtenhuijs (1971). Being in French, this work has had none of the influence which its open-minded rigour deserves. But it is by standing on the shoulders of Buijtjenhuijs and Kershaw (also Dutch by birth) that I think one can most profitably peer further. Buijtenhuijs took as his central problem the 'three Mau Maus', much as I have myself outlined them, and their presumed linkage.

He found the answer both in their link through conflict between political elites (the particular interest of Spencer), those who strove for 'political control', and those who countered them with 'direct action' by making the oath of political allegiance cheap and open to all, including women; <u>and</u> in a 'culturalist' explanation, the very interpretation favoured by the colonial government at the time and, for that reason, outlawed as a legitimate sphere of investigation by subsequent non-colonial scholars anxious not to be branded as apologists of colonialism.

Buijtenhuijs came to grips with the question of what it meant to be a <u>Kikuyu</u> peasant rather than just any peasant. He rejected the imputation of savage atavism which the colonial perspective attached to Kikuyu-ness but nonetheless, and rightly, insisted that men and women can act only within their own traditions, which provide them with an 'economy of effort' in organisation and explanation, however 'radical' their intentions may be. He emphasised three Kikuyu institutions in particular (which had not been ignored by Rosberg and Nottingham, either):

a) generational conflict, both at the level of the household and the lineage settlement;
b) disputes within and between lineages over rights of access to land;
c) the importance to the Kikuyu of fee-payment and oaths in legal disputes and in the passage of individual men through successive statuses in life in company with their age-mates; Kikuyu life was strikingly formalised.

What Buijtenhuijs did not quite do was to set these traditional institutions and disputes into a chronology of change and growing definition, a chronology which came to crystallise not only the Kikuyu as a tribe but also the political constituencies which came to fight for its control.

To carry the argument this stage further, one needs to explore four, interlinked, historical contexts. I will give here only an outline scheme:

1) The changing relationship between the colonial state (understood as both a set of politico-economic relationships and as a governing, largely bureaucratic set of institutions) and the dominant classes, white and black, which composed the political nation. In the Kenya case one needs to watch the relationshp between the growth of private proprietary power, among settlers and African notables, and the growth of state intervention to make this growing power tolerable: a combination of contradictory constraints upon fresh openings for the mass of peasantry.

2) The changing relationship between mass peasant discontent and organised political opinion (eventually competitive African nationalism), within the context of the question posed by Eric Wolf: to whom can rural populations turn for alternative patrons when faced by the 'double squeeze' between state and notables outlined above. In the Kenya case, and in all colonial situations, the alternative patrons, the 'politicians' were those based in new, often informal institutions which linked the state as a whole and the separate rural worlds, mission schools, district councils, officially tolerated traders' associations, tribal welfare associations, etc. That is, even the alternative patrons were to be found only in the advancing edge of class-formation - a very complex phenomenon which is explored further in (4) below.

3) The experience of regionally and culturally specific peasantries in socio-economic change - the particular perspective of Buijtenhuijs - but which needs a periodization best provided, I think, by:

4) The changing strategies and alliances of individual social mobility, in face of growing constraints, costs, and frustrations. This question is best explored by asking what were the (ultimately political) implications of the now conventional wisdom on the mechanism of social stratification among Africans in colonial Kenya - where, as elsewhere in southern Africa, African farm incomes were contained, but by no means destroyed, by the state's core alliance with white settlers. In this situation, African accumulation could come only by profitable 'straddling' between wage employment and agrarian investment in land, wives, and the capital goods of trade, carts, shops etc., all as outlined by Mike Cowen in many unpublished papers and Kitching (1980). My conclusion is that the strategy of upward mobility changed from individual accommodations with established notables up to 1930; to the definition of an alternative, part subversive, part conservative constituency in the 1930s; and, finally, to a determined effort to wrest the mass of the population from its establishment patrons to the insurgent ones in the 1940s. These changing strategies have much to do with the changing relationships between state and notables referred to above.

BIBLIOGRAPHY

D L Barnett and Marari Njana, Mau Mau from Within (London, 1966).

R Buijtenhuijs, Le Mouvement 'Mau Mau': une révolt paysanne et anti-coloniale en Afrique noire (Paris, 1971).

M S Clough, 'Chiefs and Politicians: Local Politics and Social Change in Kiambu, Kenya, 1918-1936' (Stanford Ph.D thesis, 1978).

F Furedi, 'The Social Composition of the Mau Mau movement in the White Highlands', Journal Peasant Studies 1, 4 (1974).

B Kaggia, Roots of Freedom (Nairobi, 1975).

T Kanogo, 'The political economy of the Kikuyu movement into the Rift Valley, 1900-1963: the case of Nakuru District' (Nairobi Ph.D thesis, 1980).

Greet Kershaw, work in progress.

M Kinyatti, 'Mau Mau: the peak of African nationalism in Kenya', Kenya History Review 5, 2 (1977).

G Kitching, Class and Economic Change in Kenya (New Haven and London, 1980).

H Ng'ang'a, 'Mau Mau: Loyalists and Politics in Murang'a, 1952-1970', Kenya History Review 5, 2 (1977).

A L Njonjo, 'The Africanization of the White Highlands: a study in agrarian class struggles in Kenya 1950-1974' (Princeton Ph.D thesis, 1977).

C G Rosberg and J Nottingham, The Myth of 'Mau Mau': Nationalism in Kenya (New York and London, 1966).

M P K Sorrenson, Land Reform in the Kikuyu Country (Nairobi, 1967).

J Spencer, 'The Kenya African Union 1944-1953: a party in search of constituency' (Columbia Ph.D thesis, 1977).

S Stichter, 'Workers, Trade Unions and the Mau Mau Rebellion', Canadian Journal of African Studies 9, 2 (1975).

M Tamarkin, 'Mau Mau in Nakuru', Journal African History 17, 1 (1976).

D Throup, 'The Kenya Governorship of Sir Philip Mitchell' (Cambridge Ph.D thesis, 1983).

The Poqo Insurrection

Tom Lodge

This paper[1] is about one of the least successful of South Africa's revolutionary movements. Several thousand Poqo insurrectionists were arrested during the course of the 1960s. The vast majority of these were detained and convicted before they had had a chance to strike a single blow. Fewer than thirty deaths can be attributed to the activities of Poqo adherents of whom nearly the same number were sentenced to death in South African courts. The history of the Poqo uprisings is a history without a climax. Its final act takes place in the courtrooms not the barricades. Perhaps for this reason the Poqo story has lacked a chronicler. This paper is an attempt to compensate for the perfunctory treatment Poqo has received from historians.[2] It provides a narrative of Poqo's development and a description of its social following. It then attempts to assess Poqo's historical significance.

After the Sharpeville crisis and a confused period during which African politicians adjusted to new conditions of illegality a variety of insurgent organisations emerged. Of these the two most important were those linked to the Pan-Africanist Congress (PAC) and the African National Congress (ANC). These were both dedicated to revolutionary transformations of society and were both prepared to employ violent measures to attain this but there the similarity between them ended. The PAC-oriented 'Poqo' movement and the ANC's military wing 'Umkhonto we Sizwe' reflected in their divergent strategies the fundamental ideological and strategic differences which had led to the fission in African resistance politics in the 1950s. As well as this the PAC insurgents were very much more numerous than the Umkhonto activists. Whilst the latter operated as an elite within the framework of a larger clandestine and sometimes less committed 'support organisation'[3] the Poqo insurgency in certain localities attained the dimensions of a mass movement. Reaching the peak of its influence in 1963, the Poqo movement was still capable three years later of inspiring violent conspiracies: in 1966 in the Eastern Cape alone, 85 men accused of PAC activity were convicted in six trials.[4] In terms of its geographical extensiveness, the numbers involved and its timespan, the Poqo conspiracies of 1962-1968 represent the largest and most sustained African insurrectionary movement since the inception of modern African political organisations in South Africa.

The word 'Poqo' is a Xhosa expression meaning 'alone' or 'pure'. The earliest known usage of the word in the context of a separatist organisation occurred when the Ethiopianist Church of South Africa was established. Its members would describe themselves as: 'Ndingum Topiya Poqo' (belonging to the Church of Ethiopia).[5] The word was used sometimes in the Western Cape in 1960 as a slogan by PAC members to describe the character of their organisation in contrast to the multiracial dimension of the Congress Alliance.[6] Leaflets allegedly circulated by PAC activists in Port Elizabeth in May 1961 opposing the ANC's call for a stay-away in protest against the governments' proclamation of a republic bore the legend: 'May demos a fraud, Poqo, Poqo, Poqo'.[7] The authorities and the press tended to employ the term to describe all PAC-connected conspiracies though only PAC supporters in the Cape identified themselves as Poqo members at first. Here, for the sake of simplicity, the state's usage of the term will be followed, though, as will become clear, different regional concentrations of PAC/Poqo affinity had quite distinct social characteristics. The first moves towards the formation of a violent organisation came in the Western Cape and it is here that the narrative will begin.

The Western Cape, and in particular the Cape Peninsula, had been one of the areas of strongest support for the PAC. This could be related to the particularly fierce effects of influx control in the Cape Peninsula, the 'repatriation' of women and children to the Transkei, the refusal of the authorities to construct adequate housing and sharply deteriorating living conditions. In addition, in the early 1960s the imposition of Bantu Authorities and land rehabilitaion measures in the Transkei also influenced the political responses of Africans in the Cape Peninsula and its hinterland. The Pan-Africanist Congress's rhetorical militancy, the incorporation into its ideology of themes drawn from traditions of primary resistance, and the immediacy of its strategic objectives made it especially attractive to the increasingly large migrant worker population of Cape Town. The Pan Africanists found an important section of their following in the 'bachelor zones' of Langa.[8] However, of the thirty-one PAC leaders who were subsequently put on trial in Cape Town after the 1960 pass campaign, only seven men were from the migrant workers' hostels in Langa and Nyanga. Unfortunately, the trial documentation only contains full details of the backgrounds of a few of the leaders: they included a herbalist, a dry cleaning examiner, a domestic servant, a university student, a tailor and a farmworker and their ages ranged from twenty two to fifty five (the majority of the accused were over thirty). At least seven were former members of the ANC and one had once belonged to the Communist Party.[9] The evidence suggests a not altogether surprising social pattern: a political movement with a large following amongst migrant workers, but with positions of responsibility held by men with at least some education, work skills and political experience.

During the 1960 pass campaign as well as before and after it, there was considerable contact between the local Pan Africanist leaders and members of the multiracial Liberal Party. This was despite frequent attacks on white radicals who had been associated with the Congress movement.[10] Local Liberals were seeking a mass base and though wary of the racialist undertones of Pan-Africanist ideology, they sympathised with and were attracted by the PAC's hostility to left wing influences within the Congress movement. Cape Town PAC leaders, whatever their private feelings about the Liberals, were glad to accept offers of assistance that appeared to be without strings, and allowed certain Liberals to play an important intermediary role between them and the authorities during the 1960 troubles in Cape Town. Whereas this relationship had certain advantages at the time, it did have the effect of isolating the leaders from rank and file membership[11] as well as the large informal following the campaign generated.

In the months following the crisis of March-April 1960, this gulf between leaders and followers was to widen and take on a factional form. Some of the main leaders, including Philip Kgosana, jumped bail and left the country towards the end of 1960. This considerably weakened the degree of influence of those who remained. Accounts by two Cape Town journalists tell of a struggle in the Cape Town locations between moderates and extremists.[12] The 'extremists' identified the 'moderates' as those PAC men who flirted with the Liberal party. They were 'Katangese, the treacherous ones who are playing the same role as Moishe Tshombe in the Congo'.[13] These accounts are substantiated by some of the trial evidence. In a trial of old age home workers two of the acccused in their statements to the police (possibly made after they had been tortured) mentioned a dispute within the PAC in Cape Town. One group was led by two Nyanga leaders, both former members of the regional executive of the legal PAC, Christopher Mlokoti and Abel Matross.[14] Mlokoti and Matross were the PAC men who made the initial contact with the Liberal Party in late 1959.[15] The other faction was allegedly led by Mlami Makwetu and Wellington Tshongayi.[16] Makwetu had been branch secretary at Langa New Flats in 1960 and was a docker.[17] Tshongayi also belonged to the PAC in 1960 and was secretary of the Crawford branch. He was imprisoned after the pass campaign.[18] What the evidence suggests is a struggle for dominance of the underground movement in early 1961 between upper and lower echelon leadership with the latter, by virtue of their stronger links with migrant hostel dwellers, becoming ascendant.

This split in the underground movement (which was accompanied by fighting between the different groups)[19] was followed by a period of extensive recruitment and organisation by the dominant faction. It seems that it was at this point that the 'cell system' was established.[20] Within Langa, and elsewhere in Cape Town, recruitment and organisation was often done by forming groups composed of men who had come from a particular rural region. Although this flowed naturally from a situation where migrant workers would often choose to live with friends or relatives from their homeplace, there was an element of self-consciousness in the way it was done. For example in Langa, there was a special 'Lady Frere' group drawn from men who lived in Zones 19, 20, 23 and 24 of the Langa single men's quarters.[21] This would have obvious advantages when Poqo began to extend its influence into the Transkei.[22] It also meant that Poqo cell members not only lived in close proximity with each other, they would also probably be employed together.[23] Theoretically, each cell was composed of ten men: in fact they were often larger and in any case individual cells would combine for larger meetings often involving over a hundred people. Similarly large groups would sometimes accompany recruiters on their rounds.[24] Each cell would have a leader.

Langa seems to have been regarded by other Poqo groups as the local head-quarters of the movement: certainly it was recruiting teams from Langa who played the most active role in spreading the influence of movement. There were recorded instances of Langa activists establishing cells or branches in different parts of Cape Town. Men living in employers' compounds seem to have been a favourite target for recruiting operations: a Poqo group at the Cape Town Jewish Old Age Home also included workers from a nearby hotel. Another trial, which collapsed through lack of evidence, involved staff from the Brooklands Chest Hospital.[25] Poqo activists fanned out from Cape Town to the smaller urban centres and the farms surrounding them, either starting new cells or reactivating PAC branches. Considerable effort seems to have been devoted to building cells among farmworkers: according to state witness evidence in a trial involving a member of Tshongayi's cell, there was an unsuccessful meeting to recruit people on a farm near Somerset West in February 1961.[26] More successful in this context apparently was the establishment of a Poqo cell on a farm at Stellenbosch in October 1961 after a visit by three Poqo men from Cape Town.[27] A Poqo group was active between March 1962 and April 1963 on a farm in the Elgin District.[28]

Poqo's message was stated in simple direct terms. In December 1961 a leaflet in Xhosa was picked up in Nyanga. It read:

> We are starting again Africans ... we die once. Africa will be free on January 1st. The white people shall suffer, the black people will rule. Freedom comes after bloodshed. Poqo has started. It needs a real man. The Youth has weapons so you need not be afraid. The PAC says this.[29]

Sometimes the message was more specific: farmworkers were told that Poqo intended to take the land away from whites and give it to Africans.[30] Men in Wellington were told that one day they must throw away their passes and take over the houses of the whites. All who did not join Poqo would be killed along 'with the white bosses'. Men in Paarl were told there was no need for whites; the factories and the industries would carry on as usual, for was it not the black people who worked in them?[31] Chiefs should be killed, for it was they who were responsible for the endorsement-out of Africans from the Western Cape.[32] Sometimes Poqo members giving evidence would repeat some of the old PAC slogans - from Cape to Cairo, from Morocco to Madagascar,[33] - but often witnesses would claim that they knew nothing of the ANC or PAC.[34] This may have been prompted by caution on their part, but what is noticeable is that many of the distinctive attributes of PAC speeches given at a popular level had disappeared: there were no references to Pan Africanism, communism or socialism and no careful clarifications of the movement's attitude with regard to the position of racial minorities. Ideological statements had been boiled down to a set of slogans: 'We must stand alone in our land';[35] 'Freedom - to stand alone and not be suppressed by whites';[36] 'amaAfrica Poqo; 'Izwe Lethu' (our land).

Poqo's lack of a 'political theory', the brutal simplicity of its catchphrases, the absence of any social programme save for the destruction of the present order and its replacement with its inversion in which white would be black, and black would be white, all this has helped to diminish its importance in the historiography of South African resistance movements. But because the slogans were simple does not mean that they were banal: they evoked a profound response from men who had been forced off the land, whose families were being subjected to every form of official harassment, as well as economic deprivation, who perceived every relationship with authority in terms of conflict: whether at the workplace, in the compound, or in the reserve. These were men who had no place to turn to. And hence the all-embracing nature of the movement's preoccupations, its social exclusiveness, and its urgency. The undertone of millenarianism, the concept of the sudden dawning of a juster era, the moral implications of the word 'poqo' (pure) - these are not surprising. For here was a group of men who were simultaneously conscious both of the destruction that was being wreaked upon their old social world, and the hopelessness of the terms being offered to them by the new order.

The strategy of a general uprising logically developed from this vision. The twenty-one farmworkers of Stellenbosch put on trial in June 1962 were found guilty on a number of charges which included making preparations to attack a farm manager and his family, to burn the farm buildings and then to march to the town firing buildings on the way. For weapons the men sharpened old car springs into pangas.[37] The initiative for this strategy was probably a local one: most of the national PAC leadership was in prison in 1961 and early 1962 and had only fully regrouped in Maseru in August 1962.[38] But by late 1962, judging from the evidence of men involved in the Poqo attack at Paarl, Poqo members were conscious of a plan for a nationally co-ordinated insurrection, the directives for which would come from above.[39] In March 1963, Potlake Leballo, the PAC's acting president, told a journalist that he was in touch with Western Cape and other regional leaders.[40] Despite this co-ordination of the Congress, there is a strong case for asserting that the insurrectionary impetus came initially from below and, as I have argued, can be directly related to the social situation of Poqo's local leaders and their followers. Certainly the violent impetus developed much earlier in PAC groups in the Western Cape than elsewhere, the first attacks on policemen or their informers beginning in Paarl in April 1961 and in Langa in April the following year. Before the end of 1962 several groups had travelled from the Langa migrant workers' quarters to the Transkei in efforts to kill the Emigrant Tembu paramount chief, Kaiser Mantazima and a full scale insurrection had taken place in the small Boland town of Paarl.

While the Western Cape Poqo cells had an internal dynamic and momentum of their own, elsewhere the movement, more systematically structured and more hierarchical than in the Western Cape, was motivated less by local causes of social tension and more by the strategic conception of those members of the PAC's national executive who remained at liberty or who had been released from prison. Partly for this reason it was less effective. Initially, with most of the main leaders in prison there were few signs of PAC activity. With the end of the emergency in August 1960 some important PAC men who had been detained along with Congress Alliance people were released. In particular, two Evaton leaders, both on the National Executive, were once again at liberty.[41] One of them, Z B Molete, was delegated the task of presiding over the underground organisation while the other office-bearers were in prison, and he together with Joe Molefi, began reviving branches.

The first indications of the re-establishment of an operating PAC leadership was the circulation of a typewritten leaflet in September in the Transkei with the heading 'A Call to PAC Leaders'. The leaflet instructed PAC branches to divide into small units, cells. Branch leaders were instructed to establish contact with the national and regional executives in Johannesburg. Finally, the leaflet exhorted PAC members to 'prepare for mass disciplined action', for a 'final decisive phase' with the object of 'total abolition of the pass laws'.[42] Obviously the leaflet's authors were still thinking of continuing the pre-Sharpeville strategy of mass civil disobedience. There was no explicit indication in the leaflet of the possibility of violence. That Molete and his colleagues did not at this stage share the insurrectionary disposition which was developing in the Cape is also signified by their initial willingness to participate in the Orlando Consultative Conference of December 1961.[43]

The Orlando Conference was prompted by a suggestion from the Interdenominational African Minister's Federation. Attending the meeting were representatives from the ANC and the PAC, as well as leading African members of the Liberal and Progressive Parties. At the insistence of PAC spokesmen whites and coloured were excluded.[44] After several speeches, including an address by Z B Molete on 'The Struggle against the Pass Laws'[45] the meeting resolved in favour of political unity, non-violent pressures against apartheid, non-racial democracy, and the calling of an 'All-in Conference representative of African people' to agitate for a national constitutional convention. A continuation committee under the chairmanship of Jordan Ngubane, a former Youth Leaguer and a member of the Liberal Party, was elected.

The work of this continuation committee was soon over-shadowed by conflict between the Liberals and the PAC on the one hand and the ANC on the other. Ngubane claimed that the ANC with financial assistance from the South African Communist Party worked to control the committee and the All-in Conference. Without consulting other committee members ANC people drafted publicity for the Conference to ensure its pro-Congress character.[46] Though Ngubane's accusations were probably somewhat exaggerated it is likely that neither the PAC nor the ANC had a particularly sincere concern for unity, not if this required making concessions to the other side. By mid-March the PAC men and Ngubane had resigned from the continuation committee and the All-in Conference held in Pietermaritzburg on the 25th and 26th March, was, despite the attendance of delegates from 140 organisations, a characteristically Congress affair. Among the 1,400 participants were whites, coloureds and Indians from the allied organisations. Traditional ANC rhetoric, songs and slogans predominated. The highlight of the event was the appearance of a recently unbanned Nelson Mandela, who made his first public speech since 1952. In his address Mandela announced the first phase of the campaign for a national convention which would take the form of a three-day stay-at-home, the last day of which would coincide with South Africa's proclamation of a republic on May 31st. Preparations for the strike would include an ultimatum to the Government to call a convention.

At the time of the Orlando Conference it seems likely that the PAC leaders at liberty did not have a very clear conception of the future role of their organisation. Hence their somewhat unrealistic adherence to the concept of a pass campaign which required forms of mobilisation unsuited to the operation of a clandestine movement. That they were initially willing to participate in the Orlando Conference and the continuation committee established in its wake was another indication of their confusion. Their withdrawal from the committee was prompted apparently by a message from their imprisoned colleagues brought to them by Matthew Nkoana, a national executive member who was released early as a result of his fine being paid.[47] Nkoana left prison with 'instructions to crush moves to unity'. Immediately he took the leadership out of the hands of Molete who, as he put it, was 'suffering from indecision' and rejected an initiative from Mandela to participate in the organisation of the anti-republic protest:

> I met Mandela at that time, he invited me to his house ... in connection with these plans for the stay-at-home, but when we parted he was in no doubt as to where he stood, we didn't (indistinct) pre-1960 tactic of demonstration - if there had to be any action it had to take off from 1961 and not pre-1960 and a three day demonstration was really going back to pre-1960.[48]

Accordingly Nkoana devoted his energies to the production of a somewhat cerebral broadsheet, Mafube, which inter alia, outlined the reasons for opposing the strike. Bundles of them were despatched to surviving PAC officials in different centres.[49] In the case of the Cape Town branches it seems they were ignored: in the Duncan papers there is a statement signed by a Langa PAC member which condemns the opposition to the stay-at-home and accuses the (coloured) Non European Unity Movement of distributing anti-strike leaflets in the PAC's name.[50] This may have been a reflection of the local rift which had at this stage developed: apparently in May 1961 an anonymous PAC official from Johannesburg visited Cape Town in an unsuccessful effort to unite the two factions.[51]

By July 1961 Nkoana's pamphleteering had come to the attention of the authorities and both he and Molete were arrested and subsequently accused of PAC activities. Both forfeited their bail (pending appeal against their sentences) and left the country in early 1962, Nkoana for Bechuanaland[52] and Molete joining the growing nucleus of PAC fugitives concentrated in Maseru. Before Nkoana's trial he visited Port Elizabeth and was most alarmed by what he witnessed there:

> I went to a meeting in the Eastern Cape where I felt those fellows ... we had great difficulty in containing our followers. I was taken to address a public meeting - of a banned organisation: a public meeting! Hidden in the bushes. As we go there we had to be guided by scouts at regular intervals along the way, and then I addressed a public meeting. That's when I came back feeling that the PAC were going to be unable to control our chaps. Those were the rudiments of Poqo.[53]

At some point between this visit in mid 1961 and early 1962 the PAC's leadership committed themselves to an insurrectionist strategy. In March 1962 a PAC leader for Johannesburg spoke to a meeting of the 'Task Force' in New Brighton chiding them for their lack of effort in recruitment and comparing them unfavourably with groups in Cape Town and East London who were 'ready for the fight' and who were just waiting 'until the day Sobukwe is out of jail'.[54] No information is available on how and when this decision was made but it is unlikely that it involved much heartsearching: the PAC's previous strategy had been geared to an apocalyptic concept and Nkoana's concern had arisen from a concern for caution and discipline rather than any moral reservations about violence. What seems most likely is that the violent impulses which were beginning to be discernible in the Cape in early 1961 encouraged if not prompted the leaders to plan a general uprising.[55]

By late 1962 the headquarters of the movement had been transferred from its rather precarious situation on the Witwatersrand to Maseru. Potlake Leballo had arrived in August[56] and armed with the authority of a letter from Robert Sobukwe established a 'Presidential Council' with himself as Acting Chairman.[57] From this point preparations for a popular insurrection began in earnest. But before examining these let us first look at the nature and the scope of the PAC's organisation and support that had developed by the beginning of 1963.

There are two main sources of information on the size and location of the PAC's organisation. These are firstly the often grandiose claims made by the PAC leaders themselves and secondly the evidence emerging from court cases. The former provide a rather exaggerated impression of PAC strength while in the case of the latter the evidence is incomplete. Despite the unsatisfactory quality of the evidence it is possible to reconstruct from it a picture of the surprisingly extensive network of PAC supporters.

PAC spokesmen in their claims about their organisation tended to depict it in terms of a formal bureaucratic hierarchy with clear lines of communication and control linking leaders with followers. In November 1962 Potlake Leballo stated in an interview that the PAC had sixteen regions, each with its own regional executive controlling a number of branches, themselves divided into cells. These regions embraced most of the country including the reserves.[58] Patrick Duncan, echoing Leballo in an article in the London Times, wrote of 150 'cells' with it being 'not uncommon' for a cell to have 1,000 members.[59] A London newsletter carried a report of twelve 1,000-strong cells in the Western Cape.[60] These figures are likely to have been inflated. In December 1959 before its banning the PAC claimed a total affiliation of 150 branches with 31,035 members.[61] Even this figure was a remarkably rapid expansion, bearing in mind the statistics given one month previously for 101 branches and 24,664 members distributed in the following fashion:

Transvaal	-	47 branches	-	13,324 members
Cape	-	34 branches	-	7,427 members
Natal	-	15 branches	-	3,612 members[62]
Orange Free State	-	5 branches	-	301 members

Even this quite modest claim should be treated with scepticism: according to the available evidence it is unlikely that membership in the Western Cape exceeded 1,000, and this seemed to be where the organisation was strongest.[63] A claim by Robert Sobukwe that at the time of the launching of the Pass Campaign PAC membership totalled 200,000[64] should not be taken seriously. If before the banning of the organisation the PAC leadership presented inaccurate information on the size of their following then their membership claims produced after April 1960 were likely to have been no more reliable. Numerical calculations of membership, though, are misleading indications of a movement's capacity to mobilise large numbers of people. As in the case of the 1960 Cape Town disturbances, relatively small numbers of activists could function as catalysts for large scale unrest in a volatile social context. More important are the questions of where the organisation's members were situated, what sort of people they were, and what kind of social environment they lived in.

It is possible to document the existence of sixty-eight Poqo groups as functioning in the April 1961 to April 1963 period (the two dates representing the period between the PAC's banning and the time of the projected uprising). These can be grouped in the following regional concentrations:

Transvaal	22
Western Cape	16
Eastern Cape	11
Transkei	14
Natal	4
Orange Free State	2

The table at the end of this paper provides a summary of the evidence upon which this data is based. Let us look at each regional concentration in turn, beginning with the Transvaal.

The twenty-two Transvaal branches listed in the table represent those on which information is available, either from first hand testimony of former activists from the Transvaal organisation, or from the records of the trials of those groups arrested by the police. Obviously the data is incomplete but because of the inadequacy of the leadership's security precautions (see below) it is unlikely that many other active groups existed. The major areas of PAC activity in this period were first in Pretoria and then in the townships of the West Rand and the Southern Transvaal. Reflecting a previous pattern these were areas where the ANC had been relatively weak or inactive. The reasons for the PAC's success in expanding its following in Pretoria is the topic of another paper.[65] Here our concern will be limited to forming generalisations about the movement's social character and quality of organisation. From the often sparse details provided by trial reports and newspaper reports it seems that the Transvaal membership was generally youthful - the vast majority being in their teens or early twenties - and if they were not still attending school were usually employed in white-collar occupations. A few examples will have to suffice. The eight men convicted of a PAC conspiracy in Daveyton included a clerical worker, a laboratory assistant, a caterer, an insurrance salesman and a schoolboy. Their ages ranged from seventeen to twenty-three years. In Pretoria at least two groups consisted entirely or mainly of school children. This was the case in Atteridgeville Township, where a PAC cell led by two teachers existed at Hofmeyr High School[66] as well as at Kilnerton High School.[67] There was also a PAC cell (or branch?) at the Hebron African Teacher Training College.[68] Four men imprisoned for their activities as part of a PAC conspiracy in Orlando, Soweto, included an unemployed clerk, an unemployed school leaver and an employee of the Municipal Pass Office. All four were aged twenty or twenty-one.[69] In Dobsonville, Roodepoort, the twenty- nine year old editor of a religious newspaper was alleged to be chairman of the local PAC branch.[70] The chairman of the PAC's Vaal region was David Sibeko, a young sports journalist.[71] Even from this very impressionistic picture there are obvious contrasts with the movement developing in Langa described earlier in the chapter. Noticeable by their absence from the list of identifiable Transvaal PAC members are industrial or service workers and hostel dwellers. Here the PAC was a movement of the young, the urbanised and the lower middle class and when educational details are available they suggest that most members had had at least a few years of primary education and that many had attended or were attending high school. The last point is worth drawing attention to in a context in which African secondary school enrolment in 1960 represented less than 4 per cent of total African school enrolment.[72] The importance of schoolchildren as an element in the PAC's following was often attested to by PAC leaders in the early 1960s.[73]

What evidence exists in the form of trials does not suggest an extensive PAC folowing in the 1960-1963 period in Natal. Efforts were made to rebuild the organisation after its banning in the Durban area in January 1961 and there were attempts to proselytise and recruit in Pietermaritzburg, Howick and Chesterville. According to an interview with Jordan Ngubane there was a PAC 'Task Force' at the Ohlanga Institute.[74] In 1963 it received instructions to set fire to surrounding cane fields as its contribution to the uprising. From the limited information available to attempt even tentative generalisations would not be justifiable. The same is also the case with the Orange Free State, where only two branches can be identified as existing before April 1960, in Welkom and Bethlehem.[75] The goldmining town of Welkom continued to be a centre of PAC activity with at least three groups being active after the banning of the organisation.[76]

The Cape Province and the Transkei contained the main centres of PAC activity. In the case of the Eastern Cape, evidence from the 1960-1963 period suggests that there were PAC branches in the two main towns, East London and Port Elizabeth, in educational institutions (Bensonvale,[77] Lovedale College[78] and Fort Hare University College[79]), and in several of the smaller towns as well: De Aar,[80] Grahamstown,[81] Herschel,[82] King William's Town,[83] Molteno,[84] Queenstown,[85] and Steynsburg.[86] With the exception of King William's Town there is very little information available on the 1963 Poqo groups in the smaller towns, though after 1963 teachers played a key role in Poqo conspiracies in those centres as well as in Middleburg[87] and may have done so earlier. Bearing in mind the concentration of important African educational institutions in the Eastern Cape and the evidence of political activity within them it is a reasonable hypothesis that some of their graduates may have functioned as political catalysts in nearby communities. In King William's Town, for instance, one of the members of the local Poqo groups had recently been expelled from Lovedale.[88] In King William's Town thirty-three men were accused in 1963 of taking part in a Poqo insurrection. They were led by three factory workers, local men who had grown up in the town's locations of Zwelitsha and Tshatshe. With the exception of seven men most of the accused were under twenty-five years of age and the oldest was only fifty.[89] A similar picture emerges from a trial concerning four men from New Brighton, Port Elizabeth: they and the various other people cited in the trial as Poqo activists were young, with at most a few years of primary education, born in the locality, and if not at school employed in unskilled capacities in various factories: a steelworks and a car spring factory are specifically referred to in the record.[90] For the Eastern Province there is most evidence of PAC activity in East London. One of the original nuclei of Africanists was in East London and the local PAC branch had been active in the 1960 pass campaign. One of the leading Pan-Africanists in the town, C J Fazzie, had been involved in Youth League politics in the 1940s. Sentenced for incitement in 1960 he was subsequently placed under house arrest though he was still understood to be active politically by the Rand based leadership.[91] During this time he was employed as a timekeeper at a local textile mill.[92] Four trials testify to a relatively high level of PAC activity in East London's Duncan Village in the period 1962-1963: once again the accused and their identified accomplices were predominantly young men or youths, power station, timber yard and car assembly workers as well as schoolboys, though one of the more important men in the local organisation, C V Mngaza was a garage proprietor in Duncan Village.[93] As with the other Eastern Provinces centres the available evidence suggests that PAC activists were people from an urban background and origin.

This last point is in contrast to the predominant social character of Poqo's following in the Western Cape which was, as we have seen, composed principally of the inmates of migrant workers' hostels, employer's compounds, as well as farm labourers. Poqo influence among Western Cape migrant workers was important in generating support for the movement in the Transkei, where many of the migrants had their homes. Significantly one finds no comparable degree of Poqo support in the Ciskeian reserves which form the immediate hinterland of East London and King William's Town.[94] In the Transkei itself out of the fourteen districts which comprise the southern half of the the territory (including Glen Grey - until 1975 part of the Ciskei though adjacent to the Transkei) nine were affected by Poqo activity. Trial evidence of Poqo cells exists in the case of Kentani, Willowvale, Mquanduli, Idutywa, Ngqeleni, Umtata, Engcobo, St. Marks and Glen Grey districts.[95] Ten out of the twenty Transkei trials mentioned in 1963 press reports involved twenty or more men who themselves only represented a proportion of those said to be implicated in conspiracies. Apart from those conspiracies which involved Cape Town migrant workers who set out from Cape Town to the Transkei to murder Chief Kaiser Matanzima the most common occupation mentioned in records and reports is 'peasant' but it is also evident that Poqo membership embraced quite a wide social spectrum: unemployed high school children, teachers, a Methodist lay preacher, a shoemaker and even a senior Tembu Chief were amongst those convicted for Poqo activity. This is not surprising: that there were several hundred people involved in some of the Poqo related incidents[96] suggests that in some rural locations the movement represented or was at least part of a fairly generalised revolt with a much wider social constituency than was the case in the Eastern Cape towns (predominantly school children and young unskilled labourers) and the Transvaal (school children and young clerical workers).

Just as the social character of the movement varied from region to region so too did the nature of its organisation. In the Transvaal it seems likely there was quite an elaborate hierarchical organisational structure whilst elsewhere organisational patterns were looser and more spontaneous in their evolution. The Transvaal arrangements came closest to the bureaucratic pattern depicted by Leballo. Here by 1963 there existed two functioning regions, the Witwatersrand (including Pretoria) and the Southern Transvaal (Vereeniging, Vanderbijlpark, etc.).[97]

There was some attempt within township based branches to divide up the membership into ten to fifteen man 'cells'.[98] These would sometimes be based on a particular institution (e.g. a school) or locality within the township. In fact 'cells' often met together in large meetings to be addressed by branch and more senior members.[99] Within each branch a 'task force' would be constituted from the younger men in the organisation. The 'task force' members would do guard duty at meetings, collect and manufacture weapons and explosives and in the event of the uprising undertake the initial attacks. Each branch would have a chairman and subordinate to him, a task force leader. There would also be 'block stewards' with recruiting functions within a certain area.[100] A block corresponded to a cell. To communicate with the Maseru leadership a clumsy code was used in which PAC branches and their activity would be described with reference to forms of popular entertainment. Branches were football teams, cinemas or dance-halls and their offices and functions would be described accordingly. The police were the 'forces of darkness' or 'skins'. The uprising itself was called 'the twist session ' or 'the jive session'.[101]

Notwithstanding its subjection to the supervision of the national leadership and despite the efforts at secrecy it seems that the organisation in the Transvaal was weak and demoralised. An insight into the general state of the Witwatersrand is given in a letter dated 30th March, 1963 to the Maseru leadership from the Witwatersrand 'Football Club Manager' (Regional Chairman?) which was intercepted by the police.[102] The letter provides a telling impression of an organisation preoccupied with personal feuds and internal suspicions, these exacerbated by the arrests of branch organisers whom the police had been able to trace through the Maseru's leadership's habit of using the post office as its main vehicle of communication:

> There has been gross negligence with most of our players here instead of them leaving addresses with other people when they were at HQ they only supplied pseudonyms with their proper addresses leaving themselves open to such dangers. They talk too much. They are emotional and not very revolutionary in their behaviour.
>
> We have withdrawn recognition of the Jabulani team. It was formed by people from Zola who did not want to respect their local leaders. Even most of the members of the team are from Zola and were being told a pack of lies into losing confidence and faith in their local management by people who do not want to be led by others. ... These people in order to destroy me dubbed me as an informer, exploiting the sensitivities of players towards skins. It is quite clear from reports I have been getting of the local intelligence that even the men I appointed as my captains believe these things. (The West Rand) ... are comparatively doing better than the central complex. They shouldn't at all be drawn into this seething cauldron of hatred and personal clashes which seems to be our disease.

Trial evidence suggests that the Witwatersrand officials accepted the uprising plans only reluctantly[103] and this is corroborated by the circulars sent to the Transvaal by Leballo in February and March reprimanding branches for the failure to prepare for the uprising.

> I must warn you very strongly that I shall not be intimidated by your failure to obtain these arrangements. The Twist MUST just go on whether you have these things or not. It is not my own fault. You are to blame for that. I am going ahead with my plans for the Twist or the Tournament. What I do not like of you is not to tell me the truth. You talk too much but you cannot live up to your claims!!! You don't do hard work sufficiently.[104]

The Eastern Cape more or less conformed to the Transvaal pattern of organisation and there were also signs of low morale in some of the branches. In New Brighton, Port Elizabeth, for instance, recalcitrant recruits (including a Task Force captain) were regularly punished with beatings for poor attendance at branch meetings.[105] As in the case of Johannesburg groups the New Brighton Task Force was reprimanded for being behind-hand in their organisation.[106] During 1961, incidentally, New Brighton's PAC members were under the leadership of Pearce Gqobose, the Eastern Cape regional chairman. Gqobose, an ex-serviceman and social worker, had been involved in Africanist politics since 1946. He fled the country in 1962 to avoid arrest and joined Leballo's 'Presidential Council' in Maseru.

In the case of the Western Cape and the Transkeian groups there is less evidence to suggest a formal defined hierarchy of leadership and the structure of the organisation was influenced by pre-existing social networks provided by 'home-boy' groups, burial associations and rurally oriented resistance movements formed in the wake of the implementation of the Bantu Authorities Act independently of the nationalist political organisations. These included the Dyakobs,[107] the Jacobins,[108] and the Makuluspan.[109] Such bodies served to transmit information and ideas between the Western Cape and the Transkei. It seems likey that in the Transkei itself the Poqo groups were started by migrant workers from Cape Town.[110] The more autonomous character of the movement[111] in these areas tended to protect it from police interference: a great deal of police information resulted from the indiscretions of the Maseru leadership and its communication system. A final distinguishing feature of these Poqo groups was their resort to magical protective measures.[112] This last point testifies to the major contrast that can be drawn between the Transvaal/Eastern Cape groups and the Western Cape/Transkei groups. In the case of the former the movement was constructed around the organisational conceptions and strategic ideas of a small and socially removed group of leaders. At base level the Poqo groups had very little vitality of their own: their members' main activity was to attend meetings at which they were alternately harangued or exhorted to make themselves ready for the great day of the uprising. Little was said at such meetings which was directly relevant to their specific circumstances. The movement's constituency was predominantly youthful, often with a limited range of social experience. In the case of the latter the movement developed organisationally from the bottom up, adapting itself to the social institutions it found around it, generating its own ideas and fuelled to a much greater extent by locally relevant anxieties and preoccupations, particularly those emanating from the countryside.

To return to our narrative, by the last three months of 1962 preparations for a national insurrection had begun in earnest. Poqo task force members were instructed by their leaders to gather materials and manufacture weapons and task force leaders and branch chairmen were urged to step up recruitment.[113] A thousand recruits were needed for each 'hall' (cell or block). The weapons were very crude. Bombs were improvised from petrol-filled bottles and tennis balls filled with ball-bearings, permanganate of potash, glycerin and match heads.[114] Swords were fashioned from filed-down pieces of scrap metal. Recruitment methods were no more sophisticated. A group in Port Elizabeth were told:

> We must organise right through the towns and in the buses. When you sit in a bus, the man next to you, you must tell him about this organisation.[115]

Perhaps to compensate for the rudimentary quality of these preparations many task force members were encouraged to believe that on the great day help would come from outside: weapons had been promised by Russia, one of the New Brighton task force leaders claimed,[116] though more commonly it was asserted that the assistance would be African:

> The African States would assist us in the Revolution by coming in aeroplanes and various war vehicles.[117]
>
> The independent states are with us - they are going to help us. Ben Bella has promised assistance. They will come with aeroplanes.[118]
>
> We would be supplied with arms and ammunition from the African States from the North and we would also be assisted by their soldiers.[119]

The promise of external aid was a recurrent theme in Leballo's talks to the groups of branch leaders who were summoned to Maseru in February and March of 1963.[120] In November 1962 Leballo had left Basutoland for a few weeks to visit the United Nations offices, stopping off on his return home in Ghana and it is possible that some of the urgency of his subsequent communications to his followers was inspired by assurances of support from Ghanaian and other African government spokesmen.

Task force members all seem to have had a broadly similar conception of how the uprising would begin. In each centre different groups would be assigned to attacks on police stations, post offices, power installations and other government buildings. Groups should then turn their attention to the white civilian population which they were to kill indiscriminately. The killing should go on for four hours and should then cease, when the insurgents should await further instructions.[121] Most of the features of this plan were attributable to the instructions contained in Leballo's talks to branch leaders and they formed the basic elements in an insurrectionary concept shared by PAC conspiracies throughout the country.[122] Exactly when this uprising was to take place was not revealed to rank and file. It would be in 1963 for that was the original date set by Sobukwe for the attainment of South African 'independence', but as for the exact date this would be appointed by the leadership in the near future. In the Eastern Cape some branches were told that the date of the uprising would coincide with Sobukwe's release from prison so that he would once again be able to direct the struggle.[123] This reflected a more generalised attribution to Sobukwe of prophet-like qualities of leadership.[124] Only in April were task force members given a definite date and this merely a day or two before the chosen time.[125] Branches and regional leaders were sent letters at the end of March giving them instructions for an uprising in early April. The addressed letters were intercepted by the police when they arrested the courier sent from Maseru to post the letters in Bloemfontein.[126]

By the end of March the police had a fairly accurate idea of the nature and scope of these arrangements. In November Poqo insurgents acting on their own initiative had staged an attack on the small Western Province town of Paarl and the following month several groups travelled from Cape Town to the Transkei to assassinate Matanzima and were intercepted by the police. In March several branch leaders returning to the Cape and the Transvaal from Maseru were arrested and detained. On March 24th Leballo gave a press conference in which he announced the PAC's intention to mount a general uprising, claiming that over 100,000 armed followers were waiting for his signal.[127] Final instructions had to be given to twenty-three branch chairmen who were now on their way back to South Africa. In the last week of March South African police, aided by the list of addresses they were able to assemble from Leballo's correspondence, began to detain key local activists in the Transvaal. On April 1st the colonial authorities in Basutoland arrested those PAC leaders they could find in Maseru and closed down the PAC's office confiscating a quantity of documentation including membership lists allegedly containing 100,000 names and addresses.[128] Leballo prudently went into hiding. According to affidavits the Basutoland police raid was carried out in the presence of South African security policy and the colonial government was later accused of supplying the South Africans with information.[129] In the first week of April hundreds of arrests took place throughout South Africa. In May the Minister of Justice announced that 3,246 Poqo suspects had been arrested.[130] Despite the arrests Poqo groups mounted attacks in several centres in the Eastern Cape and the Transvaal.

In King William's Town at 2.30 on the morning of the 9th a group of fifteen men entered the courtyard of the office building which contained the police station and Commissioner's office. Their first objective was to free Poqo suspects held prisoner before launching a general insurrection. They were part of a group of sixty men armed with incendiary bombs, knives and clubs. These men threw their bombs through the charge office windows and advanced on the cell doors before being driven back by police gunfire. They thereupon dispersed and subsequently many were arrested and tried *en masse*. One of the accused, incidentally, was called Bomwana Biko.[131]

In East London the police successfully anticipated local PAC preparations. On the same night as the King William's Town attack two to three hundred men walking in groups of four to eight congregated in the open veld outside the old section of Duncan Village. Many carried homemade swords and axes in haversacks and bags. From the moment the men began assembling, at 6.30 on the evening of the 8th, they were being watched by police several of whom had arrived at the rendezvous before them. Apparently an informer had betrayed the Poqo men. At about 10 o'clock when the last men had arrived the police watchers sent for reinforcements but the advent of these was noticed by a task force patrol which fired on the police. After an exchange of shots the meeting broke up, eleven men being arrested immediately and over a hundred later. Subsequent trials confirmed that the men were about to launch an uprising in East London according to a pre-formulated plan. The police reinforcements interrupted them while they were waiting for petrol. Children evidently played an important role in the preparations, young teenage boys being given files, hacksaws and motor springs and told to fashion these into swords (the task of producing one blade took two days). Some of the youths were recruited by women. In both this trial and the King William's Town trial there was evidence that many of the young auxiliaries were reluctant conscripts rather than highly motivated volunteers.[132]

The following night three small groups of young men travelled from Orlando to Johannesburg. Two men from one of the groups broke into a clothing store while others stood guard and using petrol bombs set alight counters in the old section of the building. A similar attack was intended on a sportswear shop but the insurgents were interrupted by a police patrol after breaking a window. A third group marched to the premises of Shell (SA) Pty which accommodated some oil storage facilities. Finding the main gates locked and on encountering a night watchman the members of the task force decided to go home. These events were part of a larger conspiracy for which there is no evidence of any comparably serious attempts to implement objectives which included the destruction of Orlando police and power stations. The targets in the Johannesburg central business districts were well chosen. They were old or by their nature highly inflammable and they were situated in an architecturally congested part of town where the likelihood of a well established fire spreading was high. These arson attempts in Johannesburg were the climax of several days of hurried preparation including several meetings being held in the week before the attack at which fresh recruits were inducted (some of whom participated in the Johannesburg task force) and an all day bomb making session on the 8th. Task forces were informed of their targets only immediately before setting out to attack them. There is evidence to suggest several other Poqo conspiracies in Soweto, and it should be remembered that many of the Rand PAC groups had already been arrested. The last minute character of the preparations, however, and the fact that the events took place one day later than in the Eastern Cape, and the manner in which the attacks were implemented, helps to strengthen the impression that many of the Rand insurrectionists were less than totally committed to the conspiracy.[133]

This view is corroborated by details from the trial of David Sibeko, the Chairman of the Southern Transvaal region. Though the evidence of state witnesses was discounted in court and Sibeko was acquitted, in exile he subsequently confirmed in broad outline the truth of the prosecution's case.[134] One witness claimed that he was nominated at a meeting in the Vereeniging area to travel to Maseru. In Maseru he was given instructions concerning the uprising. On returning to Vereeniging he was told that the date of the uprising was arranged for April 7th. On April 1st he was told to collect some bombs from a woman in Pretoria. These were going to be used in an attack on Vanderbijlpark police station and the Escom power installation. He allegedly failed to find the woman and returned empty handed. The bombs were collected on the 7th by Gabriel Sandamela, one of the members of the regional executive. The witness was informed by Sibeko on the 7th that the uprising had been postponed for a day because of the police being aware of the conspiracy. However, when he next saw Sibeko and Sandamela they were busy preparing to travel to Dar es Salaam via Bechuanaland. There was no uprising in Vereeniging.[135]

Elsewhere the story was much the same: large numbers of arrests frustrated some local conspiracies and demoralised others. The Maseru leadership was either in hiding or in prison. Robert Sobukwe, probably ignorant of the uprising plan, on completing his prison sentence was detained on Robben Island for a further six years. In June the Minister of Justice claimed that the Poqo movement had been destroyed. By June the following year 1,162 Poqo members had been convicted under the Sabotage Act.[137]

Notwithstanding the Minister's claim, Poqo groups continued to be active for some years to come, the last recorded incidence of a Poqo conspiracy being in Welkom in December 1968. There was no comparably ambitious effort by a central leadership to organise a national insurrection: Poqo activity after April 1963 was very localised in character. Until 1965 there was some effort by Maseru-based leaders to coordinate the activities of different PAC/Poqo branches. Despite a shift which developed in the course of 1964 in the external leaders' conception of strategy away from insurrectionism in favour of protracted guerilla warfare, surviving activists within the country continued to plot apocalyptic local uprisings. On the Witwatersrand, for example, a regional committee was formed towards the end of April 1963. It was led by two professional golfers and a boxing manager. It succeeded in re-establishing links with the Maseru group and conceived a plan to mount an uprising on December 16th, the Day of the Covenant. Whites attending nationalist festivities in Pretoria were to be attacked by bees. Unusually, for a Rand conspiracy, the participants intended to deploy witchcraft, though they also tried to obtain hand grenades from a man who worked at the Drill Hall in Johannesburg. The conspirators were encouraged by Edwin Makoti and Leballo (who reappeared in Maseru in September 1963) for the rising would coincide with the United Nations session at which they hoped to mobilise international support. Makoti visited Johannesburg in October to make arrangements for the the passage out of the country of recruits for guerrilla training but was informed by the committee that they had failed to find people willing to leave the country. Lack of transport facilities and a failing confidence in the powers of witchcraft persuaded the conspirators to abandon their plans.[138] Meanwhile in May 1963 a group in Lady Frere (Glen Grey district) plotted attacks on the magistrate's home and the police station followed by more generalised arson and killing.[139] Elsewhere remaining PAC groups in Cape Town, Durban and East London contented themselves with recruiting and sending men abroad for military instruction.[140]

The next phase of internal activity followed the conception of a plan in July 1964 by the Presidential Council for a Lesotho-based guerilla operation. The plan seemed to have two separate sources of inspiration. While, in conformity with previous PAC strategic thinking it argued that:

> Insurrection or even minor skirmishes of an effective nature, well planned, are sufficient to set in motion a full scale revolution any time in South Africa.

it went on to state:

> Our struggle is bound to be a protracted one. We must not reckon in terms of lightning warfare and an immediate victory. Apart from the unpredictable nature of warfare itself, the enemy is fully aware of our intentions and has been preparing himself accordingly for a number of years. Ours is a guerilla form of warfare against regular army forces. Our indispensable condition in these circumstances is to wear down the enemy systematically, hitting him hardest where he is weakest and then retreating where he is strongest.[141]

The document comprised mainly of detailed plans for launching a guerilla insurgency: it discussed escape routes, training programmes, the use of explosives, logistics, lines of communication, and the role of external diplomatic representatives of the movement. Initial operations would have two dimensions. Careful clandestine activity would complete the groundwork for a long-term rural guerilla insurgency. An operational base was to be established in Qacha's Nek, a village on the Lesotho border with the Transkei. A boat purchased in London would offload arms on to the Transkeian coast.[142] PAC trainees would form a nucleus of a locally recruited insurgent force. While these preparations were in progress,[143] support for the movement would be generated by a campaign of terrorism which would include assassinations of important white politicians, kidnapping of school children, the destruction of symbolically important buildings, as well as the seizure of gold bullion, money, arms and ammunition.

It is difficult to ascertain how seriously the Maseru group regarded this plan. Later it was suggested that the main purpose of the document outlining it was to persuade the Organisation of African Unity's African Liberation Committee to allocate funds to the PAC. The equivalent of R100,000 was handed over by the ALC to Potlake Leballo in late 1964 and subsequently Leballo was charged with fraud when he could not account for a large proportion of this sum's expenditure.[144] Despite this possible motive it seems that various efforts were made to implement parts of the plan. A Transkeian based Poqo cell active in the Mqanduli district was instructed to locate hiding places for arms and insurgents.[145] In September 1964 activists from East London were taken to various houses in the Quthing area and shown how to make firearms.[146] Two members of the Presidential Council, Letlaka and Mfaxa, were later found in a Maseru trial to have administered a guerilla training camp near Quthing. Lectures, physical training and weapons construction were part of the curriculum.[147] Cape Town based Poqo groups were delegated the tasks of reconnoitering the Hex River railway tunnel with a view to derailing the 'Blue Train' Johannesburg to Cape Town express and searching for guerilla hiding places in Namaqualand and the mountainous area near Paarl.[148] It seems that since 1963 a new regional organisation had been established in Cape Town under much closer control of the Maseru leadership than the previous Poqo network.[149] In the Eastern Cape rural centre of Molteno a PAC branch was revived in April 1964 by a local school teacher, Harry Mathebe, after he had attended a meeting with a member of the Presidential Council in Herschel. In the course of 1964 Mathebe succeeded in recruiting thirty. The branch held its first meeting in December 1964 at which plans for a local uprising were discussed. Before these were to be implemented it was resolved that a trip should be made to Johannesburg to buy guns. Conspirators were allegedly told that after the uprising they would be able to 'stay in the white houses'.[150] Most of the new branch's members were arrested in February. A group with similar intentions was discovered in Steynsburg. Once again it was led by a school teacher. His fifty-odd followers included a shop assistant and a shoemaker but mainly comprised illiterate unskilled labourers.[151]

On 29th April, 1965 the Maseru based members of the Presidential Council were taken into custody by the Basutoland authorities and shortly afterwards put on trial (Potlake Leballo was not amongst these, he had left Maseru in August the previous year and was not in Dar es Salaam). The Maseru group was acquitted on appeal (it was found its members had committed no crimes in Basutoland). Some of them subsequently joined the other PAC principals in Dar es Salaam, others fell victim to the leadership feuds which plagued the movement and were expelled by Leballo, and one, John Pokela, acting national secretary, was captured (allegedly kidnapped in Buthe Buthe, Basuto) in August 1966 by the South African authorities and convicted.[152]

From 1965 remaining PAC groups inside the country functioned independently: there were no longer any lines of communication with any leadership centre outside the country. Their activity conformed to the established insurrectionary pattern: groups in Laingsburg,[153] Graaff Reinet,[154] Victoria West,[155] Middleburg,[156] Steynsburg[157] in the Cape and Umzinto[158] and Esperenza[159] in Natal were discovered in the course of their preparations for local uprisings. In addition insurrectionary PAC cells were formed among convicts by previous Robben Island inmates of Gamkaspoort,[160] Baviaanspoort,[161] Bellville[162] and Leeukop[163] prisons. With the exception of the convicts about whom no sociological detail is available from the trial evidence, most of the other conspiracies apart from their common strategic intention had a strikingly similar social composition: leaders were usually teachers or clergymen and their following normally consisted of unskilled labourers. A few examples must suffice. In 1964 Jonathan Hermanus arrived in Graaff Reinet location as Methodist Minister. Initially he was active in efforts to improve the prevalently poor local conditions in the location. To this end he formed a Wesleyan Guild for church youth. In early 1966 increasingly disenchanted with social work he began to recruit people for a Poqo branch. He was transferred in 1967 and the movement died out.[164] As well as Hermanus, church elders and a school teacher were later tried for leading roles in a violent conspiracy.[165] In Victoria West a minister, a school principal and various service workers - garage attendants, milkmen, shop assistants, messengers and hospital labourers - were involved in plans to obtain weapons to attack police stations, cut telephone wires and poison water supplies. According to one state witness, it was said at one of the meetings:

> When the whites come to Victoria West, they soon had a house and a new car. They enjoyed better wages and privileges and that was why whites had to be killed. In this way the fatherland could be regained for the non-whites.[166]

Three of the conspiracies were composed of farmworkers, those in Natal and at Laingsburg. The Natal conspiracies were located on sugar estates and were led by a PAC activist from Durban. The Laingsburg movement was led by a lay-preacher, R Ndoylo. He appeared at a Saturday bible meeting attended by the workers from one farm and chose as his text a passage from Lamentations: 'Our skin was black like an oven because of the terrible famine'. He went on to 'explain to us that it was difficult to get food and water and that our land was being taken away from us. At Vleiland (the farm) we got very little money. We were paid 70 cents a week and that was very little ... He said according to Poqo they should be paid 70 cents a day'. Ndoylo later told his followers that after the arrival of weapons from the Congo they would participate in an 'uprising which would take place simultaneously all over the country on an appointed day. Ndoylo would tell the people at Vleiland when that day was'.[167]

In Welkom a departure from this pattern occurred in 1968 when J Ramoshaba, a former student of Fort Hare, a social worker employed on the goldfields, and a member of the Thabang Township Urban Bantu Council, presided over a revival of the local PAC branch. He and his confederates attempted to raise funds to send people abroad for military training. With their arrest PAC activity inside South Africa was to cease until the mid 1970s.

In an analysis of the Poqo movement some useful starting points can be drawn from the literature on general theories of collective action. Existing treatments of South African insurgent movements have on the whole been influenced by the social theory emerging from the United States in the 1960s. Edward Feit and Fatima Meer both seem to share the premise that 'order is the normal state of things and that disorder is very difficult to sustain'.[168] As Meer puts it: 'Revolution, though dependent on the populace, is not a popular cause. The security of a familiar system, even if limiting, is invariably preferable to the risks of change'.[169] In such a context collective violence is viewed as pathological and hence irrational:

> The picture of a mass ready for the final plunge to liberate itself is deceptive. It is observed by abstracting the motifs of rebellion scattered through a tapestry, which otherwise speaks of reasonable peace and quite. While spontaneous uprisings are clear indications of deep sores, they are certainly no indication of people's intelligent, rational and conscious awareness of these sores. They are rather symptoms of mass psychosis, and like the psychotic who is unable to see the root of his passion beyond the immediate trifle which provoked it, so too, is the vision of the mass shallow and blurred.[170]

The instigators of revolt are motivated not so much by the material grievances of the poor but the 'status incongruity' of a middle class minority.[171]

Meer and Feit's work testifies to the influence of the view which understands violence as a consequence of social breakdown. A period of rapid social change is seen to erode customary social restraints while simultaneously the material effects of change introduce into people's lives insecurity and tension. Mass protests occur with the changing political expectations resulting from economic progress. On their fringes minorities drawn form the marginal elements of society, those most psychologically and materially disoriented by the changes attendant upon industrialisation and urbanisation, express their anxieties and emotions through violence.[172] Writers in this school discern a statistical coincidence in the incidence of crime, individual violence and collective violence[173] and the latter is consequently analysed as simply another example of socially deviant behaviour. Breakdown theory has influenced the South African government's perception of civil disorder as well as that of its liberal opponents: the former is concerned to deny the possibility of violence being an expression of reasonable social and political aspirations among Africans,[174] the latter are concerned to ameliorate the social conditions which they understand to give rise to unbalanced behaviour.[175]

Another broad category in the analysis of violence drawing its insights from empirical historiography rather than social psychology perceives collective violence not as the result of social breakdown, normlessness and anomie, but rather as the expression of the conflicting interests of coherent social groups as they struggle for ascendency. George Rude's work on the French revolutionary crowd[176] and his and E J Hobsbawm's analysis of the 1830 'Captain Swing' riots in rural England are two of the best known studies in this category.[177] In their work and that of their disciples collective violence finds its constituency among social groups whose existence is tightly woven into the fabric of their community. The targets of their actions are systematically selected for their symbolic or actual function. In its outbursts the behaviour of the crowd reflects a distillation of the political and material grievances of broad swathes of society. Its violence is symptomatic of the inherent contradictions of any society characterised by profound inequalities of wealth and power.

A useful refinement of these ideas is provided by the Tillys' study of a century of collective violence in France, Italy and Germany.[178] They find the explanation for specifically violent forms of collective behaviour not so much in social change itself but rather in the impact of such phenomena as the expansion of the capacity of national states and national markets on popular conceptions of justice.[179] In their survey of riots and civil disorder in their three chosen countries they discern a shift between three different phases and types of collective action. In the first phase, competitive collective action, group violence normally takes place as a result of intra or intercommunal competition over resources. Feuds, village rivalries and ritual encounters between competing groups of artisans are expressions of competitive collective action. In a South African context faction fighting or the activities of the Amalaitas[180] at a certain phase in their development could be understood in this context. Competitive violence predominates on the fringes of the national state or economy.

When these latter start infringing on local rights and resources a second generation of popular violence manifests itself. This the Tillys term reactive violence, essentially acts of resistance to attempts from the centre to control the periphery. Tax rebellions, food riots, Luddism, and the evasion of enclosed land are examples of reactive violence. With the triumph of the state and the national market a third set of struggles ensues as groups make claims for rights and resources not previously enjoyed. Here collective action is geared to attempts 'to control rather than resist different segments of the national structure'.[181] The insurrectionary strike would be an example of what the Tillys call 'proactive' collective violence.

Ostensibly social breakdown analysis would seem easier to apply to the Poqo disturbances. The movement was drawn from groups which were peripheral rather than central to the development of a modern industrial economy, or from people who had not been totally socially encapsulated by that process. The roles of unskilled migrant labourers, farmworkers (in an increasingly capital intensive agriculture), service workers in small rural towns, and even school children can be conceptualised thus. The conjunction in the movement's constituency between groups threatened with or actually undergoing a process of marginalisation and such middle class elements as teachers, clerics and office workers might be explained with reference to both the morally disorienting effects of rapid social change for the former and a crisis of rising expectations for the latter. The inclusion of magic and witchcraft in Poqo/PAC tactics, the impracticality of its insurrectionary concept, the millenarian undertones of the movement - its belief in an apocalyptic 'great day', its investiture of Sobukwe with biblical attributes of leadership, its strategic dependence on external intervention[182] - all these features could be employed to explain the movement's emergence and following in terms of the transient social dislocations introduced as a by-product of modernisation. In such a scheme the 'irrationality' of the movement would reflect the hysteria of victims of social progress.

There are problems, though, with such an analysis. Examining the movement in its different contexts its appeal at times is far more general than such an argument might suggest. In Lady Frere, for example, in 1963, a Poqo conspiracy involved a major proportion of the adult African men in the location.[183] The superimposition of Poqo on earlier resistance organisations in the migrant society of the Western Cape and the peasant communities of the Transkei and its drawing upon well established networks and local ideology again does not suggest a movement based upon morally disoriented people in a situation of anomie. The violent Poqo conspiracies took place in a context of much wider incidence of collective violence than is obvious from the academic treatments of South African insurgencies cited above. To take one example: in the time when Poqo cells were being established among school children (and in some cases their teachers) African rural schools were periodically shaken by waves of pupil violence. In 1963, for instance, in three months there were reports of rioting, arson, strikes and mass walkouts or suspensions at five leading educational institutions in the Eastern Cape and the Transkei: Lovedale,[184] the Faku Institute, Flagstaff,[185] Bethal College, Butterworth,[186] Sigcau High School, Flagstaff[187] and Healdtown.[188] Once again, this does not suggest, at least in its local context, that Poqo's violence was that of the socially deviant.

A more helpful approach may be found in the second group of writers referred to above and in particular from the conceptions derived from the Tillys' work. Poqo's social complexity does not permit easy causal generalisations; its regional variation in both constituency and organisation embraced very different political responses which were different at least partly because they were responses to different things. The political preoccupations of migrant workers in Cape Town were to an extent shaped by events in the Transkei; despite their involvement in the urban economy they still had residual links with rural culture. In the Transkei itself peasants (who themselves often had experience of migrant labour) were engaged in defending their rights over land and their notions of land husbandry against intensifying efforts by the state to control and modify these. In such a context Poqo drew its strength largely from what the Tillys would call reactive and competitive movements though its initial inspiration was proactive as would be the case with any nationalist organisation.[189] Elsewhere I have attempted to reconstruct the movement's following in the local contexts of the Transkei and Paarl. Here the actions of its participants were influenced by a communal matrix of struggle and within the limits of the knowledge available to them their behaviour was rational enough: it can be explained without recourse to notions of mass psychosis.

But this is not the whole story. The involvement of Transvaal groups in the Poqo conspiracy did not stem from reactive concerns nor did it seem to represent such a popular constituency: here the movement's following was much more narrowly socially defined. The same too could be said for the Eastern Cape groups: unlike the Transvaal organisation they included industrial workers but these were commonly very youthful. At this point the existence of another violent insurgent movement needs to be born in mind, Umkhonto we Sizwe, which was most active in the two main Eastern Province towns, in Durban and in Johannesburg and Pretoria. Umkhonto was a much smaller organisation than Poqo, technologically more sophisticated in its methods, tactically more effective, and its strategy reflected an intellectually more complex analysis of South African society. While Poqo in its areas of strength drew on locally evolved resistance movements Umkhonto benefited from the modern organisational framework created by a much more powerful nationalist organisation than the PAC as well an allied trade union movement. Though Umkhonto was in its conception and performance an insurgent elite nevertheless it was itself the product of a decade of mass-based proactive struggles. In two centres, Port Elizabeth and East London, there is evidence of a substantial support base for the Umkhonto insurgents. The local leaders here were men who had been at the forefront of communal political assertions since the 1940s.[190] In this context the nature of Poqo's constituency in such centres as Port Elizabeth, East London or even Pretoria becomes more understandable: it was composed of people who though affected by a communal history of revolt belonged to groups which were not easily incorporated into the increasingly proletarian following of the ANC, or who were too young to have been involved in the pre-1960 struggles. In the case of young school children a study made in 1963 may be of some relevance. From samples of future autobiographies written by African high school students in 1950 and 1960 it is possible to trace a declining interest in individual economic and social aspirations and a sharp increase in commitment to political activity.[191] A survey conducted among professional people, ministers, teachers, clerks and students and school children in the Transvaal showed the PAC to be the most popular group among the sample and support for the PAC tended to correlate with acceptance of violence.[192] Within the sample endorsement of violence or some type of force reflected the view of a large minority - forty-three per cent. As in the case of the Transkei and the Western Cape, the Poqo conspiracies in the Transvaal and the Eastern Cape should not be examined in isolation, for apart from the activities of other insurgent movements, there is evidence of quite widespread sentiments which while not providing proof of a popular willingness to participate in violent revolt does indicate that violent actions were widely seen as legitimate. This will become clearer in local case studies. The comparative weakness of the Transvaal/Eastern Cape impulse to violence in contrast to the behaviour of the Western Cape/Transkeian groups can be attributed to the predominant organisational features of each. In conformity with the Tillys' thesis, the former proactive movement depended on the mobilising capacity of a modern political association whilst the latter partly reactive movement drew to a much greater extent on communal bases for political action.[193] Earlier in this chapter the contrast was described as one between an organisational structure imposed from above and a movement which had developed organically from the bottom up. Given the state imposed barriers confronting black efforts to create large scale political associations it is not surprising that the 'organic' movement provided the strongest response.

A final comment on the role of teachers in Poqo will help to underscore the argument concerning the movement's communal legitimacy. As we have seen teachers figured prominently in Eastern Cape Poqo conspiracies as well as in the Transkei. In this region teachers had been uncharacteristically active in political organisations: an example of this can be found in the political history of the Cape African Teacher's Association as a constituent of the All African Convention.[194] With its radicalisation in the late 1940s CATA could provide an organisation based on the dense network of mission schools long established in the region. Teachers themselves had their security and status threatened by the Bantu Authorities and school boards systems and may also, suggests Colin Bundy, have been radicalised by the pupil disturbances in the region which accommodated some of the largest African schools and colleges in the country.[195] Teachers were especially influential in the countryside and small towns where illiteracy rates were high and other middle class elements often absent. Bearing in mind their poor pay and recent interference by the state in their profession it is not surprising to find radical rural opposition movements gravitating around them as leaders. In the Eastern Cape small town and rural communities were unusually subject to the influence of the political organisations. As well as the narodnik dimension of the AAC's activity, Fort Hare and other colleges served as local disseminators of political ideas. Interviewed in the late 1960s Tennyson Makiwane remembered:

> Then I got to Fort Hare where the Youth League was very well established. And there was the period when the Defiance Campaign was being launched and this attracted tremendous interest among the youth and we used to go to the neighbouring villages and organise people to the Defiance ... as far as King William's Town, Adelaide, Beaufort and Port Elizabeth. We used to go to them at night and sometimes over weekends to address meetings of villages.[196] ... In our area we touched most of the villages.

Also relevant in this context were the activities of the Herschel branch of the Congress Youth League in 1949. This branch ran an education class for twenty-five herdboys in Ndunga. It also had plans for adults and children's literacy classes in the Bluegums area and administered a cooperative saving society which had accumulated £60.[197] The presence of PAC branches at a significant number of Eastern Cape educational institutions a decade later may help to explain the part played by teachers in small town Eastern Cape Poqo groups.

The historiographical neglect of the PAC can be related to the issues discussed above. The influence of social breakdown theory directly or indirectly has affected much of the analysis of Black South African politics. Movements of what might be diagnosed as collective madness are not considered worthy of sustained analysis by writers concerned with what they see as the mainstream of Black political response. Even Gail Gerhart, a scholar who handles theoretical issues with extreme caution, explains Poqo's behaviour with reference to a Fanonist-need for catharsis,[198] rather than in terms of the specific situation of socially coherent groups. For a writer whose preoccupation is with the development of a natavistic black political tradition Gerhart shows a surprising lack of curiosity in one of the few popular expressions of her chosen theme. The lack of interest of Gerhart and other authorities in Poqo is mainly attributable, though, to their preference for writing about organisations rather than social movements,[199] particularly those organisations which produce an abundance of documentation. Much of the historical writing about African politics is therefore the history of leaders, not followers. Meticulous and scholarly as some of this work is it discusses at best superficially the greater social conflicts which underlie the biographical and organisational developments which form the main focus of study. In this survey it is hoped that the historical significance of the Poqo movement is made clear. It was a response to crisis of a varied but distinctive set of social groups. Its strategy and ideology only becomes comprehensible when these groups and the situation with which they have to contend are clearly identified.

TABLE: PAC/POQO GROUPS IN SOUTH AFRICA, 1960-1968

CAPE PROVINCE (EAST)

Dates	Location	Source
1963	ALIWAL NORTH	Black Star (London), May 1963, report on 130 arrests.
1963	BURGERSDORP	Star, 5 June 1963, report on unspecified trial of 7.
1964	CRADOCK	Eastern Province Herald, 11 December 1964, report on unspecified trial of 1.
1960-1965	EAST LONDON	Daily Dispatch, 28 October 1963 - 13 November 1963, reports on State vs. Lwana and 25; Daily Dispatch, 13 November 1963 - 19 November 1963, reports on State vs. Mgoqi and 9; Dispatch, 1 April 1965, report on State vs. Loliwe and 3; State vs. Mngaza, transcript, CSAS, University of York.
1960-1963	FORT HARE University	Author's interview with former branch chairman, Neshtedi Sidzamba.
1963-1966	GRAHAMSTOWN	Rand Daily Mail, 17 May 1963, report on unspecified trial of 4; Contact, July 1966, report on State vs. Pityana and 3.
1966	GRAAFF REINET	Eastern Province Herald, 2 December 1970, report on unspecified trial of 7.
1961-1962	HERSCHEL, Bensonvale School	Bloemfontein Friend, 30 July 1971, report on State vs. Lebese.
1963	HERSHEL	Black Star, May 1963, report on 57 arrests
1963	KING WILLIAMS TOWN	Daily Dispatch, 28 August 1963 - 31 August 1963, reports on State vs. Nyobo and 32.
1962-1963	LOVEDALE COLLEGE	State vs. Mtshizana, transcript, SAIRR; Interview with Sidzamba.
1963-1965	MOLTENO	PAC Newsletter (Maseru), Report on State vs. Mathebe and 13; Evening

		Post, 4 September 1965, report on State vs. Tyali and 29.
1966	MIDDELBURG	Evening Post, 24 June 1966, report on State vs. Silwana and 2.
1961-1963	PORT ELIZABETH, New Brighton	New Age, 3 August 1961, report on PAC activity; State vs. Neconga and 3, transcript, SAIRR; Cape Times, 19 June 1963, report on unspecified trial of 24.
1963	QUEENSTOWN	Contact, 27 November 1964, report on State vs. Gwabeni and 1.
1963-1966	STEYNSBURG	Rand Daily Mail, 14 June 1963, report on unspecified trial of 19; Evening Post, 16 February 1966, State vs. Mapete and 53; Evening Post, 23 June 1966, report on State vs. Silwana and 2.

CAPE PROVINCE (WEST)

Dates	Location	Source
1965	CAPE TOWN	Contact, May 1965, report on State vs. Mkhalipi and 3.
1962-1963	CAPE TOWN, Brooklands Chest Hospital	State vs. Budaza and 3, lawyer's notes, Sachs papers, AS/70, ICS, London University.
1962-1963	CAPE TOWN, Jewish Old Age Home	State vs. Mandla and 31, lawyer's notes, Sachs papers, AS/69, ICS, London University.
1962-1963	CAPE TOWN Helmsley Hotel	State vs. Mandla and 31, lawyer's notes.
1961-1965	CAPE TOWN, Langa	State vs. Mandla and 31, laywer's notes; State vs. Ngconcolo and 19, transcript, CSAS, York University; Cape Times, 26 May 1961, report on State vs. Qumbulu; Contact, December 1966, report on State vs. Mangqangwana and 1; Cape Argus, 17 January 1967, report on unspecified trial of 8; Cape Times, 23 August 1962, report on State vs. Galela; Cape Argus, 13 November 1967 and 23 November 1967, reports on State vs. Siyothula.

1961-1963	CAPE TOWN, Nyanga	<u>New Age</u>, 9 March 1961, report on arrests; <u>Contact</u>, 6 September 1963, report on State vs. Mcapazeli and 23; <u>Cape Times</u>, 23 September 1963.
1963	CAPE TOWN, Royal Dairy	State vs. Mandla and 31, lawyer's notes, Sachs papers.
1963	CAPE TOWN, Saint Columbus House	State vs. Mandla and 31, laywer's notes, Sachs papers.
1963	CAPE TOWN, Seapoint	<u>Daily Dispatch</u>, 20 August 1963, report on State vs. Matanga and 14.
1961	CAPE TOWN, Windermere	<u>Cape Times</u>, 8 February 1962, report on police interruption of PAC meeting.
1963	CAMPS BAY, Rotunda Hotel	State vs. E Dudumashe and 1, charge sheet, SAIRR.
1963	CAPE TOWN, Wynberg	<u>Rand Daily Mail</u>, 20 August 1963, report on State vs. Roto and Zekani.
1963	DE AAR	<u>Star</u>, 9 April 1963, report on arrests of five PAC recruiters.
1962-1963	EERSTE RIVER	<u>Contact</u>, December 1966, report on State Mangqangwana and 1.
1962-1963	ELGIN district, Molteno's farm	<u>Cape Argus</u>, 17 September 1963, report on State vs. Melwane and 22.
1966	LAINGSBURG	<u>Cape Times</u>, 9 June 1967, report on State vs. Ndoylo.
1962	PAARL, Mbwekeni location	State vs. Matikela, lawyer's notes, Sachs papers, AS/35, ICS, London; State vs. Makatezi and 20 others, transcript, SAIRR; Snyman Commission, transcript of evidence, CSAS, York University.
1961	SOMERSET WEST	State vs. Xintolo, laywer's notes, Sachs papers, AS 8/14, ICS, London University.
1961	STELLENBOSCH, farms	<u>Cape Times</u>, 28 June 1962, 5 July 1962, report on State vs. Cyrus Tolibode and 20.
1963	STELLENBOSCH, Kaya Mandi location	<u>Star</u>, 9 April 1963, report on arrest of 13.

1966-1967	VICTORIA WEST	Star, 4 September 1968, Daily Dispatch, 19 October 1968, Rand Daily Mail, 4 September 1968, Cape Times, reports on unspecified trial of 10.
1962-1963	WELLINGTON, Sakkieskamp.	Cape Argus, 11 July 1963.
	WOLSELEY	Cape Times, 1 May 1963, report on unspecified trial of 57.

NATAL

Dates	Location	Source
1961-1963	DURBAN	Rand Daily Mail, 28 April 1963, report on State vs. Msomi and 3.
1964	DURBAN	Natal Witness, 10 June 1964, report on State vs. Shabalala and 3.
1961-1962	DURBAN, Chesterville township	Rand Daily Mail, 16 July 1964, report on State vs. Mohletshe and 2.
1966	DURBAN	Contact, Otober 1966, report on State vs. Mbele.
1961-1963	HOWICK	Star, 18 July 1963, report on State vs. Khanyi.
1963	OHLANGA INSTITUTE	Interview with Jordan Ngubane, Karis and Carter microfilms, Reel 13A 2 XN 32: 94.
1965-1966	UMSINTU, Jimbele Compound	Natal Mercury, 1 September 1966, report on State vs. Dlamini.
1963	PIETERMARITZBURG	Rand Daily Mail, 24 August 1963, report on State vs. Msomi and 3.
1966	ESPERENZA, sugar estate	Contact, December 1966, report on unspecified trial of 8 farmworkers which ended in acquittal.

ORANGE FREE STATE

Dates	Location	Source
1960-1965	VIRGINIA district	Star, 2 November 1965, Daily Dispatch, 4 November 1965, Contact, April 1966, reports on Sate vs. Ndoni and 3.
1960-1965	WELKOM	State vs. Tangeni, transcript, SAIRR.

1968	WELKOM	Bloemfontein Friend, 30 July 1971, report on State vs. Lebese; Bloemfontein Friend, 8 September 1971, 14 October 1971, 16 December 1971, reports on State vs. Coetzee and 5.

PRISONS

Dates	Location	Source
1965	BAVIANSPOORT Prison	State vs. Mabuso and 13, transcript, SAIRR; Contact, October 1966, for report on State vs. Bahole and 15.
1966	BELVILLE prison	Contact, March 1966 and September 1966 - reports on trial of 31.
1966	GAMKASPOORT prison	Contact, January 1966 and April 1966, reports on trial of 30.
1964	LEEUKOP prison	Contact, March 1965, report on trial of 9; Cape Argus, 7 August 1965, report on third Leeukop trial of 14.

TRANSVAAL

Dates	Location	Source
1963	BENONI, Daveyton	Cape Argus, 21 June 1963, report on State vs. Mlambo and 7.
1961-1963	CARLTONVILLE	Author's interview with former chairman of PAC's Vaal region, David Sibeko.
1961-1963	EVATON	Sibeko interview and The Times (London), 21 October 1963, report on State vs. Sibeko.
1963	EVATON, Wilberforce Institute	Cape Times, 24 June 1963, report on State vs. Mthimunye and 10.
1963	GERMISTON, Natalspruit	Rand Daily Mail, 16 August 1963, report on State vs. Mokoena and 3.
1963-1964	KRUGERSDORP, Muncieville	Star, 2 October 1963, report on State vs. Motsoahae and 3; Star, report on State vs. Majadebodu and 14, 1 September 1964.
1962-1963	PRETORIA, Atteridgeville	State vs. Masemula and 15, transcript, CSAS, York University.

1963	PRETORIA, Atteridgeville, Hofmeyr High School	Existence of a student branch of PAC mentioned in profile of Ernest Mosen-eke in Azania News (Dar es Salaam), 27 January 1966.
1963	PRETORIA, Garankua	Rand Daily Mail, 7 August 1963, report on State vs. Magashoa and 2.
1963	PRETORIA, Hebron African Teachers' Training College	Cape Times, 12 April 1964, report on State vs. Malepe and 11.
1961-1963	PRETORIA, Kilnerton High School	Author's interview with Tommy Moha-jane.
1963	PRETORIA, Eastwood	State vs. Masemula and 15, transcript.
1963	PRETORIA, Lady Selbourne	State vs. Masemula and 15, transcript; arrests reported in Rand Daily Mail, 22 March 1963.
1963	PRETORIA, Vlakfontein	State vs. Masemula and 15, Transcript.
1963	RANDFONTEIN	State vs. Ntsoane, transcript, SAIRR; Rand Daily Mail, 24 July 1963 on State vs. Mbamba and 19.
1963	ROODEPOORT Dobsonville	Star, 24 May 1963, report on State vs. Pheko.
1961-1963	SASOLBURG	Sibeko interview.
1962	SEKHUKHUNILAND	Existence of a PAC region alleged in an interview with P K Leballo, West Africa.

TRANSKEI

Dates	Location	Source
1963	ENGCOBO district	Daily Dispatch, 28 August 1963, report on State vs. Mtirara and 36.
1962-1963	ENGCOBO district, Clarkebury Area	Daily Dispatch, 28 May 1963, report on State vs. Dlwati and 1; Daily Dis-patch, 29 May 1963, 31 May 1963, unspecified trial of 24.
1963	GLEN GREY district, Lady Frere, Ngqoka location	State vs. Manisi and 2, transcript, CSAS, York University.

1963	IDUTYWA district	Daily Dispatch, 8 April 1963, report arrests.
1963	KENTANI district, Makiba location	Daily Dispatch, 21 June 1963, Star, 18 July 1963, reports on unspecified trial of 20.
1961-1965	MQANDULI district, Jixini, Hoabatshana, Mgumbe, Ngwane and Ntalanga locations	Daily Dispatch, 15-19 January 1963, 26 January 1963, Cape Argus, 29 March 1963, for reports on unspecified trial of 15 and three other unspecified trials; State vs. Nkolo and 1, transcript, York University.
1963	NGQELENI district	Daily Dispatch, 5 September 1963, 17 September 1963, for reports for unspecified trial of 38 and unspecified trial of 38 and unspecified trial of 41.
1963	ST. MARKS district, Cofimvaba, Qitsi location	Daily Dispatch, 14 February 1963, for Poqo involvement in attack on headman.
1962	ST. MARKS ditrict, Cofimvaba, Banzi location	Daily Dispatch, 11 January 1963, 15 January 1963, Contact, 31 May 1963, for reports on unspecified trial of 6.
1962	UMTATA district, Bziya location	Star, 16 July 1983, report on unspecified trial of 31.
1962-1963	UMTATA district, Mputi location	Daily Dispatch, 31 July to 12 August 1963, reports on State vs. Xhego and 29.
1963	WILLOWVALE district, Msendo location	Daily Dispatch, 18 June 1963, report on State vs. Natusela and 2.
1962-1963	WILLOWVALE district, Ntshatshungu location.	Daily Dispatch, 19 June 1963, report on unspecified trial of 10.

NOTES

1. This paper is adapted from chapter four of a Ph.D thesis entitled: "Insurrectionism in South Africa', University of York, Centre for Southern African Studies, 1984.

2. Apart from Gerhart the best published descriptions of Poqo and its development are in: Tom Karis, Gwendoline Carter and Gail Gerhart, From Protest to Challenge, Volume 3, (Stanford, 1977); Mary Benson, South Africa: The Struggle for a Birthright, (Harmondsworth, 1966); 'Sandor', The Coming Struggle for South Africa, (London, 1962); Z B Zwelonke, Robben Island, (London, 1973), is a novel based on the prison experiences of a Poqo activist.

3. For discussion of Umkhonto se Sizwe's organisational structure see Edward Feit, Urban Revolt in South Africa, 1960-1964: a case study, (Evanston, 1971).

4. Evening Post (Post Elizabeth), 28 March 1967.

5. 'On the meaning of Poqo', Interpreter's note, Albie Sachs papers, AS 31/19, ICS, University of London. In Albert Knopf, Kaffir- English Dictionary,(Alice, 1913), the meaning of Poqo is given as 'completely (adv.), a religious denomination that refuses to have anything to do with white men (noun)'.

6. 'Poqo' is used in the slogan ending a letter in Xhosa written by P Z Joli to Meshack Mampunye, secretary, Kensington PAC branch in October 1959. Karis and Carter microfilm, Reel 6B, 2 DPI: 41/10.

7. Govan Mbeki, 'An Unholy Alliance', New Age, 3 August 1961.

8. See Tom Lodge, Black Politics in South Africa since 1945, (London, 1983), 210-223.

9. Regina vs. Synod Madlebe and 31, Case no. 313/60, transcript and lawyer's notes, Albie Sachs papers, AS 31.

10. See for example notes on speeches by C. Mlokoti on 3 March 1959 and W Phuza on 11 October 1959, AS 31/6.1 and AS 31 31/6.4 in Albie Sachs papers.

11. Lodge, ibid.

12. Report of evidence submitted to Snyman Commission by Frank Barton, Cape Town editor of Drum magazine in Cape Argus, 12 March 1963.

13. Howard Lawrence, 'Poqo - we go it alone' in Fighting Talk (Johannesburg), 17, 2, (February 1963), 4-6. This account may seem to be slightly romanticised but there is evidence that recent events in the Congo were discussed in at least one Poqo

cell in Cape Town in 1961 (see evidence of state witness Sontekwa in State vs. Mandla and 31 others, defence lawyer's notebooks, Albie Sachs papers, AS 69/7).

14. State vs. Mandla and 31 others, statements by accused nos. 21 and 23, AS 69/8 and Regina vs. Synod Madlebe, AS 31/11.

15. Author's interview with Randolph Vigne, London, 1975.

16. State vs. Mandla and 31 others, statements by accused nos. 14 and 23, AS 69/8.

17. Contact, 16 April 1960.

18. State vs. Mandla and 31 others, defence lawyer's notebooks, AS 69/7.

19. Contact, 29 November 1962.

20. Drum's report (February 1963) mentions an inaugural meeting in August 1961 by 750 Poqo activists in a hall between Paarl and Wellington, very near Mbekweni. I have come across no other reports to confirm this and it is not mentioned by Snyman in his Report of the Commission appointed to inquire into the events on the 20th to 22nd November, 1962, at Paarl, RP 51/1963.

21. 'Sobukwe was Poqo leader', report in Cape Times, 4 March 1963, on Queenstown trial of men involved in unsuccessful assassination attempt on Chief Matanzima.

22. See Lodge, op. cit., pp. 283-290.

23. As in the case of the men who belonged to the Poqo cell at the Jewish Old Age Home in Cape Town.

24. State vs. Matikila and 3 others, March 1962, defence lawyer's notebook, Albie Sachs papers, AS 35/5.

25. State vs. Budaza and 3 others, August 1963, Albie Sachs papers, AS 70.

26. State vs. Xintolo, n.d. defence lawyer's notes on evidence, Albie Sachs papers, AS 83/14.

27. Cape Times reports of the trial, 28 June 1962 and 5 July 1962.

28. Cape Argus, 17 September 1963.

29. Quoted in Rand Daily Mail, 23 March 1963.

30. Cape Times, 28 June 1962.

31. Snyman proceedings, p. 348. Transcript of proceedings of Snyman Commission, CAMP microfilm held at University of York.

32. Report on trial of men involved in Matanzima assassination attempt, Cape Times, 4 March 1963.

33. Snyman proceedings, p. 329. Evidence of state witness X3 (evidence is remarkably detailed and suggests careful rehearsal of witness beforehand).

34. Cape Times, 28 June 1962 and Snyman proceedings, p. 38.

35. Ibid., p. 271.

36. Ibid., p. 297.

37. Cape Times, 5 July 1962 and 28 June 1962.

38. 'Leballo did not escape' in Cape Times, 15 August 1962.

39. Snyman proceedings, p. 283.

40. Draft of an article based upon an interview with Leballo in Maseru dated 24 March 1963 on microfilm of South African political documentation held at School of Oriental and African Studies, University of London.

41. The police refused to arrest the Evaton PAC leaders when they presented themselves at the police station on 21 March 1960. They subsequently obeyed police instructions to disperse the crowd. Z B Molete was tried for incitement in November and was fined £60. See Regina vs. Majake, Ncomane and Molete, transcript, p. 172, held at South African Institute of Race Relations.

42. State vs. Z B Molete, case no. 9/1962, transcript, exhibit DD, p. 341. SAIRR.

43. Though according to Mthimunye, one of the accused in a trial in 1963 in Pretoria (Rand Daily Mail 21 June 1963) the decision to abandon a non-violent strategy followed Z B Molete's assumption of control.

44. Contact, 31 November 1960.

45. State vs. Z B Molete, transcript, p. 15.

46. See Jordan Ngubane, An African Explains Apartheid, (New york, 1962).

47. Author's interview with Matthew Nkoana, London, 1975.

48. Ibid.

49. State vs. Z B Molete, transcript, pp. 89-90.

50. 'Let the People Know'. Leaflet signed by James Mañgqekwana of Main Barracks, Langa. Patrick Duncan Papers, 8. 42. 9, University of York.

51. Report on evidence to the Snyman Commission, Cape Argus, 12 March 1963.

52. Nkoana interview. The BOSS defector Gordon Winter suggests that Nkoana was still in South Africa in July 1964 working as a 'secret police agent'. Apart from his own testimony all the available evidence (for example the document cited in note 57 below) suggests this was not the case: for most of 1964 Nkoana was representing the PAC in Cairo after a period spent in what was then Bechuanaland. Winter's book includes a mass of unreliable detail on the PAC and the ANC and should be treated with great reserve by researchers. See Gordon Winter, Inside BOSS, Penguin: Harmondsworth, 1981, p. 94.

53. Nkoana interview.

54. State vs. G S Neconga, RC 37/65, transcript held at SAIRR, p. 44 and p. 96.

55. It seems that the decision was made independently of leaders still in prison. See note 136.

56. Because Leballo, the son of a South African Anglican priest, had been born in his father's parish at Mafeteng, Basutoland, he was entitled to Basotho nationality and residence. He was therefore permitted by the Native Commissioner at Ubumbu, Kwa Zulu, to leave his place of banishment to live in Basutoland. Cape Times, 15 August 1962.

57. Potlake Leballo and John Pokele, 'Background to Official Appointments and Policy Statement', Maseru, 20 June 1964, mimeo, Anthony Steel papers, private collection, London.

58. West Africa (London), 3 November 1962.

59. Patrick Duncan, 'Gathering Darkness in South Africa', The Times (London), 6 May 1963.

60. Africa Confidential (London), 15 February 1963.

61. National Executive Committee Report to the 1st Annual Conference of the PAC, 19-20 December 1959, Karis and Carter microfilms, Reel 6B, 2: DPI: 979/23.

62. The Africanist (Orlando), November 1959.

63. See Lodge, op. cit., p. 215.

64. The claim was made in court. See Regina vs. Majake, Neumane and Molete, 1960, transcript, p. 94, SAIRR.

65. Research for this currently in progress. Relevant factors include a very fragmented history of political organisation in the area prior to the launching of the local PAC and in particular the failure of ANC activists to capitalise on the trade union organisation accomplished by Communists during the 1940s; unrest in Pretoria's African high schools from 1960 onwards; freehold township removals which had a peculiarly disruptive effect in Pretoria on black communities; and the existence of a relatively substantial group of middle-class professional people (especially teachers) not involved in the ANC. All these contributed to the existence of a space in which the PAC could operate.

66. Cape Argus, 21 June 1963.

67. State vs. Masemula and 15, 1963, transcript, CSAS, University of York. Also author's interview with Tommy Mohajane, York, 1975.

68. Cape Times, 12 April 1964.

69. State vs. Letsoko and 4, 1963, transcript, SAIRR.

70. The Star, 24 May 1963.

71. Author's interview with David Sibeko, London, 1976.

72. R Tunmer and R K Muir, Some Aspects of Education in South Africa, (Cape Town, 1970).

73. Interview with Potlake Leballo, 9 March 1964, Karis and Carter microfilm, Reel IIA, 2: 91; Interview with Peter 'Motosi, 10 August 1963, Karis and Carter microfilm, Reel 10A, 2: XM: 120: 94.

74. Interview with Jordan Ngubane, Reel 13A, Karis and Carter microfilm, 2: N24: 91.

75. According to a draft of an article by Benjamin Pogrund dated 16 January 1960, microfilm of South African Political Documentation held at SOAS, University of London, M 749.

76. The persistence of PAC efforts to organise in Welkom might be attributable to the passage of migrants between the Free State goldfields and Lesotho which may have facilitated contact between exiles in Maseru and PAC supporters in Welkom.

77. The Friend (Bloemfontein), 30 July 1971.

78. State vs. Ntshizana, 1963, SAIRR transcript.

79. Author's interview with Neshtedi Sidzamba, Maseru, 1976.

80. The Star, 9 April 1963.

81. Rand Daily Mail, 17 May 1963.

82. According to an exile PAC publication, Black Star (London), May 1963, 57 PAC suspects were arrested in Herschel but I have found no trial evidence to indicate Herschel as a centre of PAC activity.

83. Daily Dispatch, 28 August 1963 and 31 August 1963.

84. PAC Newsletter (Maseru), 15 May 1965.

85. Contact, 27 November 1964.

86. Rand Daily Mail, 14 June 1963.

87. Evening Post, 24 June 1966.

88. He gave state evidence at the trial of the King William's Town group. Daily Dispatch, 4 September 1963.

89. Daily Dispatch, 28 August 1963.

90. State vs. Neconga and 3, transcript, SAIRR.

91. State vs. Z B Molete, 1962, transcript, p. 88, SAIRR. Nkoana and Molete sent Fazzio copies of Mafube for distribution.

92. Daily Dispatch, 27 April 1963.

93. State vs. C V Mngaza, 1967, transcript, University of York.

94. Except in Glen Grey, then adjacent to the Transkei but not part of it.

95. See table.

96. For example, nearly eighty people were accused in a series of trials in December 1962 or organising meetings attended by over six hundred people in Ngwana, Ntlanga, and Mgombe locations, Mqanduli district. Daily Despatch, 19 January 1963.

97. Author's interview with David Sibeko.

98. See State vs. Masemula and 15, transcript, pp. 269-272.

99. See State vs. Neconga and 3, transcript p. 13.

100. State vs. Jairus Ntsoane, case no. 295/63, transcript, p. 54, SAIRR.

101. Ibid., pp. 54-66.

102. Ibid., exhibit Y, pp. 271-278.

103. Rand Daily Mail, 23 May 1964. Report on State vs. Nkosi and 3. Here a state witness testified that the Witwatersrand area was

the least prepared for the April uprising. Rand Daily Mail, 21 June 1963, report on State vs. Mthimunye and 10. The accused claimed that as a member of the Wits. regional committee he had opposed Leballo's conception of an uprising.

104. State vs. Jairus Ntsoane, exhibit M, p. 242.

105. State vs. Neconga and 3, p. 53 and p. 102.

106. Ibid., p. 13.

107. Daily Dispatch, 14 February 1963.

108. Ibid., 23 February 1963.

109. Ibid., 12 February 1963.

110. This was the case, for example, with the group at Mputi location, Umtata district, responsible for the Bahsee Bridge killings. Daily Dispatch, 3 December 1963.

111. Nkoana believes that by 1962 the national leadership was no longer in control of the movement in the Cape. Nkoana interview.

112. See, for example, State vs. Siyothula, report in Cape Argus, 23 December 1967 and 13 November 1967.

113. State vs. Jairus Ntsoane, exhibit G, 'Urgent Warning', 13 February 1963, signed by M G Macdonald.

114. Examples: State vs. Letsaka and 4, transcript, p. 1550, and report on State vs. Mgoqi and 9, Daily Dispatch, 13 November 1963.

115. State vs. Neconga and 4, transcript, p. 13.

116. Ibid., p. 20.

117. State vs. Jairus Ntsoane, transcript, p. 52.

118. Ibid., p. 79.

119. State vs. Mtshizana, transcript, p. 296.

120. For example, see State vs. Masemula, transcript, pp. 166-167.

121. Ibid., p. 232.

122. Examples: State vs. Mtshizana (Lovedale), p. 295; Rand Daily Mail report, 20 August 1963 on State vs. Nqobo and 32 (King William's Town); Rand Daily Mail report, 16 August 1963, State vs. Mokoena and 3 (Germiston).

123. For example: State vs. Neconga and 3, transcript, p. 6.

124. Z B Zwelonke's novel, Robben Island, describes the Poqo men imprisoned on the island cherishing the hope that:

> the five to eight year, and nine to fifteen or life sentence would wither away when that man in the lonely house (Sobukwe) decided to act. (p. 40)

Sobukwe

> never pushed us from the rear but led us from the front like a good shepherd. (p. 106)

125. Report on Sibeko's trial, The Times (London), 21 October 1963.

126. The Star, 4 May 1963.

127. Ibid., 30 March 1963.

128. Jack Halpern, South Africa's Hostages, (Harmondsworth, 1965), pp. 26-31; Patrick Duncan, 'South Africa: How Britain Helped Verwoerd's Police', Tribune (London), 26 April 1963.

129. Affidavit by P. Gqobose before Commissioner of Oaths, Maseru, 17 April 1963, Anthony Steel Papers. For what it is worth, Gordon Winter claims that the British authorities did not pass information to the South Africans. His version of the incident has it that Leballo compiled a list of 4,000 PAC members and these had been obtained by a South African intelligence agent, Hans Lombard, with whom Leballo had developed a friendship, (Gordon Walker, Inside Boss, Harmondsworth, 1981). The Duncan Papers testify to the existence of Lombard, who, by 1964, was widely believed to be a South African spy and who had enjoyed Leballo's confidence. Perhaps on this occasion Winter may be correct. But this does not rule out the possibility of British complicity with the South Africans.

130. Race Relations News, June 1963.

131. Daily Dispatch, 28 August 1963.

132. Ibid., 28 October 1963 to 19 November 1963.

133. State vs. Napoleon Letsoko and 4, transcript.

134. Sibeko interview.

135. The Star, 21 and 23 October 1963.

136 Author's interview with A B Ngcobo, London, 1975. Benjamin Pogrund in an article in the Rand Daily Mail, 'The Paradox of Robert Sobukwe' (26 April 1969), describes Sobukwe as a 'firm believer in non-violent political action'.

137. Cape Times, 13 June 1966.

138. Rand Daily Mail, 23 May 1964, The Star, 20 May 1964, 21 May 1964, 12 June 1964.

139. State vs. Manisi and 2, case no. 326/63, transcript, CSAS, York University.

140. Natal Witness, 10 June 1964, report of Shabala and 3; Daily Despatch, 1 April 1969, report on State vs. Loliwe and 3; Contact, May 1965, State vs. Mkhalipi and 3.

141. The Star, 16 March 1965.

142. Rand Daily Mail, 19 March 1965.

143. Arrangements concerning the purchase of a second hand motor torpedo boat are detailed in the Patrick Duncan Papers, 8. 48. 61. A plan for a Basutoland-based insurgency in the Transkei is discussed in correspondence in January 1963 between Duncan and the Maseru group (Patrick Duncan Papers, 8. 43. 6). Duncan discussed the plan with Robert Kennedy in Washington later that year. See C J Driver, Patrick Duncan, South African, Pan African, (London, 1980), 229.

144. The Star, 13 February 1967.

145. State vs. Alex Nikelo and 1, transcript, CSAS, York.

146. Cape Times, 27 April 1965.

147. Contact, July 1965.

148. Contact, December 1966.

149. Africa Confidential, 9 May 1965; Contact, May 1965, New African (London), June 1965; Cape Times, 13 March 1965.

150. PAC Newsletter, Maseru, 15 May 1965.

151. Evening Post, 15 and 16 February 1966; Eastern Province Herald, 2 April 1966.

152. Cape Times, 6 May 1967.

153. Ibid., 9 June 1967.

154. Eastern Province Herald, 2 December 1970.

155. The Star, 4 September 1968; Daily Dispatch, 19 October 1968.

156. Evening Post, 24 June 1966.

158. Natal Mercury, 1 September 1966.

159. Contact, December 1966.

160. Contact, January 1966.

161. State vs. Mabuse and 13, transcript, SAIRR.

162. Contact, March 1966.

163. Cape Argus, 7 August 1965.

164. Eastern Province Herald, 2 and 15 December 1970.

165. The Star, 5 July 1969 and 2 August 1969.

166. Cape Times, 3 October 1968.

167. Cape Times, 9 June 1967.

168. Feit, op. cit., p. 17.

169. Fatima Meer, 'African Nationalism, Some Inhibiting Factors' in H. Adam (ed.), South Africa: Sociological Perspectives, (London, 1971).

170. Ibid., p. 140.

171. Feit, op cit., p. 90.

172. See, for example, Neil Smelser, 'Mechanisms of Change and Adjustment to Change', in B F Hoselitz and W E Moore, Industrialisation and Society, (Paris, 1966).

173. Ted Gurr, Rogues, Rebels and Reformers: A Political History of Crime and Conflict, (Beverley Hills, 1976), pp. 82-90.

174. See, for example, the Snyman Commission Report (RP 51/1963), paras. 161-165.

175. See, for example, SAIRR, Report by the Director on Visits to Port Elizabeth, East London and Kimberley in connection with the riots, RR 9/53, 12 January 1953.

176. George Rude, The Crowd in the French Revolution, (Oxford, 1959).

177. E G Hobsbawm and George Rude, Captain Swing, (Harmondsworth, 1973).

178. Charles, Louis and Richard Tilly, The Rebellious Century, (London, 1975).

179. Ibid., p. 85.

180. See Charles van Onselen, Studies in the Social and Economic History of the Witwatersrand, Volume 2, (Johannesburg, 1982), 54-60.

181. Tillys, op. cit., 52.

182. cf. E J Hobsbawn, Primitive Rebels, (Manchester, 1978), 57-58.

183. State vs. Fundile Maseko, EC/5/66, transcript, CSAS, University of York. Out of a black population of 200 sixty men were said to have belonged to Poqo.

184. Daily Dispatch, 7 March 1963.

185. Ibid., 23 April 1963.

186. Ibid., 21 May 1963.

187. Ibid., 9 May 1963.

188. Ibid., 21 May 1963.

189. cf. Hobsbawm, op. cit., Chapter VI for a study of the Sicilian Fascii, an illustration of the 'complete process by which a primitive social movement is absorbed into a wholly modern one'. (p. L 93).

190. For example: Raymond Mhlaba. For biographical details of this Umkhonto leader's early career see Lodge, op. cit., 51-53.

191. K Danziger, 'The Psychological Future of an Oppressed Group', Social Forces, (October 1963), 31-40.

192. E A Brett, African Attitudes, (Johannesburg, 1963).

193. Tillys, op. cit., 70.

194. Tom Lodge, 'The Parents' School Boycott', B Bozzoli (ed.), Town and Countryside in the Transvaal, (Johannesburg, 1983), 370-372.

195. Colin Bundy, 'Resistance in the Reserves: the AAC and the Transkei', African Perspective, 22, (1983), 58.

196. Karis and Carter microfilm, Reel 11A, 2: XM: 26: 94.

197. Inkundla ya Bantu, 7 May 1949, p. 5.

198. Gerhart, op. cit., 15-16. In fairness to Gerhart it should be conceded that the PAC's Matthew Nkoana also has attributed a psychological function to Poqo violence:

> ... they had to prove not so much to others as to themselves that they in fact could do things ... they had to divest themselves of fear, the almost inexplicable fear engendered by the power that was symbolised by the white colour.

Matthew Nkoana, 'The end to non-violence', The New African, (March 1963).

199. See Ghita Ionescu and Ernest Gellner (eds.), Populism, (London, 1969), 156, for the distinction.